A User's Guide for Managing Surveys, Interpreting Results, and Influencing Respondents

The Power of Survey Design

Giuseppe Iarossi

THE WORLD BANK
Washington, D.C.

ISBN 0-8213-6392-1
EAN 978-0-8213-6392-8
e-ISBN 0-8213-6393-X
e-ISBN-13 978-0-8213-6393-5
DOI 10.1596/978-0-8213-6392-8

Library of Congress Cataloging-in-Publication Data

Iarossi, Giuseppe.
   The power of survey design : a user's guide for managing surveys, interpreting results, and influencing respondents / Giuseppe Iarossi.
      p. cm.
   Includes bibliographical references and index.
   ISBN-13: 978-0-8213-6392-8
   ISBN-10: 0-8213-6392-1
   1. Social surveys—Methodology. 2. Questionnaires—Methodology. I. Title.

   HM538.I37 2006
   300.72'3—dc22

                                                      2005044618

To my father, Antonio, and my mother, Esterina Civetta

Table of Contents

Figures

Tables

Foreword

The vast majority of data used for economic research, analysis, and policy design comes from surveys—surveys of households, firms, schools, hospitals, and market participants. In today's world it is easy to go online and download all kinds of data—infant mortality rates, trends in inflation, poverty levels, degree of inequality, growth rates of investment and GDP. Most users of these data do not think very much about where they come from. But they should. Take what seems a fairly straightforward piece of information, such as the amount of gross investment in China in 2004: the real answer to this question is all of the expenditure or effort households, firms, and the government made during the year to increase or enhance the value of the land, buildings, and machinery that can be used to produce goods and services. It would be extraordinarily costly—probably impossible—to actually count all this activity. So, in practice researchers, officials, and market participants will rely on an estimate that is derived from surveys of households and firms. The accuracy of the estimate will depend on how well the survey is done.

This innovative book is both a "how-to" about carrying out high-quality surveys, especially in the challenging environment of developing countries; and a "user's guide" for anyone who uses statistical data for any purpose. Reading this book will provide users of data with a wealth of insight into what kinds of problems or biases to look for in different data sources, based on the underlying survey approaches that were used to generate the data. In that sense the book is an invaluable "skeptic's guide to data."

For the producer of data through surveys, Giuseppe Iarossi has written a straightforward, practical guide to survey design and implementation. This guide is based on his years of experience implementing surveys of firms in a variety of institutional settings in Africa, East Asia, and South Asia. It is a readable guide that covers such issues as writing questionnaires, training enumerators, testing different wordings of questions, sample selection, data entry, and data cleaning.

Users of data can skip certain sections that go into technical detail. But the broad storyline of the book is something that should be absorbed by anyone who works with statistical data. Just as anyone who visits a sausage factory never feels quite the same way again about eating a sausage, readers of this book will never quite feel the same about data that is just handed to them. The book will teach you how difficult it often is to come up with reliable estimates of important social and economic facts, and thus encourage you to approach all estimates with sensible caution.

David Dollar
China Country Director
World Bank

Acknowledgments

I owe a considerable intellectual debt to all researchers and practitioners of survey methods referenced throughout this work. I could have not written this book had I not benefited from the extensive experience of my colleagues working on Investment Climate Surveys at the World Bank, to which I am very grateful. In particular I wish to thank Rita Almeida, Demba Ba, Sergiy Biletsky, Amanda Carlier, George Clarke, Linda Cotton, Antonie De Wilde, Simeon Djankov, David Dollar, Pablo Fajnzylber, Ana Fernandes, Aurora Ferrari, Alvaro Gonzalez, Mona Haddad, Luke Haggarty, Mary Hallward-Driemeier, Sriyani Hulugalle, Philip Keefer, Thomas Kenyon, Veselin Kuntchev, Sergio Kurlat, Esperanza Lasagabaster, Ying Li, Syed Mahmood, Jean Michel Marchat, Melanie Mbuyi, Taye Mengistae, Jorge Meza, Hisaaki Mitsui, John Nasir, Axel Peuker, Ismail Radwan, Vijaya Ramachandran, Menhaz Safavian, Federica Saliola, Hyak Sargsian, Luis Serven, Stefka Slavova, Andrew Stone, Mona Sur, Giovanni Tanzillo, Tilahun Temesgen, Son Thanh Tran, Colin Xu, Yutaka Yoshino, and Albert Zeufack. I am thankful to Abuzar Asra, Gemma Estrada, V.N. Ghanathurai, Rana Hasan Kanokpan Lao-Araya, and Ernesto Pernia from the Asian Development Bank. I am also grateful to local consultants and government officials in Bangladesh, Brazil, Costa Rica, Ethiopia, Guyana, India, Indonesia, Malawi, Malaysia, the Philippines, the Republic of Korea, Sri Lanka, Thailand, and Vietnam with whom I have worked over the years. I am indebted to Mary Hallward-Driemeir, Phil Keefer, Yusuf Mohammed, Federica Saliola, Giovanni Tanzillo, and Veselin Kuntchev for useful comments on early drafts. Rina Bonfield, Polly Means, Hedy Sladovich, and Tourya Tourougui provided invaluable editorial assistance. The most important sources of moral support in the completion of this work have been my wife, Izabella, and my brother, Nicola, to whom I offer my warmest gratitude. I thankfully acknowledge financial support from the Bank Netherlands Partnership Program and the World Bank Private Sector Development Group of the Africa Region. All mistakes remain mine.

The views expressed here are entirely those of the author and do not necessarily represent the views of the World Bank, its executive directors, or the countries they represent. My hope is that this work will help enhance the accuracy of the data collected in Investment Climate Surveys and in turn improve the policy advice to developing countries on their path toward poverty reduction.

Abbreviations and Acronyms

ACS	Association for Survey Computing
BEEPS II	Business Environment and Enterprise Performance Survey II
BOSS	brief, objective, simple, and specific
DCF	discounted cash flow
DK	don't know
HQ	headquarters
IC	Productivity and Investment Climate Surveys
ID	identifier
LCU	local currency
LSMS	Living Standards and Measurement Study
NA	not applicable
NP	not provided
NPV	net present value
PPS	probability proportional to size
REF	refuse to answer
ROE	return on equity
SAS	Statistical Analysis System
SRS	simple random sampling
TOR	terms of reference
UNDP	United Nations Development Programme

Chapter 1
Taking A Closer Look at Survey Implementation

When I was a student in graduate school, I was often intrigued by the ambiguity of survey results. Whether it was politics, the economy, or even human behavior it was common to find contradicting results, sometimes from the same survey. Little has changed since then. A Latinobarometro poll in 2004 showed that while a clear majority (63 percent) in Latin America would never support a military government, 55 percent would not mind a nondemocratic government if it solved economic problems (see table 1.1).

Years have passed since I was finally able to solve this puzzle. If we were to conduct a survey today and ask, "Are you in favor of financial incentives for poor countries?" very likely many respondents would be inclined to answer yes. Yet the result of this poll would be different if the question were "Are you in favor of subsidies for poor countries?" Experiments have proven that a single word, *incentives* or *subsidies,* can sway the outcome of a poll.

The way a question is worded can often lead the respondent toward one answer or another. And this effect can be significant, in the order of up to 30 percent change in attitude. Hence, the cause of survey inconsistencies does not rest, as I originally thought, on the respondents, but rather on the question designer. Respondents are not irrational. Questionnaire designers, on the contrary, are often either skillful enough (or inexperienced enough) to exploit or to understand, respectively, the many "tricks" of the survey business. I tried one of these tricks myself while teaching a class on survey methodology at the Johns Hopkins University. On the first day of class, I randomly split the students into two groups and asked each member of the groups to answer the same question, worded differently (see table 1.2). My covert intention was to lead students of the first group toward answer A and students of the second group toward answer B. From this simple experiment, I learned how easy it is to influence respondents.

Table 1.1
Attitudes and Ambiguities toward Democracy in Latin America (Percent of Respondents)

	Under No Circumstances Would Support a Military Government	Wouldn't Mind a Nondemocratic Government If It Solved Economic Problems
Costa Rica	89	42
Panama	77	56
Dominican Republic	74	62
Uruguay	72	33
Venezuela, R.B. de	71	48
Nicaragua	70	70
Ecuador	69	49
Bolivia	67	49
Argentina	64	46
Chile	64	45
Mexico	60	67
Colombia	58	64
Brazil	56	54
Guatemala	54	57
El Salvador	48	56
Honduras	47	70
Peru	47	64
Paraguay	41	75
Latin America	63	55

Source: The Economist 2004.

Response artifacts are not limited to question wording. The international comparison of survey results is today a common occurrence. When this comparison happens, however, it is important to consider the way the survey is implemented in each country and how this might affect each country's survey results. For example, we are all aware that underreporting occurs when questions on corruption or taxes are asked by a government official. Therefore, if we wish to obtain a meaningful international comparison of these phenomena, we must investigate and control any such survey fixed effect. Survey results are often used, com-

Table 1.2

Same Question (Leading to) Different Answers

Group 1	Group 2
With which of the following statements do you agree most?	
a. Democracy is the best form of government preferable to any other kind of government	a. Democracy is the only system of government in any circumstance
b. An authoritarian government is preferable to a democratically elected government	b. In some limited circumstances and for a short period of time, a nondemocratic government could be temporarily installed if it solves deep economic and/or political crises.

Source: Author.

bined, and presented without due attention to the methodology employed in the data collection. People do not pay attention to *who* is asking the question or *how* the question is asked and hence they combine different answers. Unless these fixed effects are properly identified and corrected, survey results might be misleading. Contrary to what Transparency International reports, for example, El Salvador appears to be more corrupt than China if we simply combine data from the Investment Climate Surveys in these two countries. Once we account for the underreporting, because the survey in China was conducted by government officials, the adjusted ranking of El Salvador and China corresponds to that of Transparency International.[1]

And this is the goal of this book: to show the host of survey fixed effects that play a subtle but critical role on survey results. This work is presented in manuscript form and is directed to two audiences: those who *use* survey data (the majority) and those who *produce* survey data. The former group should read the chapter on questionnaire design (chapter 3) and the last section of the chapter on sampling (chapter 4). Too often survey results are loosely presented as representative of the broad population, while the subset of the population they really represent is not

---

[1] See http://www.transparency.org/cpi/2004/cpi2004.en.html, retrieved on June 13, 2005.

clearly identified and the levels of precision and confidence are not always disclosed.

For those directly involved in the production of survey data, this work is a unique and concise source of information on all the steps of survey implementation from planning to data cleaning. Although written with an eye on business surveys, and in particular the Investment Climate Surveys conducted by the World Bank and other international financial institutions, anyone who manages surveys will find this book extremely useful.

Chapter 2 on survey management provides an overview of the main organizational hurdles that must be addressed when planning a survey. The chapter on training (chapter 5) includes an interesting discussion on one of the most difficult tasks for the interviewer, convincing the respondent to participate in the survey. It highlights the psychological factors contributing to the decision to participate. Finally, the chapter on data cleaning (chapter 6) is, to my knowledge, the first attempt to present, in a systematic way, a methodology aimed at improving data accuracy after the field work has been completed.

Whether we like it or not surveys are part of our life. Even the inhabitants of the most remote village are affected by surveys as long as they care about inflation because price changes are monitored through surveys. After reading the chapter on questionnaire design, you will be able to detect how skillful question designers can lure respondents toward one answer and you will be more cautious in pooling results from different surveys. Additionally, you will acquire a critical eye in interpreting results from polls reported in the media.

Box 1.1

One Poll, Multiple Interpretations

On January 19, 2005, BBC News published the results of a world poll following the U.S. elections. The highlight of the poll was that "More than half of people surveyed in a BBC World Service poll say the reelection of U.S. President George W. Bush has made the world more dangerous." According to the results of this poll, "only 3 countries out of 21 polled believed the world was now safer" (see box table 1.1.1).

Box Table 1.1.1

BBC World Poll Results

Question: As you may know, George Bush has been reelected as president of the United States. Do you think this is positive or negative for peace and security in the world? (percent respondents)

Country	Positive	Negative	No Effect Either Way	Don't Know/NA
Argentina	8	79	4	9
Australia	31	61	5	3
Brazil	17	78	3	2
Canada	26	67	2	5
Chile	19	62	6	13
China	27	56	5	12
France	13	75	4	7
Germany	14	77	8	2
Great Britain	29	64	4	4
India	62	27	2	8
Indonesia	21	68	5	6
Italy	34	54	3	9
Japan	15	39	31	15
Korea, Rep. of	36	54	7	3
Lebanon	23	64	9	4
Mexico	4	58	28	10
Philippines	63	30	2	5
Poland	44	27	7	23
Russian Federation	16	39	32	13
South Africa	35	57	3	5
Turkey	6	82	6	7
United States	56	39	1	4
Total	27	57		

(continued)

Box 1.1 (continued)

Are these results really true? Two basic questions should be asked: Do these countries represent the world community? Do the people interviewed represent the world population?

To determine whether this sample is representative of the world, the sample of countries should have been random. Nowhere in the article, or in the methodology, does it appear as though the sample of 21 countries was randomly chosen from among the world's 191 countries.

Even assuming that the selection was random, we next need to ask ourselves the following question: What level of confidence have we obtained from these results? A sample of 21 elements in a population of 191 gives a level of precision of +/−20 percent (at 95 percent confidence). This implies that the true share of respondents with negative attitude could be anywhere between 37 percent and 77 percent. Similarly, the true share with positive attitude could be anywhere between 7 percent and 47 percent. Because the two confidence intervals overlap, we cannot conclude that the observed difference in attitude is statistically significant.

Although the poll is not representative of the countries in the word, it can be argued that it is representative of the world population. If we follow this argument, however, we need to weight each country by its share of the world population. It would not be correct to give China, with a population of 1.2 billion inhabitants, the same weight as Lebanon, with 5 million inhabitants. By weighting the results of the poll, we can see that the difference between negative and positive perceptions persists, even if at a lower level, with 49 percent of respondents having a negative attitude versus 36 percent having a positive attitude.

There is, however, another interesting survey fixed effect to keep in mind. From the methodology, it appears that, in some countries, the survey has been conducted by phone while in others it was conducted through a face-to-face interview. To the extent that the question asked is considered sensitive by the respondents, the mode of interview can influence answers. In particular, we would expect that the nonresponse rate in the face-to-face interviews would be higher than in the phone survey. If we look at the data from the BBC poll, this is exactly what happened. In the face-to-face surveys, the share of nonresponse is double (20%) that of the phone survey. Such a high nonresponse rate might have an impact on the results of the survey itself, unless it is assumed that the distribution of nonresponses in each mode is the same (but this is a strong assumption given the sensitivity of the question). Hence, if we look at the survey results by mode of interview, we can see that, if the survey is conducted by face-to-face interview, then the difference between positive and negative attitude vanishes. Hence, it appears that the results of the survey are dependent on the mode of interview (see box table 1.1.2 and box figure 1.1.1). Not a conclusive result for a world opinion poll.

Box 1.1 (continued)

Box Table 1.1.2

BBC Polls by Mode of Interview and Weighted Results

Country	Positive	Negative	No Effect	DK/ NA	Population (thousands)	Weight	Positive Weighted	Negative Weighted
			Face to Face					
Argentina	8	79	4	9	38,377	0.018	0.14	1.43
Brazil	17	78	3	2	176,596	0.083	1.41	6.48
Chile	19	62	6	13	15,774	0.007	0.14	0.46
India	62	27	2	8	1,064,399	0.501	31.05	13.52
Indonesia	21	68	5	6	214,471	0.101	2.12	6.86
Japan	15	39	31	15	127,210	0.060	0.90	2.33
Korea, Rep. of	36	54	7	3	47,912	0.023	0.81	1.22
Lebanon	23	64	9	4	4,498	0.002	0.05	0.14
Mexico	4	58	28	10	102,291	0.048	0.19	2.79
Philippines	63	30	2	5	81,503	0.038	2.42	1.15
Poland	44	27	7	23	38,195	0.018	0.79	0.49
Russian Federation	16	39	32	13	143,425	0.067	1.08	2.63
Turkey	6	82	6	7	70,712	0.033	0.20	2.73
Total face to face	26	54	11	9			41	42
			Phone					
Australia	31	61	5	3	19,890	0.010	0.32	0.63
Canada	26	67	2	5	31,630	0.016	0.42	1.09
China	27	56	5	12	1,288,400	0.666	17.97	37.28
France	13	75	4	7	59,725	0.031	0.40	2.31
Germany	14	77	8	2	82,551	0.043	0.60	3.28
Great Britain	29	64	4	4	59,280	0.031	0.89	1.96
Italy	34	54	3	9	57,646	0.030	1.01	1.61
South Africa	35	57	3	5	45,294	0.023	0.82	1.33
United States	56	39	1	4	291,044	0.150	8.42	5.86
Total phone	29	61	4	6			31	55

Source: Author's calculations.

Box 1.1 (continued)

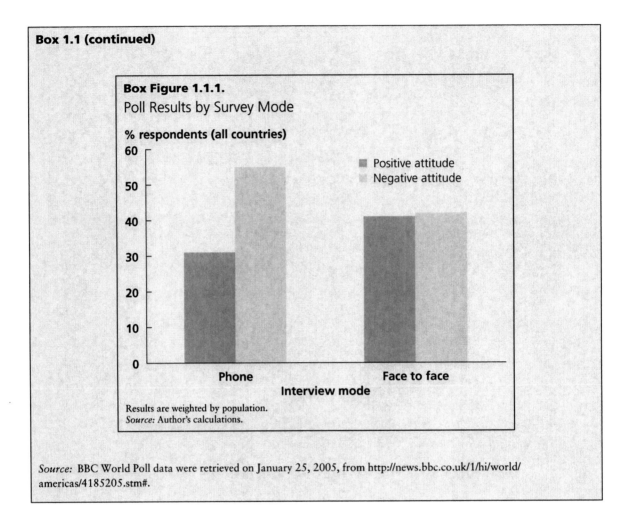

Box Figure 1.1.1.
Poll Results by Survey Mode

Results are weighted by population.
Source: Author's calculations.

Source: BBC World Poll data were retrieved on January 25, 2005, from http://news.bbc.co.uk/1/hi/world/americas/4185205.stm#.

Chapter 2

Survey Management: An Overview

Careful planning is vital to the timely completion of any project, yet the task of planning and managing a survey is subject to everything from cultural vicissitudes to weather conditions (Warwick and Lininger 1975). Given the endless number of factors (cultural, economic, ethnic, linguistic, political, psychological, sociological, and religious) that influence the implementation of any survey, managing such a project is as much art as science. Hence, the survey manager must have experience in survey implementation and a clear understanding of the objectives of the study.[1] As in all projects, the survey manager must plan, organize, lead, and control the development of the survey (Weeks 2003).

Throughout the survey process technical and organizational decisions must blend the theoretically desirable with the practically feasible (Moser and Kalton 1971). Within this realm the survey manager is responsible for the following:

- Preparing the overall survey program;
- Designing the questionnaire and data entry form;
- Conducting the pilot;
- Selecting the survey firm[2] and defining the financial arrangements;
- Drawing the sample;
- Training the interviewers; and
- Monitoring the fieldwork and developing data quality control procedures.

Often there is the temptation to skip on [survey] preparation in order to move to the field too rapidly. This temptation should be avoided.

—Ghislaine Delaine and others, "The Social Dimensions of Adjustment Integrated Survey"

---

[1] We assume the survey manager to be a single individual. Although it is possible for a team of staff to take on this role, this is less desirable. Given the functional links among the key steps of any survey, there are obvious externalities that favor a single individual to be the survey manager. Furthermore, a clearly identified and experienced survey manager can ensure that the survey adequately covers policy issues of interest to the data users (Delaine and others 1991).

[2] The survey firm is contracted to do the fieldwork and enter the data.

The chronological sequence and overlap of each activity as well as their functional links must be carefully synchronized. After one step is completed, going back will compromise the next step and, thus, either the timely conclusion of the survey, the accuracy of the results, or both. The survey manager is generally assisted in these tasks by a statistician and a data processing coordinator, but the manager remains responsible for overseeing the collection of accurate information in a timely manner and within budget (Delaine and others 1991). A good survey manager has the ability to anticipate possible sources of error (interviewing, wording of questions, editing, and coding) and delays (national or seasonal holidays, weather conditions, religious festivities, or sample frame inaccuracy) (Moser and Kalton 1971).

Overall Program Design

The early stages of a survey should include a careful review of the literature and talks with experts in the country. This helps conceptualize potential problems. Similarly, a review of previous survey work and discussions with local survey practitioners will help determine what approach works best, what hypotheses have been tested, and which question items are best suited for the specific survey (Warwick and Lininger 1975). This stage also includes an assessment of the survey infrastructure, a careful search for potential partners in implementing the fieldwork and sponsoring the survey initiative, and finally the design of plans for data gathering and entry, reports, presentations, and dissemination.[3]

Questionnaire Design, Pilot, and Data Entry Form

After the research objectives have been identified, the difficult challenge of translating them into a well-conceptualized and methodologically sound questionnaire begins (Warwick and Lininger 1975). In Investment Climate Surveys[4] the core[5] questionnaire represents the starting

---

[3] It is good practice to address issues of data entry software and coding from the very beginning, although a more detailed discussion and implementation of these issues comes only after the questionnaire is finalized.

[4] Productivity and Investment Climate Surveys, or Investment Climate Surveys, in short, are business surveys conducted by the World Bank. These surveys identify key features of the business climate that foster productivity in a way that allows regional and subregional benchmarking (World Bank 2003).

[5] The core questionnaire is a set of standard questions implemented across countries to enable international benchmarking. Retrieved on June 13, 2005, from http://www.ifc.org/ifcext/economics.nsf/Content/IC-SurveyMethodology.

point. The development of the questionnaire starts soon after general plans have been drawn and ends just days before the start of the field-work. Focus groups can identify concerns and experiences of the target population, as well as evaluate questions and clarify definitions (Gower 1993). The initial questionnaire is usually revised many times.

The pilot test in the field is a critical component of questionnaire design. Similarly, the training sessions for enumerators should be considered the last step of questionnaire design, because it often helps identify problems with wording and translation.

As soon as the questionnaire has been finalized, it must be immediately coded and the data entry form developed.[6] A variety of data entry software programs are available, some at no charge.[7] A well-designed data entry form will have two basic characteristics. First, it will have an interface that is a replica of the paper questionnaire. Second, it will include a number of built-in consistency checks to disallow invalid entries. The development of a data entry form is a delicate and complex process. A number of intricate cross-references and checks must be included, which requires a professional programmer. It remains the survey manager's task to determine and identify which, and to what extent, within- and cross-question consistencies should be embedded in the form.[8] The inclusion of too many or too stringent consistency checks will make data entry almost impossible, even when there are errors that can be easily corrected. Conversely, a lax system of consistency checks will defeat the purpose of the data entry form. A delicate balance between these two alternatives must be found.

Once completed the data entry form must be tested, if possible before the beginning of the fieldwork. Testing is of critical importance and attempts to short cut this step could result in delays at later stages of the survey.[9] In the World Fertility Survey, more than 80 percent of

---

[6] Coding a questionnaire stands for assigning a name to each variable in the questionnaire corresponding to each field in the data set.

[7] A variety of commercially available software programs (Microsoft Access©, SPSS©, and so on) can be purchased, depending on the desired level of sophistication. Simpler but equally effective data entry programs can be downloaded for free from the U.S. Centers for Disease Control and Prevention (www.cdc.gov/epiinfo/) or the U.S. Census Bureau (www.census.gov/ipc/www/imps/index.html). Additionally, the U.K. Association for Survey Computing (ACS) has links to software that can be used for data capture and the different stages of survey implementation (http://www.asc.org.uk/Register/index.htm).

[8] The complexity of the form automatically excludes the use of simple software such as Microsoft Excel©. Excel is data management software and, therefore, not appropriate for this purpose.

[9] Form development and testing generally takes two to four weeks.

all errors found at the first check were due to specification errors and programming errors (Rattenbury 1980).

Survey Firm Selection

Depending on the intricacy of the questionnaire and the complexity of the sample elements, the selection of a survey firm is one of the most difficult and critical tasks. It affects both the *timing* of the survey and the *quality* of the data collected. The survey infrastructure is usually difficult to assess in developing countries and an informed selection usually involves evaluating a wide range of factors, from the geographic distribution of local offices to the number of personal computers owned (box 2.1). An experienced survey manager can easily infer the technical ability of a prospective firm (Grosh and Muñoz 1996) from the quality of written documents, such as survey manuals and recently implemented questionnaires, as well as from the complexity of surveys completed over the past two to three years and those planned in the near future.[10]

Box 2.1
Criteria to Look at When Selecting a Survey Firm

Experience
Questionnaire
How difficult is the content?
How coherent is the content?
How good is the formatting?
How much time does the interview last?
How are sensitive and memory questions addressed?

Sampling
What is the unit of observation?
How difficult is to interview the respondent?

---

[10] Opinion polls and market research surveys are much easier to administer than the typical Investment Climate Survey.

Box 2.1 (continued)

How large was the sample?
Was the sample nationwide?

Fieldwork
What was the ratio of supervisors to enumerators?
How many reinterviews were conducted?
How good were the supervisor and enumerator manuals?
What was the nonresponse rate due to refusal?

Data management
What kind of data quality assurance did they adopt?
What type of data entry software did they use?
How did they organize data editing and checking?

Resources
Personnel
How many people are on staff in relevant positions (supervisors,
    interviewers, data entry, programmers)?
What is their level of education?
What is their age range?
How much experience do they have?
Do staff who worked in previous complex surveys still work there?

Equipment
Do they have offices throughout the country?
Do they have computer capabilities?
What software do they use?
Do they have their own e-mail accounts?

Client orientation
What is their data access policy?
What is their reputation?
What are their business affiliations?

Source: Based on Grosh and Muñoz 1996.

Another important factor to consider in the selection process is the organization of the fieldwork. The collection of high-quality data in a timely manner depends on how well field operations are organized. Coordinating and timing the interactions of tens if not hundreds of people at different levels and stages of the survey becomes a vital and yet complex task. The way the prospective implementing agency deals with staffing, scheduling, and coordinating simultaneous activities should therefore be given the appropriate weight in the selection process (Weeks 2003). A survey in which each individual is clearly identified as a part of a team, in which all members are clear about their responsibilities and accountabilities, and in which a well-organized structure facilitates the flow of information and quickly resolves possible conflicts and doubts will definitely have a positive impact on the timing and quality of the data collection process. Key actors in a typical Investment Climate Survey and their functional relationship are shown in box 2.2.

As in all other steps, the procurement process requires a great deal of attention to details. Even when a highly recommended and seemingly well-qualified agency exists less noticeable factors should inform the selection process:

- How unexpected problems are anticipated and addressed;
- What steps are taken to ensure quality;
- Which approach is used to handle the expected bias associated with sensitive questions;
- What strategies are adopted to elicit participation; and
- Which characteristics interviewers and supervisors have (in terms of age, education, experience, and occupation).[11]

The terms of reference (TOR) developed by the survey manager provides guidance on the "technical" requirements of competing proposals. Inadequate TORs have frequently been a source of error in contracting out the fieldwork (Grosh and Muñoz 1996). Thus it is preferable to follow a two-stage strategy. Initially, the TOR should indicate the project objectives and provide a copy of the draft questionnaire as well as a description of the basic minimum data quality requirements. Bidders should be left free to formulate a detailed methodology to achieve the survey objectives. Given the cultural, political, religious, and ethnic characteristics of each country, it is not advisable to apply the same

---

[11] See chapter 5 for a more detailed treatment of the interviewer's characteristics.

Box 2.2

Key Actors and Their Functions in a Typical Investment Climate Survey

Box Figure 2.2.1.

Typical Organizational Structure of Fieldwork

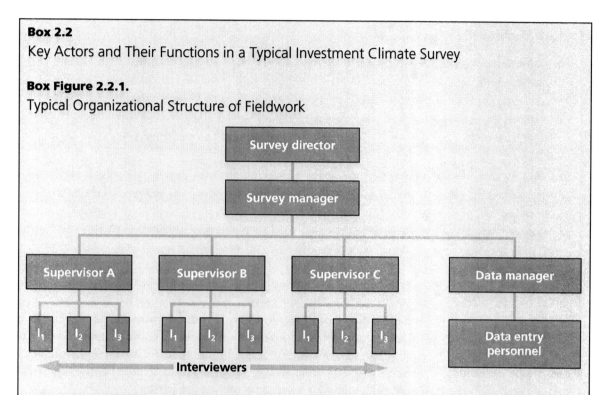

- The *survey director* generally is the head of the agency in charge of the fieldwork. He or she provides professional leadership, coordinates with the survey manager on organizational and financial issues, and provides support to survey implementation especially through community awareness.
- The *survey manager* coordinates with the survey director on more technical aspects of the survey work. He or she helps in designing the sample, plans and supervises the field operation procedures, and contributes to the training session. He or she will also oversee the field supervisors and the data manager (Grosh and Muñoz 1996).
- The *supervisors* assign respondents to interviewers, coordinate their assignments, and ensure that they work efficiently. It is part of the supervisors' responsibilities to monitor and review the quality of the fieldwork, to conduct unannounced field interviews, and to make call-backs as deemed necessary while personally visiting some respondents. Supervisors must review the quality of completed questionnaires, ensuring that interviewers' writing is legible and skip patterns are followed. Unreasonable answers must be flagged and returned to the interviewer for correction, if necessary, through an additional visit. Finally, supervisors facilitate the exchange of information between survey manager and interviewers, make sure that all instructions from the central office are relayed to field workers, and

(continued)

Box 2.2 (continued)

ensure that the central office is regularly updated on the progress of data collection (Grosh and Muñoz 1996).

- *Interviewers* set up appointments with the sampled respondents and conduct the interviews following the rules, techniques, and protocols highlighted during the training sessions and indicated in the survey materials. They re-interview respondents, when necessary, to rectify incorrect or incomplete entries.
- The *data entry manager*, along with the survey manager, designs the data entry quality control protocol and oversees the development of the data entry form. He or she supervises data entry personnel and liaisons with the field manager.
- *Data entry staff* code and key-punch electronically the questionnaires completed in the field.

Source: Author's creation.

---

methodology in every country. Thus, for instance, in Indonesia it appears unnecessary to require call-backs given that standard practice calls for each form to be signed and stamped by the respondent. Once a survey firm has been selected, a second more detailed and comprehensive TOR should be agreed on among the parties.

An often-overlooked criterion in the procurement process refers to the potential measurement error associated with each type of implementing agency. The type of agency conducting the fieldwork—*government agency* or a *private survey company*—can have a different effect on data accuracy depending on the kind of question asked. Sensitive questions about bribes, for instance, are consistently underreported when the interviewer is a government employee.[12] Although the magnitude of the bias varies depending on the specific question, the impact of the underreporting appears to be in the order of 0.3 to 0.6 standard deviations when a government agency is conducting the survey.[13] Nonetheless the survey manager should not rush to the conclusion that private survey companies are always to be preferred. As a matter of fact, the same data shows that using government officers as interviewers has a positive effect on data accuracy by reducing measurement errors for nonsen-

---

[12] A more detailed description of this phenomenon is presented in chapter 3, on questionnaire design, in the discussion on sensitive questions and subjective questions.

[13] See appendixes 2 and 3 for a description of questions and a complete set of regressions results.

sitive questions. The manager's estimates of sales growth were more accurate[14] when government officials conducted the interview. This is not surprising, because statistical officers generally are better trained and more experienced in conducting business interviews. The magnitude of the underreporting (measured in terms of standard deviations) of corruption questions when government officials conduct the interviews appears similar to the magnitude of accounting data inaccuracy when the survey is fielded by a private firm (see figure 2.1).[15]

Over the years, the financial resources needed to conduct a firm-level survey in developing countries have varied. Once again a number of country-specific factors apply, each having a different impact on the survey budget: a 7-page questionnaire will be priced differently than a 20-page instrument, travel costs are unlikely to be the same in Brazil and in Eritrea, and survey experts are harder to find and more expensive in Africa than in East Asia.

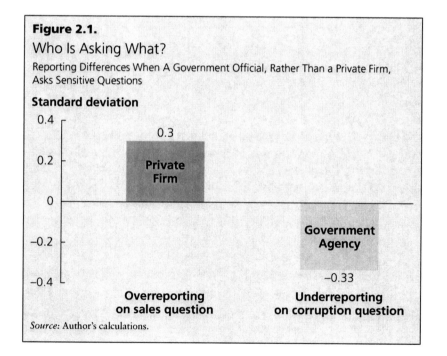

Figure 2.1.

Who Is Asking What?

Reporting Differences When A Government Official, Rather Than a Private Firm, Asks Sensitive Questions

Standard deviation

Source: Author's calculations.

---

[14] The absolute value of the error was more than 17 percent for a private company and close to 1.5 percent for a government agency.

[15] Data accuracy is measured as deviation between the manager's reported value of sales growth last year and the same values calculated from company books.

Household surveys experience shows that 70 to 90 percent of the total survey cost goes to field implementation, while personnel and travel represent the two most important cost categories (table 2.1). Particular attention must also be paid to the internal composition of these two items. Determining the appropriate salary levels across different professional categories is always problematic. The survey job requires months of intense work and it is unrealistic to assume that this can be done without appropriate incentives, particularly for the interviewers. Travel costs, including per diems, will also be a source of resentment if not appropriately estimated. This is clearly a country-specific problem. Nonetheless, accurate planning in terms of the estimated number of visits necessary to complete an interview is essential.

Survey managers must use creativity, diplomatic skills, and expertise to find a solution that is tailored to the country characteristics while being fair to all parties (Grosh and Muñoz 1996). An issue that occasionally surfaces is not only the appropriate rate of pay, but also the relative merits of paying interviewers on a piece rate or by the hour. Supporters of piece rate payment point out the strong economic incentive for field staff and the more efficient use of time. Hourly wage advocates criticize the former approach for providing an incentive to prefer quantity over quality and to "fabricate" answers (Warwick and Lininger 1975). A combination of the two approaches might be the best solution. In this case, for each completed questionnaire, a flat rate would be paid, augmented by variable components, mainly related to travel costs and per diem expenses, with a decreasing weight when the number of visits reaches a predetermined limit. It remains in the survey manger's interest to relate the cost of the survey to the quality of the data collected, and the final rate agreed with the implementing agency should reflect this.

The Sample

Soon after the decision to undertake the survey has been reached, a number of critical decisions must be taken regarding the following:

- The identification of the sample unit;
- The localization of the population list;
- The design of the sampling procedure; and
- The determination of the sample size.

Preparations to draw the sample should start at the earliest possible time given how difficult and time-consuming it is in many developing

Table 2.1

Share of Survey Cost in Household Surveys

| | Percentage Weight of Accounting Categories | | | | | |
	Personnel	Transport	Equipment	Consumables	Other	Sample Size
Angola	63	22	10	1	4	6,000
Botswana	79	0[a]	10	4	7	7,000
Eritrea	64	0[a]	28	5	3	4,000
Kenya	62	23	3	5	7	7,000
Lesotho	75	5	6	2	12	7,500
Madagascar	31	7	33	13	16	6,500
Malawi	32	17	24	22	5	6,000
Mozambique	61	12	3	12	11	
Somalia	44	18	5	1	33	2,200
South Africa	69	24	2	4	2	30,000
Swaziland	30	4	2	1	63	4,500
Tanzania	78	13	2	1	7	3,000
Zambia	82	5	2	6	5	8,000
Overall	63	15	7	6	9	7,054

| | Percentage Weight of Survey Activities | | | |
	Preparation	Implementation	Data Processing	Reporting
Angola	—	84	6	10
Botswana	10	59	22	9
Kenya	—	94	3	4
Lesotho	—	73	19	9
Madagascar	0	79	3	18
Malawi	5	63	16	16
South Africa	1	93	3	3
Swaziland	63	23	8	6
Tanzania	23	72	4	1
Zambia	0	92	6	1
Overall	7	81	6	6

Source: Keogh 2003.

Note: Data refers to household surveys. — = Not classified.

a. Amount included in the personnel costs.

countries to identify a reliable sampling frame. At the end of the field-work, the estimated weights must be adjusted to account for frame problems and nonresponse.

Training

When everything is ready for the start of the fieldwork, training should take place. No matter how complex the questionnaire is, and given the average interviewer's quality in developing countries, training remains fundamental to ensure a consistent interpretation and implementation of questions. The survey manager, having extensive experience and a clear understanding of the analytical objective of each question, is the best person to conduct the training. In this process, training manuals are particularly useful, containing detailed information on the general purpose of the survey, instructions on the conduct of the interviews, detailed explanations of the questions, and references to the methodology for recording answers.

Fieldwork and Data Quality Control

The fieldwork is the most time-consuming part of the survey. Although the interview cycle itself must be clearly defined and responsibilities clearly identified (box 2.3), the more complex the questionnaire, the more difficult it is to estimate the exact timing of survey completion.

A host of factors influence the chronological implementation of the survey. Apart from some obvious "objective" features such as the *length* of the questionnaire, the *size* and *composition* of the sample, and the *number* of interviewers, a host of other intangible factors, some quite subtle, come into play. For example, *how well* a questionnaire is designed will definitely impact the timing of the interview. The appropriate use of skipping patterns and the clarity of definitions and sentences will not only speed up the interview process but also ensure accurate data. The *quality* of the interviewers, and more generally of the survey firm, is another factor influencing the timely completion of the survey. Interviewers with an unambiguous understanding of the questions, with experience in similar surveys, and with the ability to establish a clear relationship of trust with the respondents will foster higher cooperation and complete the interviews in a shorter period of time. Similarly, if the fieldwork is thoroughly organized, delays are minimized. The *accuracy* of the population list is yet another factor. If the list is up to

Box 2.3

Responsibilities Must be Clearly Identified in the Interview Cycle

Box Figure 2.3.1.

Typical Interview Cycle

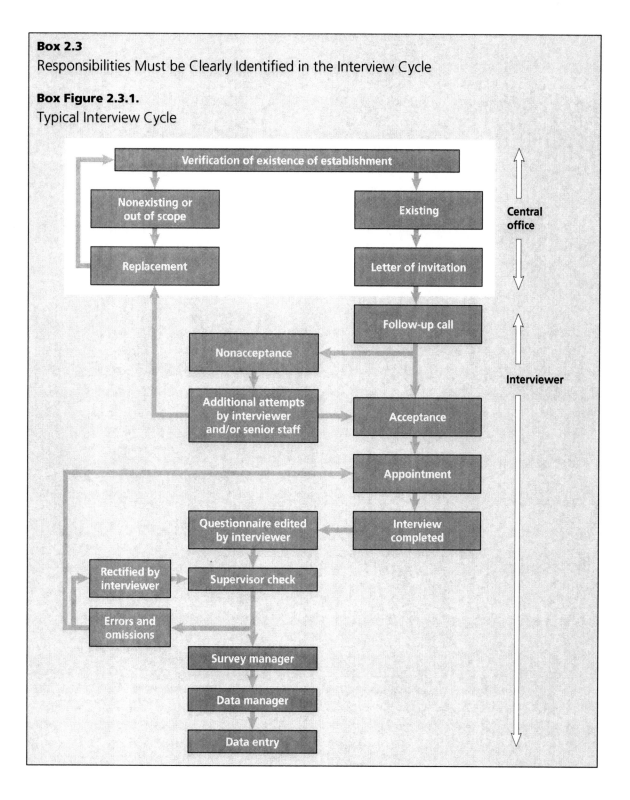

date, time will not be wasted in locating respondents that relocated or establishments that no longer operate. Last but not least the predetermined level of *response rate* considered acceptable will also impact the duration of the survey. A survey with 50 percent of item nonresponse will no doubt be completed faster than a survey with 90 percent of all questions appropriately answered.

The beginning of the fieldwork marks the start of a number of headquarter (HQ) activities coordinated by the survey manager. As soon as interviewers are in the field, the survey manager should start planning for quality control and data cleaning. While the development of a response rate control program is relatively fast, the development of a cleaning program takes longer. The response rate control must proceed almost contemporaneously to the fieldwork and should be used to feed back instructions to the field manager about how to improve the quality of the data collection process. To achieve this efficiently, data must be sent back to HQ in batches at regular intervals. Data cleaning, on the other hand, should start during the fieldwork but can only be completed after the end of the collection process.[16]

One critical aspect of the survey manager's job is to anticipate potential bottlenecks and take remedial actions before they compromise the timely completion of the whole project. No matter how many factors have been taken into account in the preparatory stage of the survey, the experienced survey manager must be on the lookout for the

---

[16] Depending on the length of the questionnaire and the degree of accuracy of the cleaning protocol, the development of the cleaning program can take from three to six weeks.

unexpected. Two useful tools are at the survey manager's disposal—one for monitoring the design of the whole project, the other to supervise the progress of the fieldwork.

A first tool used in planning and managing the timing of a survey is the Gantt Chart (see figure 2.2). Defined as a graphic representation of the sequence and link of activities, it can be used to detect slacks and the critical path of the whole project.[17] This chart is a useful tool in identifying what options are available if problems occur during the implementation of the survey. For example, if the survey is behind schedule, the following alternatives could be employed to make up time (Weeks 2003):

- Start earlier critical path activities by overlapping with predecessor activities.
- Shorten the duration of critical path activities by (1) adding resources if they are resource-driven, or (2) internalizing the loss (that is, lower quality) if not resource driven. This approach works best if employed on earlier activities.
- Move resources from noncritical to critical path activities.

The second tool designed to aid field supervision is the weekly report (table 2.2). This simple form allows the survey manager to effectively monitor the progress of interviews from invitation to completion and to estimate a number of fieldwork performance indicators, such as cooperation rate, response rate, coverage rate, refusal rate, and completion rate.

[17] The critical path is the series of activities that determines the duration of the project. Slack is the amount of time that an activity can be delayed without delaying the project completion date. By definition, the critical path has zero slack (Project Management Institute 2000).

Figure 2.2.

Gantt Charts Illustrate Timing of Survey Activities

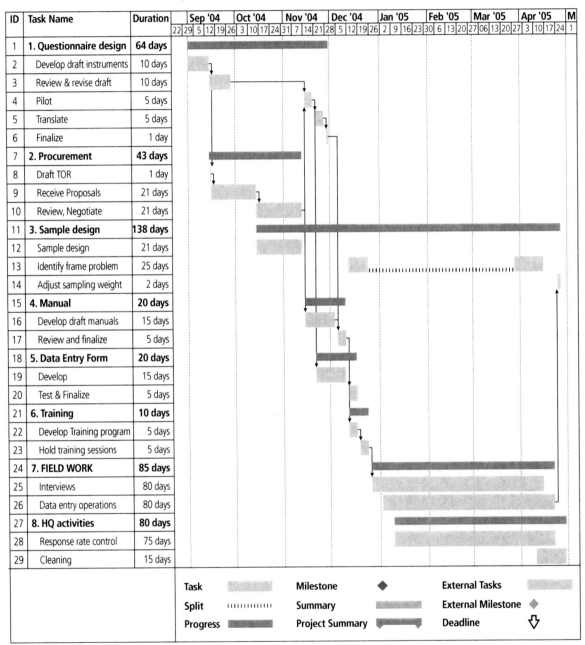

Source: Author's creation.

Table 2.2.

Weekly Reports Enable Managers to Monitor Progress

| Supervisors | Target Sample | Nonresponse | | | Total Sample[c] Visited | Respondents | | | | | | |
		Refusals[a]	Out of Scope	Non-contact[b]		Agreed to Participate	Form Partially Completed	Form Fully Completed	Forms Validated	Forms Entered	Sample Left
Supervisor 1	133	8	2	0	143	78	56	39	22	18	16	115
Supervisor 2	100	3	9	0	112	76	58	53	51	41	40	59
Supervisor 3	130	1	10	0	141	94	78	56	53	50	47	80
Supervisor 4	299	0	25	0	324	207	164	161	157	111	99	188
Supervisor 5	73	0	1	0	74	28	23	47	31	21	15	52
Supervisor 6	265	5	50	0	320	202	140	118	75	74	63	191
Total	1,000	17	97	0	1,114	685	519	474	389	315	280	685

Source: Author.

a. No more attempts.

b. Nonexisting, moved outside study area, wrong address.

c. Target sample + Replacements (refusals + out of scope + noncontacts).

Chapter 3
How Easy It Is to Ask the Wrong Question

Improving question design is one of the easiest, most cost-effective steps that can be taken to improve the quality of survey data" (Fowler 1995, vii), yet it is frequently one of the most disregarded. While many people focus a lot of attention on sampling where the discussion of errors often deals with few percentage points, "experiments suggest that the potential range of errors involved in sensitive or vague opinion questions may be twenty or thirty percentage points" (Warwick and Lininger 1975, 126).

Although there is no formal theory on the wording of a question, a general principle exists to substantially improve its design. That is, two basic rules make a good question: relevance and accuracy.

Relevance is achieved when the questionnaire designer is intimately familiar with the questions, knows exactly the questions' objectives, and the type of information needed. To enhance accuracy, the wording, style, type, and sequence of questions must motivate the respondent and aid recall. "Cooperation will be highest [. . .] when the questionnaire is interesting and when it avoids items difficult to answer, time-consuming, [or] embarrassing" (Warwick and Lininger 1975, 127). A question is relevant if the information generated is appropriate for the purpose of the study. The objective of the question defines the information that is needed and models the words to be used. Sometimes this task is easy, for example, when asking the respondent's age. Other seemingly simple tasks, such as estimating the respondent's level of income is trickier. Hence, the questionnaire designer must force the analysts to be very specific about what they want to measure and why. "Until researchers decide specifically what their goals are it is impossible to write an ideal question" (Fowler 1995, 11).

A question is accurate if it collects the information sought in a reliable and valid manner. It serves no purpose to ask the respondent about

The goal is to have differences in answers reflect differences in where people stand on the issues, rather than differences on their interpretations of the questions.

—Floyd Fowler,
*Improving Survey Questionnaires:
Design and Evaluation*

Relevance

Accuracy

something he or she does not understand clearly or that is too far in the past to remember correctly; doing so generates inaccurate information. As discussed later, respondents rarely admit ignorance. Rather, for a number of different reasons (the desire to be helpful or not appear ignorant), they tend to answer any question, even if they are not informed or barely understand the matter at hand. Because surveys query a variety of respondents, the questionnaire designer must always pose these questions only to people who are able to provide an accurate answer (Moser and Kalton 1971).

It is not always easy to determine whether the respondent has sufficient information to provide an accurate answer. The questionnaire designer should not fall into the trap of thinking easier questions give more accurate answers. This is especially true for opinion questions. By asking opinions on the budget deficit, for instance, we can not distinguish between whether the policy is wrong or the respondent is uninformed. Opinion questions require a validity check to screen "informed" respondents. This is accomplished by resorting to data on measurable behavior available from other sources (Moser and Kalton 1971) (that is, asking the current level of budget deficit) or by asking similar questions in different parts of the questionnaire to check the consistency of answers.[1]

Willingness   Finally, unless the respondent is *willing* to provide an answer, asking the right question to the right respondents still may not produce the desired outcome. In most surveys, respondents are not obliged to participate and are generally reluctant to do so.

> Many forces motivate people to participate in a survey: an interest in the topic, a desire to be helpful, a belief of the importance of the survey, a feeling of duty. . . . Other forces influence people to refuse: difficulty in understanding the questions, fear of strangers, the feeling of one's time being vested, difficulty in recalling information, and embarrassment at personal questions. (Plateck, Pierre-Pierre, and Stevens 1985, 17)

The way the survey is presented, how difficult the questionnaire is, and how sensitive questions are addressed influences the willingness of a prospective respondent to participate.[2]

---

[1] This second approach is the hardest to implement and not recommended.
[2] Issues of survey participation are addressed in the section on survey interview (chapter 5).

Practical Guidelines in Questionnaire Design

Constructing effective questions is an art in which field experience, along with a basic knowledge of linguistic and cognitive psychology plays a critical role (Peterson 2000). Although practitioners have developed techniques to help assess the level of readability and difficulty of questions, the ability to design a question cannot be learned from a book.[3] There is no substitute for experience of personally piloting and conducting interviews.

"A good rule to remember in designing questions [. . .] is that the respondent has probably not thought about these questions at the level of detail required by the survey" (Warwick and Lininger 1975, 158). When developing a question, the designer should first of all put himself "in the position of the typical, or rather the least educated, respondent" (Moser and Kalton 1971, 320). He or she must have a sense of the cognitive abilities of respondents and design the questions accordingly. Hence, while South Asia and East Asia are the regions with the highest share of businessmen with university training, in Sub-Saharan Africa less than half of the businessmen hold a university degree. Similarly Sub-Saharan Africa and Latin America are the only regions where approximately 10 percent of businessmen have not completed secondary education (figure 3.1).

Last but not least the mode of the interview[4] must also be taken into account when designing questions. The same word may generate confusion if spoken but be unambiguous if written. Homophonic words might elicit different interpretations in oral interviews, whereas in some languages different *intonations* of the same word will educe a completely different meaning (Peterson 2000).[5]

Question Wording

A number of studies have irrefutably shown that changing even a single word in a question can significantly alter the response distribution and accuracy. Three decades ago Loftus and Zanni (1975) reported the

---

[3] See Homan, Hewitt, and Linder 1994; Stevens, Stevens, and Stevens 1992; Gallagher and Thompson 1981; McConnell 1983.
[4] Possible modes include face-to-face, telephone, and mail interviews.
[5] The survey mode has a clear effect on a number of survey issues well beyond wording. Table 1 in Tourangeau and Smith (1996) shows survey mode effects on sensitive topics.

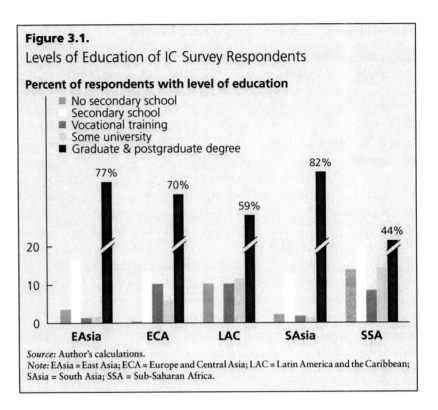

Figure 3.1.
Levels of Education of IC Survey Respondents

Percent of respondents with level of education
- No secondary school
- Secondary school
- Vocational training
- Some university
- Graduate & postgraduate degree

Source: Author's calculations.
Note: EAsia = East Asia; ECA = Europe and Central Asia; LAC = Latin America and the Caribbean; SAsia = South Asia; SSA = Sub-Saharan Africa.

results of two experiments in which a short movie is shown to two in-dependent groups followed by a series of questions, some referring to events not even present in the movie. Figure 3.2 shows how changing one word for another—one group was asked, "Did you see *the* broken light?" the other group was asked, "Did you see *a* broken light?"—has a significant impact on the response distribution. In the mind of the respondent, "a" increases uncertainty about the existence of the event and consequently boosts (by more than half) the number of non-responses. By contrast, "the" leads the respondent to infer the presence of an event, even if the event is nonexisting, hence encouraging false recognitions.

Because of the unique needs of each question, there is no universally accepted theory on question wording. There is, however, a general agreement on what constitutes good and bad questions. Four criteria should be followed when wording any question: it must be *brief, objective, simple,* and *specific* (or BOSS).

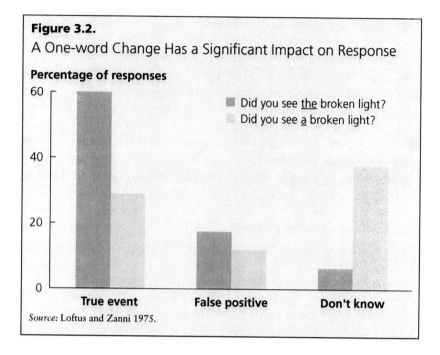

Figure 3.2.
A One-word Change Has a Significant Impact on Response

Percentage of responses

Legend:
■ Did you see <u>the</u> broken light?
■ Did you see <u>a</u> broken light?

X-axis: True event, False positive, Don't know

Source: Loftus and Zanni 1975.

Be Brief

All practitioners would agree that "unless a question is relevant to the research being conducted, it should not be included in a question-naire. Likewise, unless a word is relevant to a question, it should not be included in the question" (Peterson 2000, 52). Questions should be short. Longer questions quickly become more complex and confusing for the respondent as well as the interviewer. Presser and Zhao (1992) show how a shorter question helps the interviewer do a better job by decreasing the tendency to misread it. Furthermore, the complexity of a long question is magnified by the intricacy of the subject matter covered.

As a rule of thumb, a question should not exceed 20 words (Payne 1951) and should not have more than three commas (Peterson 2000); however, brevity should not only be judged on physical appearance but also on contextual simplicity. In this sense, brevity means asking one question at a time. The designer must avoid the use of hidden questions, that is, questions that implicitly determine their relevance on another question. So asking "what interest rate are you paying on your loan?" implies the hidden question of "having a loan." More reliable data can be collected if we ask the questions separately: Do you have a loan? What interest rate are you paying? (Foddy 1993).

While brief questions are simpler, a question that is too short may also generate confusion. So the issue of brevity is not to reduce the length of a question by itself, but to choose the shortest way to pose the question without jeopardizing the intended meaning (see example 3.1). Likewise, a complex topic should not be phrased in one single question in the interest of brevity. This will only magnify its complexity and result in inaccurate answers.

The exception to the brevity requirement involves questions probing memory or sensitive topics. Experiments show that longer questions provide more accurate answers when memory or sensitive topics are covered (Peterson 2000).

Be Objective

"Nonobjective questions share a common characteristic: they tend to suggest an answer" (Peterson 2000, 57). The questionnaire designer should pay close attention to the neutrality of the words, because the question's objectivity can be subtly violated unintentionally. Hence he or she must be aware of the following:

Avoid leading questions. Leading questions are those questions that—by their content, structure, or wording—push the respondent in the direction of a certain answer by implication or suggestion (Warwick and Lininger 1975). So, for instance, a question that begins "Shouldn't something be done about . . . ?" leads to a positive answer. Similarly, when a question suggests only some of the alternatives, it leads in the direction of those alternatives, particularly if the respondent is not sure or does not understand the question properly (see example 3.2).

Response options   The set of response options have been proven to influence the answers given by the respondent in at least three different scenarios. First, failure to give equal weight to all options has the effect of suggesting what the usual or expected answers should be. Schwarz and others (1985) showed that compared with the true distribution on television viewing, respondents who were given a set of low-range categories to chose from were more likely to underreport. Similarly, respondents who were given a set of high-range categories did overreport television viewing (table 3.1).

Second, the actual set of options offered act as a source of information. This happens because respondents are reluctant to go beyond the list to avoid reporting behaviors that might appear unusual in the context of the range offered, or because respondents follow the easier path

Example 3.1

Does Brevity Mean Short?

Brevity in this case is achieved at the expense of clarity.

Original question: How frequently does your consignment arrive late at the gateway port and final destination in comparison with your planned schedule?

	Gateway port	Final destination
Average delay in the last year	(days)	(days)
Maximum delay in the last year	(days)	(days)

This question is extremely complex for a number of reasons:

a) it combines 4 different questions in one sentence. Generally, questions in table format are easy to write but extremely difficult to administer in a survey;

b) part of the question is not even included in the main text (average and longest delay);

c) it uses a general term, "frequently." Questions need to be specific; since we expect an answer in days we are to ask for "days";

d) There is no clear time reference. When? How long ago? Over what time period?

e) It assumes that the respondent experienced such an event. Filtering is missing.

A better way to ask this question(s) is:

Revised question:

In the last year, did you experience delays in delivering your goods from the factories to the gateway port?   Yes / No

If yes, what is the average and maximum number of days that your export shipments arrived late at the gateway port in comparison with your planned schedule?

	Gateway port
Average delay in the last year	(days)
Maximum delay in the last year	(days)

In the last year, did you experience delays in delivering your goods from the gateway port to the final destination?   Yes / No

If yes, what are the average and maximum number of days that your export shipments arrived late at the final destination in comparison with your planned schedule?

	Final destination
Average delay in the last year	(days)
Maximum delay in the last year	(days)

Example 3.2

Can I Ask You a (Leading) Question?

"How well is the Prime Minister managing monetary policy?"
1. Extremely well **2.** Very well **3.** Pretty well **4.** Well **5.** Not so well

This question has three elements that are designed to lead the respondent toward a favorable answer:

(1) The explicit inclusion of the word "well" in the main text of the question has the concealed intent of pulling the respondent toward a positive attitude. This is even more so if he or she is not aware of the event asked (see point 3).

(2) The range of options provided is not balanced, with all the choices referring to a different degree of positive attitude. Even the least favorable option rates the Prime Minister conduct of monetary policy as "not so well." A more balanced rating would include "Poor," "Very poor," and "Extremely poor."

(3) Finally there is no opt-out option (Don't Know). Because it is easier to influence the un-informed respondent, this is another way to lead him or her toward one of the "well" options reported.

Table 3.1

Reported Behavior Using Low and High Category Ranges

Hours	Percentage of Estimated TV Usage		
	True Distribution[a]	**Low Category**	**High Category**
up to 0.5	0	11.5	
0.5 to 1	19.2	26.9	
1 to 1.5	15.4	26.9	70.4
1.5 to 2	46.2	26.9	
2 to 2.5	0	7.7	
2.5 to 3	19.2		22.2
3 to 3.5	0	0	7.4
3.5 to 4	0		0
4.5 +	0		0
Mean	3.7	2.8	3.7

[a] Answers to an open-ended question.
Source: Schwarz and others 1985.

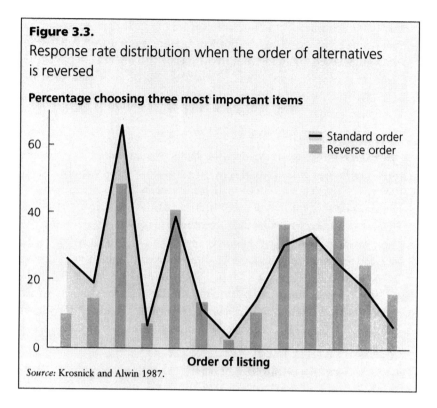

Figure 3.3.
Response rate distribution when the order of alternatives is reversed

Percentage choosing three most important items

Standard order
Reverse order

Order of listing

Source: Krosnick and Alwin 1987.

of answering closed questions rather than recalling specific information (Foddy 1993). Third, the actual list of options provided will influence the respondent. Options that appear at the beginning of a long list seem to have a higher likelihood of being selected, which is known as the primacy effect (figure 3.3). Research on the primacy effect appears to show that this phenomenon is inversely correlated with the respondents' level of education (Krosnick and Alwin 1987). Furthermore, the interview's mode also plays a critical role. When the list of options are read to the respondents, there is evidence that that respondents tend to favor the ones they hear last (known as the recency effect). Conversely, when the respondent reads the list himself or herself (that is, when using show cards), the primacy effect seems to dominate (Foddy 1993).

Another case of a nonobjective leading question occurs when some information is withheld from the respondent. This would be case of asking "Are you in favor of a new road that would reduce rush hour traffic by 50 percent?" without mentioning that the road would be financed with a new tax (Peterson 2000). Finally, leading questions might

Withholding information

generate the so-called "politeness or courtesy bias," when respondents, in their desire to be well-mannered toward the interviewer, might lean toward an answer that they think will please the interviewer (Plateck, Pierre-Pierre, and Stevens 1985).[6] This bias can be mitigated by using lead-in statements on both desirable and undesirable events, that is, "Many believe that . . . while others think that. . . . What is your opinion?" (Warwick and Lininger 1975).

Avoid loaded questions. Loaded questions bias answers through emotionally charged words, stereotypes, or prestige images such as "fair," "honest," "experienced," "colonialism," and so on. "Do you work?" is an example of a simple but emotionally charged question. Sometime this effect is more subtle. To describe the same phenomenon—for example, government help—the words "welfare" or "subsidy" are used if we refer to something we oppose, but the word "incentives" is used if we refer to something we favor (Browne and Keeley 2001). The "question designer must be continually on the alert for options which either flatter the respondent's self image or injure his pride" (Warwick and Lininger 1975, 144), because these options are a clever way to push the respondent in the desired direction.

Be wary of built-in assumptions. Generally speaking, questions should not take for granted that the respondent has familiarity with or carries out the activity asked in the question (Moser and Kalton 1971). The need for this awareness is even greater if the question refers to specific issues such as immigration laws or trade policy. Such questions could embarrass or annoy respondents who might claim knowledge they don't have so that they do not look ignorant or the respondents might refuse to continue with the interview (Plateck, Pierre-Pierre, and Stevens 1985). In these cases, filters should be used.

In fairness to some practitioners, it must be said that there are exceptional cases in which *not* using leading or loaded questions would bias the results. When you ask people whether they engage in certain disapproved practices (that is, paying bribes), they tend to lie and say no. However, if you provide more background information on the sensitive behavior[7] and then ask directly when, where, and how often

---

[6] This phenomenon is not limited to leading questions: it can very well occur with loaded questions.

[7] This to reduce the threatening nature of the question (see section on sensitive questions later in this chapter).

brides are paid, it is more likely that respondents will answer truthfully (Warwick and Lininger 1975).

Be Simple

The questionnaire designer should use language and terminology that exploits the simplest words and phrases. He or she should do the following:

Use words and expressions that are simple, direct, and familiar to all respondents. He or she must refrain from adopting "consider, initiate, purchase, or state," and use instead "think, start, buy, or say." He or she should not ask "Is it your opinion . . . ?" but simply "Do you think . . . ?" Similarly, the designer should refrain from employing slang expressions, because not everybody understands these expressions in the same way, if at all. It is not sufficient to ensure that all respondents understand the words used, it is necessary that they all understand the words in the same way (Moser and Kalton 1971). Take for instance the apparently simple and familiar expressions "majority" and "minority." What percentage value would you associate to these two commonly used expressions? Scipione (1995) asked this of a group of respondents and discovered that the average values associated with majority and minority were, respectively, 56.50 and 24.12 percent.[8]

Avoid technical jargons or concepts that are common only to those with specific and specialized training. The problem with technical terms, such as return on equity (ROE), discounted cash flow (DCF), and net present value (NPV), is determining whether the respondent understands the question or simply provides an answer in order not to appear ignorant. Furthermore, it is difficult to know whether the interpretation of the technical term is the same across respondents. Therefore, in these instances, if a technical term must be used and there is no simple correspondent concept, the technical term must be explained *before* the question is asked. Doing so may prevent the respondent from mentally framing the answer to the question based on his or her own interpretation of the technical term (Plateck, Pierre-Pierre, and Stevens 1985). After the respondent has framed the answer in his or her mind he or she will not listen to the definition provided afterward.

Adopt the same definitions throughout the form. If respondents are to answer accurately, the same definitions should be applied consistently

---

[8] With a wide standard deviation of 18.55 and 20.63, respectively. More examples are provided in table 3.7.

across all respondents. This is the only way their answers can be aggregated and compared not only within a country but also across regions. Although most practitioners agree with this predicament (that is, consistency in terminology), not all realize this also means avoiding the use of different terms with the same meaning. Unfortunately, we occasionally find that different definitions are used interchangeably to mean the same thing, such as when the same unit of investigation (the establishment) in a business survey is referred to as establishment, plant, factory, company, mother-company, firm, enterprise, or outlet (see example 3.3).[9]

If different terms are meant to indicate the same thing, then the questionnaire designer should use one term consistently throughout the whole document. Failure to do so will inevitably generate confusion in the respondents. If different terms do have different meanings, then all the definitions must be clearly explained in the questionnaire. This avoids possible confusion among respondents and ensures that the respondent answers questions on the basis of a consistent definition. Failing to take this into account in the questionnaire design is a major source of error (Fowler 1995).

When definitions are complex, it can become difficult to communicate a common definition to all respondents. In this case, it may be preferable to divide the single complex definition into a series of simple components. Hence, when asking for the geographic distribution of exports, it might be easier, and more accurate, for respondents to indicate the specific country of destination rather than the region (see example 3.4).

This approach has a number of benefits. First, it makes the question unambiguous because it is not necessary to communicate a common complex definition. Second, it makes the respondent's task easier because he or she does not have to add up or use the assigned definition to give an answer. Finally, this approach will provide the researcher with user-friendly data.

Avoid negative or double negative expressions. Double negatives not only generate cognitive complexity but also lead the respondent toward one answer. Suppose we ask a respondent whether he or she agrees or not with the following statement: "I am not satisfied with my job."

---

[9] Others examples of different terms used with the same meaning are (1) product, main product, main product line, most important activity, leading product, main line; (2) workforce, employees, workers; and (3) loan, term loan, line of credit, overdraft.

Example 3.3

To Whom Are We Talking?

Q 87 We have heard that **establishments** are sometimes required to make gifts or informal payments to public officials to "get things done" with regard to customs, taxes, licenses, regulations, services, etc . . .
Would you say this is true:

Always	1
Mostly	2
Frequently	3
Sometimes	4
Seldom	5
Never	6
Refuse	99
NA	100

Q 88 On average, what percent of annual sales value would such informal expenses cost to a typical **firm** like yours?
_____%

Q 89 Recognizing the difficulties many **enterprises** face in fully complying with taxes and regulations, what % of total sales would you estimate the typical establishment in your area of activity reports for tax purposes?
_____%

Q 90 Has your **company** been inspected or by or required to attend meetings with officials of national government, provincial, or municipal authority agencies during last 12 months?

Yes	1 Go to Q90b
No	2 Skip to Q91

This real case example shows how four different terms referring to the same unit of investigation (the establishment) are used interchangeably in four consecutive questions.

Note: Words in bold italic type emphasized here only; not on survey form.

Disagreeing with this statement of not been satisfied is a complex way of saying that he or she is satisfied (Fowler 1995). Similarly if we ask "You are going to do X, aren't you?" we imply the expectation of a yes answer. Conversely, if we ask "Aren't you going to do X?" we imply the expectation of a no answer (Foddy 1993). Experiments show that affirmative questions that are equivalent to superfluous negative questions take less time to answer (−7 percent) and prompt fewer requests for repetition or clarifications (−6 percent) (figure 3.4).

Simplicity is achieved when the level of cognitive effort the respondent is called on to perform in answering the question is minimized. This is not to say that difficult questions cannot be asked. Answers to

---

Example 3.4

Is Hong Kong Part of China?

X9. Please provide information on the percentage distribution of your plant's exports by destination regions:

Regions of export	Percent of annual exports of *your plant* per year		Which year did *your plant* export to this region for the first time?
	2001	2000	Year
a. West Europe	_____ %	_____ %	_____
b. East Europe	_____ %	_____ %	_____
c. North America (USA & Canada)	_____ %	_____ %	_____
d. Russia & Former Soviet Union countries	_____ %	_____ %	_____
e. China	_____ %	_____ %	_____
f. Rest of Asia (excluding China)	_____ %	_____ %	_____
g. Others specify	_____ %	_____ %	_____
TOTAL	100%	100%	

This example shows how difficult it is for the respondent to answer the question in the way presented. Exports to Hong Kong should be included in "China" or in "Rest of Asia"? Unclear definitions generate inaccurate answers.

---

complex questions can be obtained from surveys, but their accuracy will depend on the ability of the designer to match the level of cognitive complexity of the question with the respondent's level of cognitive ability.

Be Specific

Being specific means asking precise questions. Vague queries will generate vague answers or, as is often the case in business surveys, will generate a sense of frustration in the respondent and lead to a perception that the study is not legitimate. Elite respondents do not like oversimplification of complex issues and when this happens they tend to ask detailed questions putting the interviewer in a difficult or embarrassing position (Zuckerman 1972).

Indefinite words

The questionnaire designer should avoid items that are too general, too complex, or too ambiguous. Indefinite words used in everyday con-

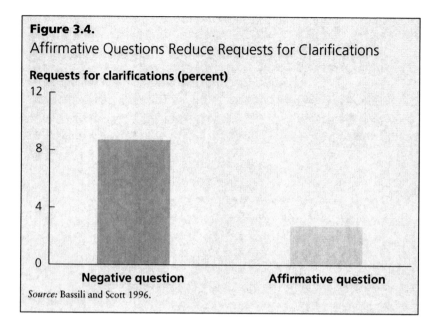

Figure 3.4.

Affirmative Questions Reduce Requests for Clarifications

Requests for clarifications (percent)

Source: Bassili and Scott 1996.

versation such as *often, occasionally, usually, regularly, generally, rarely, normally* or *good, bad, approve, disapprove, agree, disagree, like, dislike* should also be avoided because they lack an appropriate objective dimension. For one person *often* may mean once a day, for another once a year (Warwick and Lininger 1975). The more general the question the wider the range of interpretations it invites (Converse and Presser 1986). If you ask "What kind of car do you have?" you should not be surprised to hear "a foreign car," or "a four-wheel-drive car," or "a sports car," or even "a very nice car."

Particular attention should be placed on the usage of words that imply great specificity, such as *ever, always,* and *never.* The meaning of these words extends the time horizon of the questions to the utmost limit and thus might render meaningless any answer because of its (almost) complete invariance. It might be legitimate to use these expressions when the phenomenon is rare or when respondents tend to answer randomly or untruthfully (Peterson 2000).

Abbreviations should equally be avoided. Using MNC[10] can cause confusion for the respondents who might assume a different meaning

Abbreviations

[10] Instead of Multi-National Corporations or Manila National Company.

Example 3.5
Are You from New Delhi or from India?

III.4 Do you expect to make a substantial increase in investment in order to increase capacity or improve quality?
  code: Yes=1; No=2; Firm is closing=3

  In 2003
  In 2003–2005

In this example the question includes two options not mutually exclusive. Hence if one respondent intends to invest in 2003 and in 2004 while another intends to invest only in 2003, they will both answer YES to both questions and we will not be able to discriminate among them.

---

than intended by the interviewer. The use of abbreviations may also generate confusion for the interviewers, especially when interpersonal relations are tense. Abbreviations should be spelled out clearly unless they are common to all respondents or have already been defined in the questionnaire (Plateck, Pierre-Pierre, and Stevens 1985).

Answer alternatives

In closed-ended questions, the selection of answer alternatives, in itself, could become a source of confusion for the respondent unless they are mutually exclusive and collectively exhaustive (Peterson 2000). This apparently simple requirement is sometimes overlooked (example 3.5) and it is occasionally hard to fulfill. In some instances, in fact, the set of possible alternatives is too broad and their "neutral" classification in groups hard to determine.[11]

Double-barreled questions

Another typical example of ambiguity is generated by double-barreled questions, that is, questions covering two or more issues at once. These questions cause uncertainty and confusion, particularly when both parts of the question apply to the respondent in different ways, and they usually require additional explanations (figure 3.5) As a consequence, they must be avoided. These type of questions should be divided into two questions or the choices provided for answering should cover all possible answer combinations.

Ability to answer

Finally, in evaluating the appropriate level of specificity to apply in a question, the designer should not ignore the ability of the respondent to answer. While it is important to ask specific questions, it is

---

[11] In this case, one possible solution is to adopt an open-ended question.

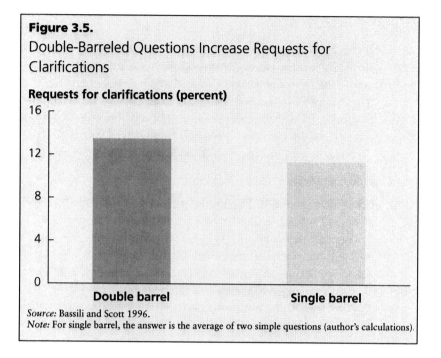

Figure 3.5.
Double-Barreled Questions Increase Requests for Clarifications

Requests for clarifications (percent)

Source: Bassili and Scott 1996.
Note: For single barrel, the answer is the average of two simple questions (author's calculations).

equally essential to give the respondent an answer task that he or she can perform (Fowler 1995), as in example 3.6. It is very likely that the respondent knows the village where he or she sells his or her products, but at the same time, he or she might have no idea of its current population.

Example 3.6
Can You Tell Me How Many People Live in Pisa?

Sales and Supplies
13. a) What percent of your establishment's sales are:
   i) sold domestically
      a) to towns with 50,000 inhabitants or more   ____%
      b) to towns with < 50,000 inhabitants   ____%
   ii) exported directly   ____%
   iii) exported indirectly (through a distributor)   ____%
                                            TOTAL = 100%

Question Style

Unless respondents clearly understand a question, they will not be able to provide meaningful answers (Peterson 2000). Hence two fundamental concerns must be in the designer's mind when developing any question: will respondents be able to *understand* the question and will they be able to *answer* it? A well-understood question will not only increase the accuracy of the answers, but also their frequency. Two characteristics have a direct impact on these abilities: legibility and relevance.

Use Legible Questions

Ask questions that read well. This implies that conditional clauses, qualifications, and all other less important information must come ahead of the key content of the question. This placement prevents the respondent from jumping to an answer before the full question has been laid out. Likewise, punctuation should loosely follow proper grammatical rules and be more tailored to the flow of ideas stemming from the question. Thus, clarity is more important that grammatical correctness. This allows the interviewer to pause at the right time and place during the questioning. Similarly, words that need to be emphasized during the interview must be properly identified in the questionnaire and interviewers must be trained to recognize the identifiers. Finally, all words should be spelled out (Warwick and Lininger 1975).

Questions should not be formulated in a complex structure. Questions organized in a table format may appear well designed, and they give the impression of being easy to answer. However, they are extremely difficult to administer in a face-to-face interview and they put a big burden on the respondent's memory.

Similarly, the longer the list of questions the lower the quality of the data. "It is possible that respondents and/or interviewers recognize the 'production line' character of this survey strategy and that this promotes carelessness in the way questions are asked and answered" (Andrews 1984, 431).[12] Two types of errors can result from this behavior: acquiescence bias and position bias.

Acquiescence bias   Acquiescence bias is the tendency of respondents to choose a certain response category regardless of the item's content. For example, in questions with "agree-disagree," "yes-no," "0–5," and so on, respondents continually check "agree," "yes," or "2" even when the content of the

---

[12] Further experimental evidence has shown that these types of questions generate a higher tendency for the interviewer to misread them (Presser and Zhao 1992).

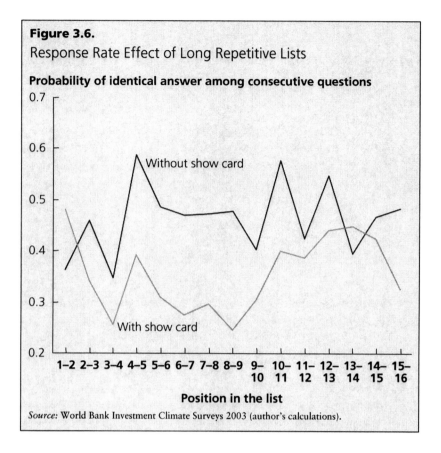

Figure 3.6.

Response Rate Effect of Long Repetitive Lists

Probability of identical answer among consecutive questions

Source: World Bank Investment Climate Surveys 2003 (author's calculations).

question is reversed. This is particularly true when a long sequence of questions in exactly the same order[13] is asked. This approach infringes conventional conversational norms and can easily become boring and irritating, pushing the respondent to answer mechanically without thinking carefully about the individual alternatives (Plateck, Pierre-Pierre, and Stevens 1985). When repetitive questions need to be asked, data accuracy can be improved by using show cards. Figure 3.6 illustrates how the adoption of show cards reduces the probability of obtaining the same answer (answering mechanically) among consecutive questions. When show cards are not used, evidence shows that consecutive questions are answered more mechanically (the probability of obtaining the same answer is higher). This effect appears to pick up when the list contains

---

[13] For example, questions like (1) How big of a problem is Telecommunication? (2) How big of a problem is Electricity? (3) How big of a problem is Transportation?

more than four repetitive questions. Using show cards instead helps eliminate this "contagion" effect, although only up to a point: when the list reaches 10 items the same "mechanical" effect reappears.[14]

One proposed solution to this bias is to give specific content to each response option. So instead of asking, "Do you agree or disagree that your current company is efficient in delivering packages?" you might want to ask, "Do you think that your current company is efficient or inefficient in delivering packages?" (Moser and Kalton 1971; Warwick and Lininger 1975). Yet a different possible strategy is to have two forms of the questionnaire in which the order of the alternatives is reversed or to have as many forms as the possible combinations of alternatives (Warwick and Lininger 1975).[15]

Position bias

In other cases, when the respondent is asked to select from a list of alternative answers, their choice may be affected by the order in which the alternatives are presented rather than true relevance to the respondent. When a set of alternatives is ordered, such as a set of numerical variables, respondents may consistently lean toward the middle, right, or left irrespective of the meaning of the order. Experiments have shown that the alternatives presented at the beginning or at the end are favored (Moser and Kalton 1971; see also figure 3.3). This phenomenon is more likely to occur when the list of alternatives is long, so the best solution is to use a short list of alternatives (no more than eight) or to elicit a response from each individual alternative. If it is not possible to reduce the list of alternatives, another useful approach is the filter-unfolding method. With this technique, major categories are first presented to the respondent. Then on the basis of his or her choice, a set of more specific alternatives are shown or the interviewer moves on to the next major category (example 3.7). This method optimizes the use of time by focusing only on the choices perceived by the respondent as most relevant. A less efficient solution is to use separate versions of the questionnaire, allowing each alternative to appear in a given position with equal frequency or use different show cards in which the order of the alternatives is different to make its position neutral.[16]

---

[14] This figure is based on question 18 of the Investment Climate Surveys' core questionnaire (see appendix 1 for exact wording of the question). Data refer to pooled answers from Bangladesh2002, Brazil2003, Cambodia2003, China2002, Ethiopia2002, Honduras2003, India2002, Kenya2003, Nicaragua2003, Nigeria2001, Pakistan2002, Peru2002, Philippines2002, Tanzania2003, and Uganda2003.

[15] Avoid, however, using different orders within the same form. This could be misleading for the interviewer and the respondent.

[16] The last two alternatives carry a higher risk of error during data entering and coding.

Example 3.7
Filter-Unfolding Method

In this example, instead of asking questions d(1)–d(7), the interviewer first asks question d and only if the response is a 3 or 4 are options d(1)–(7) asked. Question d works as a filter for the more detailed questions d(1)–(7). This approach saves time and maintains focus during the interview.

V.2. Please tell us if any of the following issues are a problem for the operation and growth of your business. If an issue poses a problem, please judge its severity as an obstacle on a four-point scale where:

0 = No obstacle   1 = Minor obstacle   2 = Moderate obstacle   3 = Major obstacle   4 = Very severe obstacle

	No Problem	Degree of Obstacle			
a. Telecommunications	0	1	2	3	4
b. Electricity	0	1	2	3	4
c. Transportation	0	1	2	3	4
d. Access to land for expansion/relocation	0	1	2	3	4
1) Procurement process	0	1	2	3	4
2) Cost of land	0	1	2	3	4
3) Availability of infrastructure	0	1	2	3	4
4) Disputed ownership	0	1	2	3	4
5) Small size of land ownership	0	1	2	3	4
6) Government ownership of land	0	1	2	3	4
7) Others (please specify _____)	0	1	2	3	4
e. Tax rates	0	1	2	3	4
f. Tax administration	0	1	2	3	4
g. Customs and trade regulations	0	1	2	3	4
h. Labor regulations	0	1	2	3	4
1) Minimum wages	0	1	2	3	4
2) Mandatory non-salary benefits	0	1	2	3	4
3) Restrictions on employment of local staff	0	1	2	3	4
4) Visa/work permit for foreign staff	0	1	2	3	4
5) Hiring and firing regulations	0	1	2	3	4
6) Labor dispute settlement	0	1	2	3	4
7) Others (please specify _____)	0	1	2	3	4
i. Skills and education of available workers	0	1	2	3	4
j. Business licensing and operating permits	0	1	2	3	4
1) Constructing operational facilities	0	1	2	3	4
2) Fire department	0	1	2	3	4
3) Environmental clearance	0	1	2	3	4
4) Intellectual property, trademark registration	0	1	2	3	4
5) Company registration	0	1	2	3	4
6) Others (please specify _____)	0	1	2	3	4

Example 3.7 (continued)

k. Access to financing (e.g., collateral)	0	1	2	3	4
l. Cost of financing (e.g., interest rates)	0	1	2	3	4
m. Economic policy uncertainty	0	1	2	3	4
n. Macroeconomic instability (inflation, exchange rate)	0	1	2	3	4
o. Corruption	0	1	2	3	4
p. Crime, theft and disorder	0	1	2	3	4
q. Anticompetitive practices	0	1	2	3	4

Source: Author's creation.

Use Relevant Questions

Ask questions applicable to all respondents. Few things are more irritating than to be asked a question that is not applicable like "where did you complete your doctorate?" or "how many children do you have?" This is even more frustrating when elites are interviewed. As a matter of fact, while ordinary respondents are more willing to discuss issues about which they have little information, elites are quickly irritated if the topic of the questions is not of interest to them (Zuckerman 1972). Inapplicable questions are not only irritating but also potentially misleading. The individual who is not a parent may still give a positive answer to save embarrassment or simply to oblige the interviewer (known as false positives) (Warwick and Lininger 1975). One solution is to add proper lead-in questions and devise various skip patterns, filters, or conditional questions.

Hypothetical questions

Hypothetical questions, especially, should be avoided. People cannot reliably forecast their future behavior in a hypothetical scenario. Thus, the questionnaire designer should make careful use of this style of questioning. First, it is advisable to ask a question related to a hypothetical situation *only* of those who have already experienced the phenomenon in the past. For example, ask "Would you like to live in an apartment or in a house?" only of those who have lived in both. Otherwise you run the risk of picking up the answers of those who would like to try new things. Second, the designer should be wary of asking hypothetical questions in which the answer is obvious, such as "Would you like a reduction of metro fares?" In this case, answers are biased because the respondent is asked to get something for nothing (Moser and Kalton 1971).[17]

---

[17] Or, put differently, the question is not objective.

Use Painless Questions

Finally, the question asked should require the least possible effort to be answered. As the level of cognitive complexity of the question increases, the respondent is more likely to reply "I don't know" or, worse, inaccurately. If the researcher suspects that the respondent might not be candid in his or her answer, the researcher should not ask the question in the traditional way but rather adopt alternative strategies to elicit a truthful answer (Peterson 2000).

Question Type

Avoid Sensitive Questions

A sensitive question refers to a behavior that, when answered truthfully, is judged by society as undesirable or illegal, or when the question itself is perceived by the respondent as an invasion of privacy. Sensitive questions should be avoided. Two types of respondent's behavior can threaten the accuracy of answers to sensitive questions: nonresponse and response error. Respondents might refuse to answer sensitive questions, thus biasing the results because "the very persons with the most sensitive information to report may be the least likely to report it" (Tourangeau and Smith 1996, 276). Likewise, research on response accuracy has shown that respondents are prone to distort answers in ways that will make them look better (known as *social desirability bias*). Responses on illegal or immoral behavior, such as corruption, are consistently underreported not because respondents have forgotten them but rather because the behavior does not conform to social norms (Fowler 1995).

When compared internationally, sensitive questions are subject to another often overlooked source of potential measurement error associated with the type of survey firm conducting the interviews. The survey literature clearly identifies the interviewer's sponsoring agency as a potential source of measurement bias. Moreover, research has demonstrated that sensitive questions are answered more or less candidly depending on the person conducting the interviews. Evidence from the Investment Climate Surveys not only confirms this, but also it allows the estimation of such bias. The type of agency conducting the fieldwork—government agency, a private local survey company, or a private international survey firm— has a different effect on data accuracy depending on the sensitivity of question asked. Sensitive questions on corruption and taxation show a

Survey firm bias

different pattern than questions on red tape. Not surprisingly, when the interviewer is a government employee, sensitive questions on bribes and sales are consistently underreported.[18] Although the magnitude of the bias varies depending on the specific question, the impact of underreporting appears to be up to 60 percent of one standard deviation (table 3.2). This phenomenon is present also with questions on the perception of corruption.[19] Hence, respondents interviewed by a government employee are 13 percent less likely to rate corruption as a major concern (figure 3.7). On the contrary, when the same objective sensitive questions are asked by an international survey firm, no underreporting effect appears in the data. Again only the perception question on corruption shows the same magnitude of underreporting (11%).

When questions on red tape are asked, however, whether the survey firm is a government agency or an international company, a similar pattern of under- or overreporting appears in the answers. Such a bias seems even higher for the latter than for the former (table 3.2).

When designing and analyzing survey data, it is important to keep in mind that people may vary in what they consider sensitive. Questions on apparently nonsensitive issues, such as questions on infrastructure, are subject to the same measurement bias discussed above. When the interview is conducted by a government employee, respondents tend to underreport such constraints, although the impact is most of the time relatively small (table 3.2).

Strategies to minimize bias

When sensitive questions are asked, two major forces operate to produce a distortion in the reported answer: the desire to avoid responses that could pose a threat and the tendency of respondents not too look bad (Fowler 1995). A number of different steps can be taken to minimize these forces. First, the level of detail of the question can be tailored to address sensitivity concerns. It might be easier for respondents to provide answers in categories or percentages rather than in absolute values. When following this approach, however, the questionnaire designer should be aware of the fact that changing the format of the question has an impact not only on response rate but also on response accuracy. Peterson and Kerin (1980) have shown that while the refusal rate for an open-ended question on income was higher (8%) than that

---

[18] Compared with a private local survey company.

[19] See appendix 2 for exact wording of objective questions and appendix 3 presents the parametric results. Appendix 1 reports the perception questions. All questions are from the "core" questionnaire of the World Bank Investment Climate Surveys.

Table 3.2

Interviews Conducted by Government Agencies and International Private Firms Affect Survey Responses

	Government Agency		International Private Firm	
	Coefficient	Effect on Standard Deviation	Coefficient	Effect on Standard Deviation
CORRUPTION				
Unofficial payments to get things done (% sales)	−1.854**	−0.33	ns	−0.43
Gifts expected as % value government contracts	−1.974**	−0.41	ns	0.26
Estimated % of total sales declared for tax purposes	−17.854**	−0.60	ns	−0.34
RED TAPE				
% of management's time dealing with gov't officials	−0.709*	−0.05	−6.256**	−0.43
Total days spent with officials from tax inspectorate	2.307**	0.13	4.803**	0.26
Days on average to claim imports from customs	ns		−4.150**	−0.34
Days on average to clear customs for exports	1.815**	0.22	ns	
Optimal level of employment (% of current level)	2.769**	0.06	30.147**	0.64
INFRASTRUCTURE				
Days of power outages from public grid	−31.998**	−0.49	−16.366**	−0.25
Days of insufficient water supply	−2.673**	−0.05	ns	
Days of unavailable mainline telephone service	−3.69**	−0.12	ns	
% of sales lost because of power outages	−0.229*	−0.03	ns	
% of sales lost because of insufficient water supply	0.653**	0.08	ns	
% of sales lost because of unavailable telephone service	−0.844**	−0.15	ns	
% of average cargo value lost in transit	−0.176*	−0.04	−1.629**	−0.33

Source: World Bank Investment Climate Surveys 2003. (Author's calculations.)

Note: See appendix 2 and 3 for description of questions and a compete set of regression results. Results are in comparison with private local survey company.

ns = Not significant.

* Significant at 5%.

** Significant at 1%.

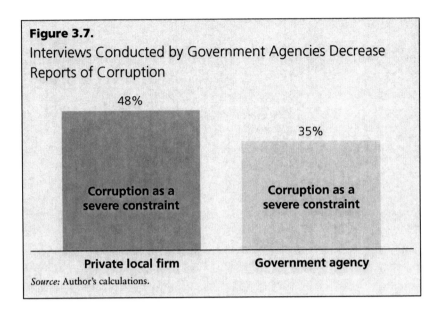

Figure 3.7.

Interviews Conducted by Government Agencies Decrease Reports of Corruption

48%

35%

Corruption as a severe constraint

Corruption as a severe constraint

Private local firm   **Government agency**

Source: Author's calculations.

on a closed-ended question (2%) the quality of the answers to narrative questions was higher (table 3.3).

Second, as mentioned earlier, the length of the question itself can also mitigate the threatening nature of the topic. Longer questions seem to have a positive impact on the accuracy of sensitive questions on behavior, while the opposite appears true for attitudinal questions (Sudnam

Table 3.3

Accuracy is Higher for Open-Ended Questions

	Percent of Respondents	
	Open-Ended Question	Closed-Ended Question
Overreported	26.7	29.7
Accurate	47.4	43.8
Underreported	25.9	26.5
Actual-reported correlation coefficient[a]	0.93	0.70

Source: Peterson and Kerin 1980.
a. Using midpoint of range category.

and Bradburn 1974). A similar approach is to moderate the extent to which respondents feel that their answers will be used to put them in a negative light. With this strategy, the question is asked in a way to explain to the respondent that there are various reasons why people behave in one way or the other so that he or she feels more relaxed in providing an unbiased answer to the sensitive topic. In other cases, it might be appropriate to ensure the confidentiality of responses and communicate effectively that protection measures are in place. This implies that no association between respondents and answers should be apparent during the interview, that sensitive questions should be asked only when the respondent is alone with the interviewer, and that, if they exist, specific laws protecting the confidentiality of answers should be mentioned and clearly stated in the questionnaire. Explaining the appropriateness of the question to the research objectives of the survey is yet another way to reduce resistance in respondents (Fowler 1995). Sometime respondents consider a question sensitive because they don't see the link between the goal of the survey and the question itself, or they don't see the usefulness of their answer. Likewise there are instances in which it is advisable to use words that imply the same sensitive behavior by others. Finally, another possible way of dealing with sensitive questions is to put the threatening topic in a list of less threatening topics or to use a randomized response technique (Plateck, Pierre-Pierre, and Stevens 1985).[20]

In business surveys, the inclination not to disclose information considered critical to the business activity should be taken into account when developing a survey instrument. Questions on taxes, profits, and names of suppliers or clients could be the subject of distorted answers or outright refusal. Conversely, questions on bribes are generally answered, unless the admission of this behavior is in itself condition for criminal prosecution. This was the case in Ethiopia where, although it was not possible to ask the amount of bribes paid by entrepreneurs, because this would have guaranteed jail time, 60 percent of the respondents were still willing to discuss how big of a problem corruption was. The pre-test is critical in detecting the respondent's reaction to a delicate question.

---

[20] With this technique, the respondent chooses to answer either the sensitive question or a nonsensitive question. The process of choosing uses a random mechanism. The interviewer is not aware whether the respondent is answering the sensitive question or the nonsensitive statement. In this way, we expect the respondent to be more truthful. At the same time, the probability of selection of each statement must be known so that it is possible to calculate the aggregate value of the sensitive question as a weighted average of the probability of selection of each statement (See Moser and Kalton 1971, 328).

Memory Questions

Retrospective questions are those questions drawing on long-term memory. Although past events are not really forgotten, their recall might be very memory intensive and therefore incorrectly reported. How many of us can remember the exact number of days we were sick two years ago? Or how many classmates we had the first year of high school? Recall questions should hence be avoided.

Because "little is known about how time-related information is mentally encoded, stored, and retrieved [and] the effect of mood or motives on memory" (Peterson 2000, 93) retrospective questions are subject to "recall bias." Survey research has identified three types of memory errors: respondents might forget the recalled events (omission), might recall events that did not occur (commission), or might correctly report events but place them at the wrong time (telescoping) (Gaskell, Wright, and O'Muircheartaigh 2000).[21]

Recurring event   Behavioral frequency questions such as "How many times last year did you visit a doctor?" are a common occurrence in many surveys. Because frequency questions rely heavily on the respondent's mnemonic ability, they require a deep understanding of the cognitive process behind it. Questions that ask respondents to recall events in the past are an increasing source of error the farther back in time the event is located and the less important the event was in the respondent's life. Research shows that recall errors are associated with the interview mode and that there is always a trade-off between the accuracy of the event reported and the length of time of the event recalled (Fowler 1995). As one would expect, self-administered questionnaires appear more vulnerable to these errors than face-to-face interviews (figure 3.8) (Sudnam and Bradburn 1974).

How far back in time can a question go without seriously compromising the accuracy of the data collected? This depends on three factors: the *saliency of the event, its frequency, and how the question is designed*. More relevant events will be recalled more accurately. Unfortunately, the reality is that "contrary to what many researchers [. . .] might think (or desire!) much of what is investigated is not significant to study participants. Thus, the container size of toothpaste used in

---

[21] Telescoping can be "backward" if the event is reported to happen before it actually did, or "forward" if the event is reported to happen after it actually did. Telescoping occurs when the memory of the past event is so detailed that the respondent mistakenly blends recency with clarity (Bradburn, Rips, and Shevell 1987).

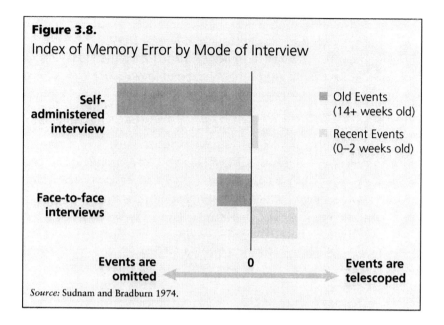

Figure 3.8.

Index of Memory Error by Mode of Interview

- Old Events (14+ weeks old)
- Recent Events (0–2 weeks old)

Self-administered interview

Face-to-face interviews

Events are omitted ← → Events are telescoped

0

Source: Sudnam and Bradburn 1974.

1991 is probably long forgotten" (Peterson 2000, 20). Three factors influence the saliency of the event: the emotion generated by the event, the marking of a turning point, and its financial impact on the respondent's life (Auriat 1993).

In addition to saliency, another factor influencing the cognitive abilities of the respondent is the frequency of the event to be recalled. Respondents use different protocols to answer frequency questions: episode enumeration, rule-based estimation, availability estimation, automatic estimation, and various combinations of these protocols.[22] In deciding which protocol to use, respondents balance the level of accuracy they feel must be achieved with the level of effort required by the cognitive process itself. Empirical evidence shows that the accuracy of recall can be improved if episode enumeration is adopted. However, respondents will use episode enumeration only if there are not too many events to recall (Burton and Blair 1991). Because more distant events are harder

---

[22] Episode enumeration implies recalling and counting the occurrences of the event; rule-based estimation involves the use of some sort of rule, such as decomposing the time period in shorter time periods or in subdomains; availability estimation involves estimation on the basis of the ease of recalling; and automatic estimation involves resorting to some sort of innate or normative sense of frequency (for example, once a week).

to locate and to retrieve, the longer the time frame, the fewer respondents will adopt episode enumeration (Blair and Burton 1987).

While the questionnaire designer cannot change the frequency of the event, he or she can adjust the wording of the question to facilitate the use of episode enumeration. The National Crime Survey and the National Health Survey improved the accuracy of data by asking about six-month reporting instead of one year (Fowler 1995). But what time period would most likely promote the adoption of episode enumeration? Blair and Burton (1987) show that respondents are less inclined to use episode enumeration if the event happens more than 10 times during the reference period (table 3.4). Consistent with this result, Burton and Blair (1991) show that when holding the time reference constant an increase in the number of events within that period appears to be associated with a decrease in the accuracy of responses (table 3.5). This demonstrates that it is not time reference

---

Table 3.4

As Frequency of Event Decreases, Use of Episode Enumeration Increases

	Percentage of Respondents Using	
	Episode Enumeration	Other Enumeration
Frequency of event		
1	100	0
2	68	32
3	93	7
4–5	63	37
6–10	15	85
11–25	0	100
26–100	0	100
100+	0	100
Time frame		
2 weeks	56	44
2 months	25	75
6 months	4	96

Source: Blair and Burton 1991.

Table 3.5
Higher Event Frequency Has a Negative Effect on Accuracy

	Number of Events Reported[c]	Correlation Between Reported and Recorded Data
Checks[a]	16.3	34%
ATM[b]	4.2	67%

Source: Burton and Blair 1991.
a. Number of checks written.
b. Number of ATM withdrawals.
c. Average value over a 3-week period.

that increases accuracy but rather the number of events to be recalled. Thus, the time referenced in the question should cover approximately 10 episodes of the event to be recalled. For example, if there are five power outages every week, the question should ask how many power outages have there been in two weeks.

The wording of the question has also an impact on the ease of recall. One way to stimulate recall is to ask a long, rather than short question. This means adding an introduction that helps the respondent to put his or her state of mind in the time period of the event recalled. A second approach is to ask multiple questions or to ask questions that trigger associations with the event recalled (called a landmark). These methodologies have been proven to facilitate recall because the respondent is asked to dig into his or her memory (Fowler 1995). Furthermore, it has been shown that communicating to respondents the importance of the accuracy of their answer has a positive effect. Thus, using specific phrases like "please take your time to answer this question," or "the accuracy of this question is particularly important," or "please take at least 30 seconds to think about this question before answering" has a positive impact on the accuracy of responses (table 3.6) (Burton and Blair 1991). Similarly, asking "how often" as opposed to "how many times" might discourage episode enumeration in favor of rule-based estimation (Blair and Burton 1987). Finally, if the recall question asks the respondent to provide a list, it is desirable to provide him or her with a comprehensive and mutually exclusive list of events (Moser and Kalton 1971).

Table 3.6

Response Time and Episode Enumeration Have a
Positive Effect on Accuracy

Time Given	Correlation Between Reported and Recorded Data	No. of Respondents Using Episode Enumeration
10–20 seconds	0.58	60%
35–50 seconds	0.81	80%
70 seconds	0.86	84%
unspecified	0.46	

Source: Burton and Blair 1991.

Unique event   While the questionnaire designer can, to some extent, improve the accuracy of the recall through a careful question design, there are cases in which his or her ability is severely limited. This happens when the past event to be recalled is unique, such as "How many employees did you have when you started your business?" In this case, the questionnaire designer cannot adjust the time reference of the question to facilitate recall nor can episode enumeration be encouraged. In this case, accuracy rests solely on the recall ability of the respondent. Saliency remains the only critical factor to which the designer must appeal. A number of experiments have attempted to determine the accuracy of such a recall. A first experiment shows that between 10 and 20 percent of details are irretrievable after only one year, and as much as 60 percent can be lost after four years. In any case, even salient events are very hard to access and retrieve after 10 years (figure 3.9) (Sudnam, Bradburn, and Schwarz 1996). Even higher nonresponse rates were reported in a study carried out by the U.S. National Center for Health Statistics. That study shows the percentage of underreporting errors is more than 40 percent after just one year (figure 3.10)

Subjective (or Objective) Questions

"Subjective phenomena are those that, in principle, can be directly known, if at all, only by the persons themselves. [. . .] Objective phenomena are those that can be known by evidence that is, in principle, directly accessible to an external observer" (Duncan, Fishhoff, and

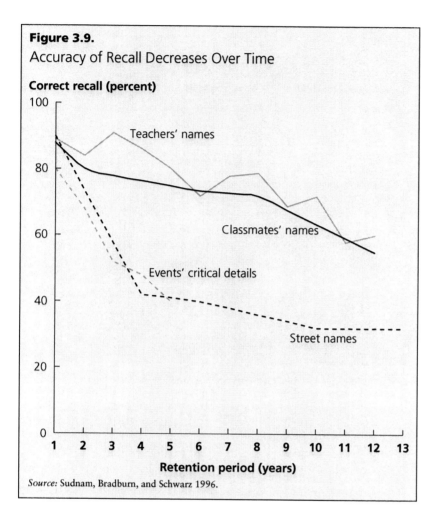

Figure 3.9.
Accuracy of Recall Decreases Over Time

Correct recall (percent)

Teachers' names

Classmates' names

Events' critical details

Street names

Retention period (years)

Source: Sudnam, Bradburn, and Schwarz 1996.

Turner 1984, vol. 1, 8). Subjective questions are questions tailored to measure people's subjective states (that is, their opinions, knowledge, feelings, and perceptions).[23]

One of the most popular ways of asking a subjective question is to use rating scales, that is, a single, well-defined continuum in which the answer is expected to be placed (see example 3.8) When employing this type of questions two issues must be addressed: how many scale

Rating scales

---

[23] That is why they are often referred to as perception or opinion questions.

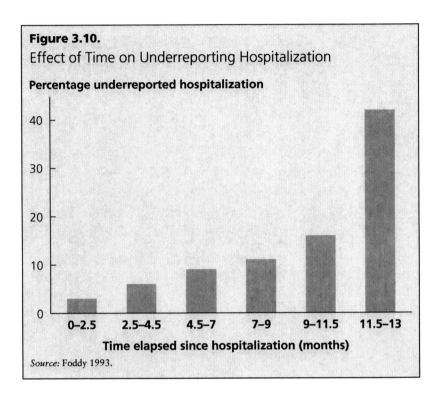

Figure 3.10.
Effect of Time on Underreporting Hospitalization

Percentage underreported hospitalization

Time elapsed since hospitalization (months)

Source: Foddy 1993.

categories should be used, and what words or numbers should be associated with each scale category.

There is no consensus in the literature on the optimal number of categories to use. Using too few categories gives less-refined information while using too many categories makes the question very hard to administer (Fowler 1995). The choice of scale frequency must be guided

Example 3.8
Rating Scales in Subjective (or Perception) Questions

Q.42 To what extent do you agree with this statement? "I am confident that the legal system will uphold my contract and property rights in business disputes."

Strongly Disagree	Disagree in Most Cases	Tend to Disagree	Tend to Agree	Agree in Most Cases	Strongly Agree
1	2	3	4	5	6

Example 3.9

Do You Agree or Disagree with "The Government is Providing Good Services"?

A.

| _____ | _____ | | _____ | | _____ |

Strongly Agree   Neither Agree Nor Disagree   Strongly Disagree

B.

Strongly Agree   Neither Agree Nor Disagree   Strongly Disagree   No Knowledge or No opinion

---

by the mode of the interview, the respondent's ability to interpret the categories, and the research goal.[24] Although some scales adopt up to 12 categories, experiments show that it is preferable to use between 5 and 9 categories (Cox 1980; Finn 1972; Leigh and Martin 1987; Miller 1956). Related to this is the decision whether to adopt a middle category. Here again no one choice fits all. It is not clear whether the presence or exclusion of a midpoint improves data quality (Andrews 1984). The content and the analytical purpose of the question will determine the optimal choice. If a neutral answer is a possibility, a midpoint should be included. If the researcher wants the respondent to take one side or the other, an even number of categories can force the respondent away from the middle alternative (Peterson 2000). The researcher, however, should be extremely careful in the latter case. Forcing respondents to choose an alternative with which they are not familiar has little analytical value and introduces bias into the data.

More important, the questionnaire designer must ensure that the scale categories are sufficient to discriminate between and "indifferent" response and "no opinion" answers. As example 3.9 shows, allowing respondents to "opt out" if they lack the required information (option B) improves the quality of the data because it avoids the risk that respondents with no opinion on the subject might otherwise select the middle alternative.

---

[24] In telephone interviews and in self-administered surveys, it is advisable to adopt a lower number of categories. The same is true if we interview a child rather than an adult. If, on the other hand, there is reason to believe that respondents are homogeneous, a higher frequency of categories should be adopted (Peterson 2000).

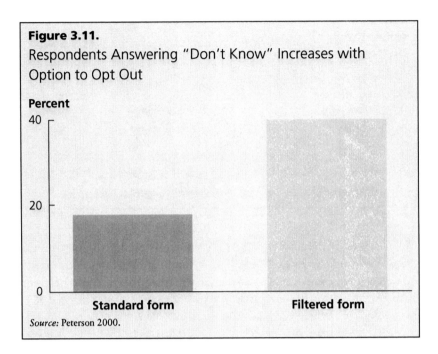

Figure 3.11.
Respondents Answering "Don't Know" Increases with
Option to Opt Out

Source: Peterson 2000.

An experiment conducted by Peterson (2000) demonstrated that more than 20 percent of respondents venture an answer although they would have chosen "don't know" if given the option (figure 3.11).

Once the optimal number of categories has been determined, there are numerous ways respondents can be asked to assign answers to a position on a continuum. Generally adjectives (that is, good, fair, poor) or numbers[25] (that is, 1, 2, 3) are used. The ongoing debate is whether to use one approach or the other, and whether to label all categories in the continuum or only some of them. What seems an apparently trivial task can have a substantial effect on the data collected. As a matter of fact, far from being "neutral measurement devices," the response categories offered are used by respondents to interpret the question and therefore can influence the answers. Thus, asking the same question but using an 11-point rating scale from 0 to 10 or from −5 to +5 can generate different results (figure 3.12).

---

[25] Peterson (2000) reports a number of different verbal stimuli most commonly used: comparison stimuli (much more . . . much less), endorsement stimuli (definitely true . . . definitely not true), frequency stimuli (always . . . never), influence stimuli (major problems . . . minor problems), and intensity stimuli (strongly agree . . . strongly disagree).

Figure 3.12.

Impact of Numeric Scales on Response Patterns

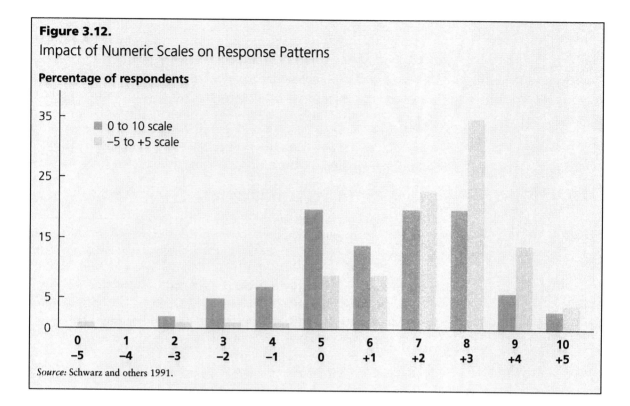

Source: Schwarz and others 1991.

Accordingly, Schwarz and others (1991) conclude that scales intended to measure bipolar concepts should use negative to positive values, while scales intended to measure the intensity (or absence of intensity) of a single attribute should use zero to positive values. In general, evidence shows that adjectives are better because they improve consistency of interpretation (Wildt and Mazis 1978), and because it might generate cognitive complexity in the respondent, it is not preferable to label all categories. It is preferable to label only the extreme values and the middle point (Andrews 1984).

Rank ordering

A second approach used by researchers in designing qualitative questions is the use of rank ordering. Respondents are asked to compare objects on some dimension. They are provided with a list of items and asked (1) to rank all of them from most to least important; (2) to identify the most (second, third) important; or (3) to rate each of the items using some scale. The first task is the easiest only if the list is short (four to five items). The second one is preferable if the list is long, but it becomes difficult if the list grows too long (more than 10 items). The third alternative is the easiest to perform and provides more information, but it is the most time-consuming (Fowler 1995).

Agree-disagree format

If the goal of a question is to measure respondents' feelings about policies or ideas, then the agree-disagree format is probably the best option. Respondents will agree or disagree if their opinion falls within a reasonable distance from the point where they see the statement's opinion is located. Sometimes this type of question is employed to spread the responses along a continuum, differing from the previous category in that the continuum is simply bipolar (Fowler 1995).[26] Attention should nonetheless be paid when developing this type of question. First, the designer must ensure that the contextual environment is appropriate for this format. Cognitive complexity is increased when we ask someone whether they agree or disagree with the statement "My health is good" instead of asking directly "How do you rate your health? Good, Fair, or Poor." Second, the designer must ensure that the wording of the question is unequivocal so that disagreeing can be interpreted unambiguously. If a person disagrees with "I am sometimes depressed," we don't know whether he or she is never depressed or always depressed. Finally, the designer must not overlook the tendency among less-educated respondents toward acquiescence, that is, to consistently answer "agree" even when they don't know whether they do or don't (Fowler 1995).

The questionnaire designer should pay particular attention to this type of question because it is very easy to be misled by its apparent simplicity. Suppose we ask a respondent whether he or she agrees with an increase in taxes to improve parks. The respondent's role, implied by this type of question, is to figure out whether the policy alternative is close enough to his or her views to "agree" with the statement. This, however, is based on a subtle but critical assumption: that the respondent has some general opinion about this specific issue. The risk of this question is that if the respondent has no opinion about this issue, but he or she is generally opposed to raising taxes *for any reason*, then he or she will "disagree," in effect answering a different question (Fowler

---

[26] Sometime four categories are used, such as strongly agree, agree, disagree, strongly disagree. In many cases, however, the answers are usually analyzed in two response categories, so such questions do not yield much more information. Some researchers also consider a question so worded as emotionally charged, violating the objectivity rule of good question design (Fowler 1995).

1995). This violates the fourth criteria of good question design, specificity: respondents should all answer the same question. Put differently,

> Respondents read meaning into the question and answer in terms of some general predisposition toward the [issue. . . .] When people rely on such a predisposition they are showing ideological or constrained attitudes, since they are using general attitudes to supply responses to specific questions. (Smith 1984, 223)

Consequently extraordinary care must be taken when designing and interpreting subjective questions. There is no doubt that questions of this type are easy to administer and easy to answer. Their response rate in Investment Climate Surveys tops 99 percent. However, what is easy to get is not necessarily easy to use. Researchers should be wary that subjective questions have the following three analytical limitations:

Limitations of subjective questions

Plausibility of the answers. A key feature of these questions is that there are no right or wrong answers independent of what respondents tell. While we can, to some extent, measure errors in reporting the percentages of sales that went to bribes, there is no way to assess the accuracy of answers on a six-point scale on the severity of corruption. There is, in fact, no objective standard against which to measure the rightness of that answer (Fowler 1995).

Comparability of the responses. No matter whether we use adjectives or numbers to define the continuum, different respondents may interpret the same categories differently. Hence, when Scipione (1995) conducted an experiment in which a group of respondents were asked what value each associated to "majority," the answers ranged from 38 percent to 76 percent with a mean value of 57 percent (table 3.7).

Furthermore, the researcher cannot be sure that the same answer from different respondents has the same weight, or that the same reply to different questions by the same respondent has the same meaning. In other words, there is no guarantee that "agree" from one respondent is different from "strongly agree" from another respondent. If we ask respondents to rate their social standing on a 1 to 10 scale, we cannot concluded that those rated 9 are three times as high as those rated 3 (Fowler 1995). Finally, the analyst should not "confuse the 'extremity' of judgments with the 'importance' of topics for respondents and with the 'certainty' or 'sureness' of their responses" (Foddy 1993, 160). In answering these types of questions, people put their perceptions up

Table 3.7
Perceived Percentage Values Associated with Descriptive Words

Expression	% Value	Standard Deviation
An overwhelming majority	74	19
A substantial majority	67	20
A large majority	62	21
A majority	57	19
A large minority	41	21
A substantial minority	32	16
A minority	24	21
Most	69	21
Hardly anyone	12	20
Much more than	33	22
Somewhat more than	31	25
Somewhat less than	30	25
Much less than	26	13
A slight change	20	28

Source: Scipione 1995.

against a self-imposed standard unknown to the analyst rather than an objective standard. What one respondent perceives as "good" may be considered only "fair" or even "poor" by another (Fowler 1995). This is because opinions on virtually any issue are often many sided, with cultural, moral, religious, legal, medical, professional, or even geographic dimensions. So an inhabitant of Canada will have different perceptions on what constitutes a cold winter from an inhabitant of Indonesia. During a pilot test in Ethiopia in December 2001, I interviewed the manager of the St. George's Beer factory. He was extremely interested in our project and he answered many questions, often looking at his laptop to provide the most accurate information. When I asked him about the severity of corruption in Ethiopia, he told me that corruption was a minor problem. Given the previous discussions I had had with other managers and experts in that country, his answer surprised me. Later on during the interview I found out why he rated corruption as minor. He had just moved from Nigeria where corruption was rampant. To him the level of corruption in Ethiopia was low because he used a different standard of reference: Nigeria's corruption level. This practically meant that in his mind the question I asked him was "How do you rate corruption in Ethiopia *compared to Nigeria?*"[27] "If respondents adopt different perspectives when answering a question, it can be argued that they are not answering the same question. If this happens, the answers that they give cannot be meaningfully compared" (Foddy 1993, 79). All this implies that,

> answers to questions about subjective states are always relative [and] never absolute. The kinds of statements that are justified, based on answers to these kinds of questions, are comparative. It is appropriate to say that Group A reports more positive feelings than Group B. It is appropriate to say that the population reports more positive feelings today than it did a year ago. It is not appropriate [. . .] to say that people gave the president a positive rating [or] that they are satisfied with their schools. (Fowler 1995, 72–73)

Reliability of the respondent. Questions based on the subjective assessment of the event are subject to idiosyncratic factors, such as the respondent's mood at the time of the interview, the wording of the question, or even external events that might cause the respondent to present only one aspect of his or her reaction to the object of the question (Dexter 1970; Narayan and Krosnick 1996). Words that appear to be the same to researchers often are not so from the point of view of the respondent. When respondents were asked, "Do you think that one should generally *forbid* the use of salt?" or "Do you think that one should generally *allow* the use of salt?" 62 percent of respondents sided in favor of forbidding it and 79 percent in favor of not allowing it (Hippler and Schwarz 1986). See figure 3.13 for an analogous example.

Similarly, using words like "dealing with drug addiction" rather than "drug rehabilitation" elicits a more active stance on the issue (Rasinski 1989).[28] Different words might stimulate different feelings and generate different reactions. In 1940 Cantril and Wilks showed that the percent-

---

[27] This example is additional proof that using the same rating scale to compare answers across countries creates serious methodological problems.

[28] This is one of the reasons why enumerators should read the question exactly as it is stated in the questionnaire.

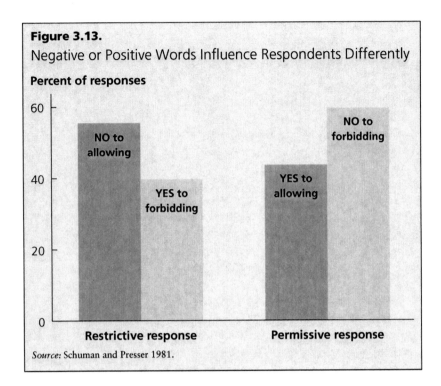

Figure 3.13.
Negative or Positive Words Influence Respondents Differently

Percent of responses

Source: Schuman and Presser 1981.

age of people supporting U.S. involvement in World War II almost doubled if the word "Hitler" appeared in the question.[29] Half a century later, following a controversial opinion poll commissioned by the European Union, the European Commission stated that "it would *change this unfortunate perception by asking the question differently* in future"[30] (*The Economist* 2003, 8).

An external factor that can "influence" answers to subjective questions is, once again, the affiliation of the interviewer. Perception questions appear to be more subject to this bias than objective questions. Furthermore and contrary to what happens with objective questions, this measurement error is more evident if the interview is conducted by an international survey firm than by a government agency. Evidence from the Investment Climate Surveys shows that, on average, compared to a private local survey agency respondents interviewed by an international

[29] Thirteen percent in favor without "Hitler" and 22 percent in favor with the word "Hitler."
[30] Italics added by the author.

survey firm are 10 percent less likely to rate any bottlenecks as a major constraint. A similar bias, although lower in magnitude (4%), is present when a government agency is conducting the interviews (table 3.8). The presence of this different fixed effect makes the international comparison of perception questions much harder.

Table 3.8

Interviews Conducted by Government Agencies and International Private Firms Reduce Probability of Rating Major Constraints

	Government Agency	International Private Firm
A. Telecommunications	2%	−5%
B. Electricity	0%	−14%
C. Transportation	0%	−12%
D. Access to Land	6%	−3%
E. Tax Rates	1%	−9%
F. Tax Administration	3%	0%
G. Customs and Trade Regulations	−4%	−8%
H. Labor Regulations	0%	−10%
I. Skills and Education of Available Workers	2%	−8%
J. Business Licensing and Operating Permits	3%	−3%
K. Access to Financing (e.g., collateral)	−9%	−13%
L. Cost of Financing (e.g., interest rates)	−16%	−18%
M. Economic and Regulatory Policy Uncertainty	−12%	−12%
N. Macroeconomic Instability (inflation, exchange rate)	−1%	0%
O. Corruption	−13%	−11%
P. Crime, theft, and disorder	−18%	−17%
Q. Anticompetitive or informal practices	−12%	−27%
R. Legal system/conflict resolution	−2%	−17%
Average effect	−4%	−10%

Source: Calculations based on World Bank Investment Climate Surveys 2003.
Note: 0% change means no significant difference; negative sign means less likely; positive sign means more likely.
All results presented are significant at 1% or 5%.
Results are in comparison with the results of the interview being conducted by a private local survey agency.
Results for international private firms refer only to East Europe and Central Asian countries.
The exact wording of the questions is presented in appendix 1.

One approach researchers have come up with to address the funda-mental problem of subjective questions, and their inability to provide quantitative measures that can be compared across individuals, is to use magnitude estimation. With this technique, the respondent is asked to rate a phenomenon by comparing it with another phenomenon for which a rating has already been assigned. For example, one such ques-tion for a physician would be as follows:

> Suppose we want to compare the amount of work involved in a splenectomy with the amount of work involved in a tonsillectomy. If we assume that the amount of work involved in a splenectomy is 10, what number would you assign to the work involved in a tonsillectomy?

This approach produces more reliable responses because it introduces an objective point of reference for respondents to rate the phenomenon. However, this technique has its limitations. First, it cannot be used for many of the subjective states that researchers want to measure. Second, the respondents must be able to understand the technique itself, a task that requires a certain level of cognitive ability. And, finally, it takes a fair amount of training by respondents, which is time-consuming. As a re-sult, this approach is not commonly used in surveys (Fowler 1995).

The best solution is to move away from subjective questions. In some cases, this is easier than it may seem. Consider, for example, the sub-jective question in example 3.10.

The question is better addressed by the corresponding objective question in example 3.11.

Example 3.10
Subjective Question

Business-Government Relations
34. How would you generally rate the efficiency of government in delivering services (e.g., public utilities, public transportation, security, education, and health). Would you rate it as (*read 1–6*)?

1. Very inefficient
2. Inefficient
3. Somewhat inefficient
4. Somewhat efficient
5. Efficient
6. Very efficient

Source: Investment Climate Surveys.

Example 3.11

Objective Question

H3. What is the share of government officials that deliver efficient services (e.g., public utilities, public transportation, security, education, and health)?

_____%

Source: Investment Climate Surveys.

When a subjective question is the only way to ask a question, the researcher should refrain from rushing into the analysis without first looking at the possible factors that might influence the respondent. Thus, it is important for the same subjective issue to be addressed from different angles. The presence of inconsistencies among answers to subjective questions by the same respondent remains the only critical source of information on their "quality."

Narrative Questions

What characterizes a narrative or open-ended question is the freedom enjoyed by respondents to answer with their own words. Because open-ended questions do not force respondents into a set of predetermined answers, this is the only type of inquiry that allows them maximum spontaneity of expression. Furthermore, not being influenced by predetermined alternatives allows the researcher to identify the respondent's level of knowledge and information, the salience of the event, the strength of his or her feelings, and his or her motivational influences while avoiding format effects (Foddy 1993).

Open-ended questions have their own set of drawbacks. They take more time and effort than closed questions. As a consequence, they have a higher refusal rate and a higher cost per completed questionnaire. Secondly, the freedom they give to respondents generates a higher variability of answers. "Because of different word choices, verbal skills, and the like, study participants seldom give identical answers, even though they may be saying essentially the same thing" (Peterson 2000, 33). The associated diversity of answers results in a great variety of interpretations making the analysis extremely labor intensive (Peterson 2000). Finally, narrative questions rely more heavily on the interviewer's ability and experience. The more expansive and complex the respondent's answer (verbosity effect) the more important the interviewer's ability to probe and the greater the risk that only those aspects of the response that the interviewer considers interesting and relevant will be reported (Warwick and Lininger 1975).

There is nevertheless a general agreement among all practitioners—both those for and against open-ended questions—that the open format of a question generates a different distribution of results from a closed version (table 3.9), although there seems to be no evidence that one form is preferable to the other (Foddy 1993).

Table 3.9
Open- and Closed-Question Formats Generate Different Responses

Most important thing for children to learn to prepare for life (percentage of respondents).

Answer	Closed Format	Open Format
1 To obey	19.0	2.4
2 To be well liked or popular	0.2	0.0
3 To think for themselves	61.5	4.6
4 To work hard	4.8	1.3
5 To help others in need	12.6	0.9
6 To be self-reliant		6.1
7 To be responsible		5.2
8 To have self-respect		4.1
9 To have respect for others		6.7
10 To have self-discipline		3.5
11 To be honest		7.4
12 To have other moral qualities		3.0
13 To be religious		5.4
14 To love others		2.0
15 To get an education		12.8
16 To learn a trade of job skill		0.9
17 To get along with others		5.0
18 Multiple answers not classifiable		16.1
19 Other	0.0	9.3
20 DK	0.0	1.3
21 NA	1.8	2.0

Source: Schuman and Presser 1979.
Note: DK = don't know; NA = not available.

In an open-ended format, the respondent puts forward a set of information (the answer to the question) and an "expert" filters out the relevant answer on the basis of some detailed instructions (stimuli). In the closed format, the expert provides the "stimuli" and the respondent filters the information to extract the relevant answer. The decision to adopt a closed or open question is fundamentally a decision about who will interpret the information and extract the relevant answer. Given the same set of "stimuli" and the same set of information, using either of the two formats leads to the same relevant answer. Should the two formats lead to different answers the difference is attributable only to the agent who performs the interpretation of the information set. It is reasonable to assume that for a given set of stimuli the best agent to interpret the set of information provided by the respondent is the respondent himself or herself. This consideration, along with the benefits highlighted earlier and the realization that respondents might voluntarily or involuntarily not reveal all relevant information for the expert to extract the right answer, provides justification for a well-designed closed format over the open format.

Because it is not always possible or feasible to construct a well-designed closed question, narrative questions retain an important role in survey research. When information about a potentially complicated phenomenon is sought, when the range of possible alternatives is so extensive that it is practically impossible to list them,[31] or when the possible answers cannot be reduced to few words, the use of open-ended questions is recommended. If knowledge is being measured, then a narrative question is better than a multiple choice question, because in the latter case some correct answers may occur by chance. Similarly, when the reasoning behind a behavior or preference is of interest, the best way too learn it is through the respondent's own words (Fowler 1995). In other cases, when there is reason to suspect that external events might affect the respondent's answers, open questions should be used. So when asked about the most important problem facing the country following the 1977 winter storm, which generated a worry about food shortages, the closed question was unable to detect this shift in public opinion (figure 3.14) (Schuman and Presser 1979).

Finally, it is good practice to use narrative questions during the pilot test to ascertain how the respondent reacts to the question, to identify the optimal set of response categories, and to determine whether the

---

[31] As mentioned earlier, good closed question design requires that the list of alternatives be exhaustive and mutually exclusive (Peterson 2000).

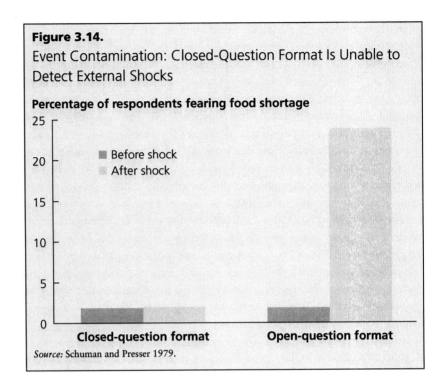

Figure 3.14.

Event Contamination: Closed-Question Format Is Unable to Detect External Shocks

Percentage of respondents fearing food shortage

Source: Schuman and Presser 1979.

closed question is itself appropriate. Notwithstanding their limitation and apart form the above-mentioned limited circumstances, research has shown that providing people with a list of answers to chose from gives more reliable responses than using the open-ended format (Fowler 1995; Schuman and Presser 1979).

Question Sequence

Question sequence should not only facilitate the administration of the interview but also "arouse the respondent's interest, overcome his suspicions and doubts, [. . .] facilitate recall, and motivate [him] to collaborate" (Warwick and Lininger 1975, 148). Therefore, questions should flow in an orderly sequence, with exact instructions on how to move ahead without having to look back and forth throughout the form (Warwick and Lininger 1975).

Three main aspects of the question sequence need attention: opening questions, flow of questions, and location of sensitive questions (Warwick and Lininger 1975).

Opening Questions

At the start of an interview, respondents are a bit suspicious about the study and unsure about their role as informants. Thus, the first questions should be easy, pleasant, and interesting. It should allow them to build up confidence in the survey's objective, stimulate their interest and participation, and eliminate any doubt that they may have about being able to answer questions (so-called motivation and confidence building). Good opening questions are conversational and encourage the respondent to express himself or herself in positive terms, while remaining within the purpose of the study (Warwick and Lininger 1975). Questions such as "What do you do in your free time?" or "Which school do your kids attend?" are irrelevant to the purpose of a business survey, might immediately generate suspicion, and should be avoided. A much better opening is "Can you tell me a little bit about your company?" In any question originating from the interviewer, even the most conversational one, the respondent must be able to see the relationship between the question asked and the purpose of the study. This is the only way to build and keep trust.

Question Flow

The sequence of questions in the body of the form should be tuned to a good flow of ideas and to the logical reasoning of the respondent. Once a general topic has been addressed, all related questions should come up before a second topic is raised. Similarly, if a long list of events is asked, each with dependent questions, it might be confusing for the respondents to go back and forth to each event to provide additional details each time.[32]

It is a good practice, especially in business surveys, not only to start with a narrative question but also to add open questions at regular intervals throughout the form. Elites "resent being encased in the straightjacket of standardized questions" (Zuckerman 1972, 167) and feel particularly frustrated if they perceive that the response alternatives do not accurately address their key concern (Dexter 1970).

---

[32] In this case, however, the designer must keep in mind that the respondent might understand the structure of the question itself and modify his or her answer to avoid the dependent questions to speed up the interview. For this reason, it is suggested to ask the main questions in their entirety first and then proceed with the dependent questions (Atkinson 1971; Moser and Kalton 1971; Plateck, Pierre-Pierre, Stevens 1985).

Illogical jumps or an abrupt change of topic should also be avoided because it will create confusion, and possibly frustrate the respondent and compromise the accuracy of the data. It is good practice to divide the survey subject in different topics linked in the interview by transitional explanations, such as "Okay, let's now move to . . ." or "All right, I am now going to ask you a few questions on. . . ." These transitions play a critical role in the sequencing of questions in both introducing a new topic and showing how a new topic relates to the purpose of the study. More important, transitional phrases help respondents foresee what type of questions they are going to be asked. This will focus their minds and help them relax. Furthermore, transitional explanations exert a positive psychological effect on respondent by giving a sense that we are moving toward the end of the interview (Atkinson 1971). Finally, the use of bridging remarks, such as "You mentioned earlier that . . . ," should be encouraged because it shows that the interviewer is attentive and interested in what the respondent has to say.

The order of questions can also be used to aid individual's memory or to gradually introduce respondents to unpleasant or embarrassing topics.[33] For example, questions on awareness of a program should precede questions on their use. Questions with a common reference period should be grouped together, with the most recent period coming first (Warwick and Lininger 1975). Easier questions should be asked at the beginning or the end of the interview.

Filter questions and conditional questions should be used to guide the interviewer and exclude respondents from a question sequence that does not apply to them. It is time-consuming and annoying for a respondent to be asked "How many days did it take you to export your goods?" if he or she does not export at all. Filter questions are more efficient, and therefore should be preferred over conditional questions. They allow us to discriminate between "not applicable" and "nonresponse." As a matter of fact a "not applicable" response to the question "If you have a loan, what is the interest rate?" could mean that the respondent does not have a loan or that he or she simply does not pay interest on an existing loan.

---

[33] To some extent, the actual order of questions might affect respondents. Although the literature is split on this issue (Benton and Daly 1991; McAllister and Wattenberg 1995; McClendon and O'Brien 1988; Sigelman 1981), it seems that "question order effects occur only when a prior question establishes a response set to a subsequent question; that is, that the order effects are selective or conditional on the substance of specific questions" (Crespi and Morris 1984, 580).

The importance of filter questions cannot be stressed enough, especially for attitude or knowledge questions. Respondents are reluctant to admit ignorance. They are open to offering opinions not only on subjects they know little about, but also on fictitious information presented as fact.

> Gallup [. . .] finds that while 96 percent [of respondents] had an opinion on the importance of a balanced budget, 25 percent did not know whether the budget was currently balanced, 8 percent wrongly thought that it was balanced, 40 percent knew it was un-balanced but didn't know by how much, 25 percent knew it was unbalanced but overestimated or underestimated the amount by 15 percent or more, and 3 percent knew it was unbalanced and knew the approximate level. (Smith 1984, 221)

When asked about a fictitious "Public Affairs Act" one-third of re-spondents volunteered an answer in a form without a filter (Bishop, Oldendick, Tuchfarber, and Bennett 1980; Bishop, Tuchfarber, and Oldendick 1986) Filters are extremely important because they can screen out from 5 to 45 percent of responses, depending on the word-ing of the filter and how familiar or emotive the issue covered is (Bishop, Oldendick, and Tuchfarber 1983).[34]

Location of Sensitive Questions

While all agree that sensitive questions should not come at the begin-ning of the interview, when the main goal of the interviewer is to gain trust from the respondent, the belief that these questions should not be placed at the end is not unanimous either. Some practitioners in fact favor the "hit-and-run" method, in which as many sensitive questions as possible are asked toward the end of the interview until the respon-dent becomes unwilling to continue.[35] This method shows a poor under-standing of the psychology of the interview process and leaves the respondent with negative attitudes toward the study (Warwick and Lininger 1975). In the worst case, the respondent may reject the whole interview and ask the interviewer to hand over the questionnaire.

Sensitive questions should be introduced only at a point of the inter-view at which the respondent is likely to have developed confidence in

---

[34] Examples of filters include the following: "Do you have an opinion on this or not?" "Have you been interested enough in this to favor one side over the other?" "Have you thought much about this?" and "Where do you stand on this issue, or haven't you thought much about it?" (Bishop, Oldendick, and Tuchfarber 1983).
[35] See Moser and Kalton (1971, 346).

the purpose of the study and trust in the interviewer. They should be placed where they are least likely to be sensitive, such as where the topic being discussed is the most appropriate. Finally, to mitigate the perceived threatening nature of sensitive questions it is good practice to introduce them gradually by a series of warm-up questions (Warwick and Lininger 1975).

Questionnaire Length

While the literature investigates extensively the relationship between question length and data accuracy, few authors have analyzed the effect of questionnaire length on data quality. A review of the literature by Bogen (1996) finds no clear association between questionnaire length and survey participation. While she blames a lack of experimental research on this issue, she points out that the existing evidence does not lead to the assertion of a negative relationship between questionnaire length and response rate. Most of the papers reviewed in this article refer to mail and telephone interviews and, in the few papers on face-to-face interviews, the average interview length is one hour. For longer interviews, like Investment Climate Surveys interviews, which can run between one and two hours, very little experimental research can be found.

As discussed in chapter five, the existing literature suggests that survey participation is only marginally associated with questionnaire length. Evidence form the Investment Climate Surveys confirms that questionnaire length[36] has no impact on response rate (figure 3.15).[37]

---

[36] The number of pages is only an imperfect measure of questionnaire length. The real length is a function of three components: the length of individual questions, the number of questions, and the format of questions included in the form. A questionnaire of only 10 questions, but with each of them in a table format, is more difficult and time-consuming than a questionnaire with the same amount of information asked in a sequence of questions with appropriate skip patterns. To account for this, we "standardized" the definition of questionnaire length by counting the words of each questionnaire and calculating the number of pages, assuming 422 words per page. All figures and analyses in this book assume this standardized definition.

[37] The response rate is calculated as the percentage of "core" questions answered to control for question effect. A copy of the core questionnaire used in the investment climate surveys is available at: http://www.ifc.org/ifcext/economics.nsf/Content/IC-SurveyMethodology. Countries included in the figure are: Bangladesh2002, Brazil2003, Cambodia2003, China2002, Ecuador, Ethiopia2002, Honduras2003, India2000, Kenya2003, Kyrgyzstan 2003, Moldova2003, Nicaragua2003, Nigeria2001, Peru2002, Philippines2002, Poland2003, Tajikistan2003, Tanzania2003, Uganda2003, Uzbekistan2003. The data on Investment Climate Surveys used throughout this book are available online at the following URL: http://iresearch.worldbank.org/ics/jsp/index.jsp.

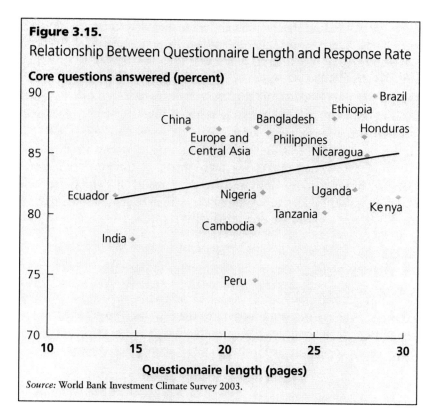

Figure 3.15.
Relationship Between Questionnaire Length and Response Rate

Source: World Bank Investment Climate Survey 2003.

Questionnaire length has a significant impact on data accuracy. Longer questionnaires put an unfair burden on the time and memory of the respondent and will inevitably result in higher response errors. Although respondents may not appear to refuse to answer a question, they may provide any answer to complete the interview more quickly, hence providing biased information. The problem is that we cannot control for this bias.

Sudnam and Bradburn (1974) suspected that interviews over two hours might endanger response accuracy. They affirm that fatigue does not jeopardize data quality in interviews up to one-and-a-half hours long, while pointing out that "a fatigue factor [. . .] could become a serious problem in interviews lasting more that two hours" (Sudnam and Bradburn 1974, 90). Andrews (1984) also found a similar association by demonstrating that on a questionnaire with up to 348 items "better data quality comes from items that fell in the 26th to 100th positions" (432).

Notwithstanding this evidence it is hard to determine the optimal length of a questionnaire. In face-to-face interviews there is a general agreement that the interview should take no longer than 45 to 60 minutes.[38] After 75 minutes, the managers manifest clear signs of fatigue (uncomfortable on the chair, watching the clock, looking around the room, asking more often for the question to be repeated). Data from the Investment Climate Surveys also seems to confirm that data accuracy starts to suffer when the questionnaire reaches 20 pages. Allowing for the fact that only part of the whole Investment Climate Surveys questionnaire is administered through a formal face-to-face interview,[39] evidence seems to show that in general face-to-face interviews should not exceed 14 pages (or approximately one-and-a-half hours).[40]

Questionnaire Layout

Often not enough attention is paid to the physical layout of the questionnaire, which results in a greater likelihood of errors by interviewers, editors, coders, key operators, and ultimately respondents.

> A common reason for poor layout is the desire to fit all of the questions in a single page, even if the type has been reduced to miniscule proportions and the items crammed together. [. . .] Though such forms mean savings on paper and printing expenses, they are ultimately wasteful if they reduce the quality of the information obtained. (Warwick and Lininger 1975, 151)

A number of principles should be followed to ensure that the questionnaire is convenient for the interviewer and respondent, as well as easy to identify, code, and store.

---

[38] See Rea and Parker 1997.

[39] The Investment Climate Surveys questionnaire is usually divided into two parts. The first is administered through a face-to-face interview with the chief executive officer or manager of the selected establishment. The second part is to be filled in by the accountant and human resources manager under the supervision of the interviewer, and requires referencing books and records. Although the questionnaire length is measured for the whole questionnaire, the time to complete the face-to-face interview refers only to the first part.

[40] In determining the actual length of the interview, the survey manager should keep in mind that a host of other factors beyond the questionnaire length play a role, not the least being the interviewer's ability.

Identification

Each form should contain one or more unique identifying numbers assigned in advance and marked on each questionnaire. It is good practice to have the same number assigned to each sample unit be the identifier of its paper questionnaire as well (Warwick and Lininger 1975).

Numbering

Questions should be numbered sequentially throughout the instrument without omissions or repetitions. Even if the questionnaire is divided in sections or parts it is preferable to use progressive numbers throughout the form.

Space

Sufficient space between questions should be left to facilitate questionnaire administration. Saving space will ultimately be uneconomical if it compromises data accuracy. It is advisable to print only on one side of the page and to leave enough space for notes from interviewers, editors, or coders on both sides of the questions. To facilitate data entering, it is good practice to align the answer boxes to the margin of the pages. If it is not practical to do so (that is, when questions are of varying length) then it might be appropriate to use a table format in which questions are spread across the page in an orderly fashion allowing the justification of answer categories (example 3.12). Finally, if it is not feasible to place the answer boxes next to the question it is advisable to use dotted lines to connect them (Plateck, Pierre-Pierre, and Stevens 1985).

Open-ended questions should have sufficient space for the expected average answer length. For questions that need to be coded at a later stage, "For Official Use Only" space should be clearly allowed in the questionnaire.

Instructions

Instructions are critical both for the administration of the form as well as for the collection of accurate data. Two types of information must be readily distinguishable in the questionnaire: questions to be read and instructions to be followed.

One effective way to eliminate confusion between instructions and questions is to use different formats or to put one of them in a box. So, for instance, all verbatim questions can be typed in regular font while instructions are typed in capital letters. Instructions should be placed

Example 3.12

Questionnaire Layout

Language	Education

Language

11. WHAT IS THE LANGUAGE . . . FIRST
    LEARNED IN CHILDHOOD AND STILL
    UNDERSTANDS? (Mark all that apply)
    English..O
    French ....O
    Other..O

12. CAN . . . SPEAK ENGLISH OR FRENCH
    WELL ENOUGH TO CONDUCT A CON-
    VERSATION?
    NO—Neither English nor French ...O
    YES—English only...........................O Go to 14
    YES—French only............................O
    YES—Both English and French.......O Go to 13

13. IN GENERAL, WHICH OF THESE TWO
    LANGUAGES DOES . . . PREFER TO SPEAK?
    English ....O
    French..O
    Neither...O
    Don't know.....................................O
    No preference................................O

14. WHAT LANGUAGE DOES . . . SPEAK MOST
    OFTEN AT HOME? (Mark all that apply)
    English ....O
    French..O
    Other ....O

Education

15. HAS . . . (EVER) ATTENDED A UNIVER-
    SITY, COMMUNITY COLLEGE, OR
    OTHER POSTSECONDARY INSTITUTION
    AS A FULL-TIME STUDENT?
    Yes O   No O   Go to 20

16. WHAT IS THE HIGHEST LEVEL OF
    EDUCATION . . . COMPLETED?
    [ ][ ] Enter code
         If code 99 Go to 20

17. IN WHAT YEAR WAS . . . 'S LAST DEGREE,
    DIPLOMA, OR CERTIFICATE GRANTED?
    [1][9][ ][ ] Year

18. IN WHICH PROVINCE, TERRITORY, OR
    OTHER COUNTRY WAS THIS DEGREE,
    DIPLOMA, OR CERTIFICATE GRANTED?
    [ ][ ] Enter code

19. WHAT WAS . . . 'S MAJOR FIELD OF
    STUDY?
    [ ][ ] Enter code

20. HAS . . . LIVED IN ANY OTHER PROVINCE,
    TERRITORY, OR OTHER COUNTRY SINCE
    JUNE 1, 1976?
    Yes O   No O   Go to 48

Example 3.12 (continued)

Migration History

21. IN WHICH PROVINCE, TERRITORY, OR OTHER COUNTRY DID . . . LIVE ON JUNE 1, 1976?
[ ] Enter code

22. TO WHICH PROVINCE, TERRITORY, OR OTHER COUNTRY DID . . . FIRST MOVE AFTER JUNE 1, 1976?
[ ] Enter code

23. WHEN DID . . . MAKE THIS MOVE?
Mo. [   ] Yr.

24. TO WHICH PROVINCE, TERRITORY, OR OTHER COUNTRY DID . . . MOVE NEXT?
[ ] Enter code
If code 99 (No other moves) go to 34

25. WHEN DID . . . MAKE THIS MOVE?
Mo. [   ] Yr.

26. TO WHICH PROVINCE, TERRITORY, OR OTHER COUNTRY DID . . . MOVE NEXT?
[ ] Enter code
If code 99 (No other moves) go to 34

27. WHEN DID . . . MAKE THIS MOVE?
Mo. [   ] Yr.

28. TO WHICH PROVINCE, TERRITORY, OR OTHER COUNTRY DID . . . MOVE NEXT?
[ ] Enter code
If code 99 (No other moves) go to 34

29. WHEN DID . . . MAKE THIS MOVE?
Mo. [   ] Yr.

30. TO WHICH PROVINCE, TERRITORY, OR OTHER COUNTRY DID . . . MOVE NEXT?
[ ] Enter code
If code 99 (No other moves) go to 34

31. WHEN DID . . . MAKE THIS MOVE?
Mo. [   ] Yr.

32. TO WHICH PROVINCE, TERRITORY, OR OTHER COUNTRY DID . . . MOVE NEXT?
[ ] Enter code
If code 99 (No other moves) go to 34

33. WHEN DID . . . MAKE THIS MOVE?
Mo. [   ] Yr.

Source: Plateck, Pierre-Pierre, and Stevens 1985.

Example 3.13
Different Emphasis Implies Different Answers to the Same Question

Overt Emphasis on		Implied Emphasis on	Possible Replies
<u>*Why*</u> did you buy this book?	→	motivation	(gift, self interest)
Why did <u>*you*</u> buy this book?	→	person	(self, other)
Why did you <u>*buy*</u> this book?	→	action	(rent, borrow)
Why did you buy <u>*this*</u> book?	→	object	(other book, magazine)

Source: Peterson, 2000.

---

directly above the question concerned or the section of the question-naire to which they apply. It is not advisable to put instructions at the beginning of the questionnaire or in the manuals (Plateck, Pierre-Pierre, and Stevens 1985).

Fonts and Formats

Given that the same question can educe different meanings if different words are emphasized (see example 3.13), critical words should be underlined or printed in bold to ensure uniform emphasis by inter-viewers and uniform interpretations by respondents.

Similarly, when the time reference changes from one question to the next, it is particularly important to ensure uniformity of interpretation. Using bold when asking "**In the last two weeks,** how many . . ." focuses the respondent's attention on the new time reference (Plateck, Pierre-Pierre, and Stevens 1985).

In a multicultural survey in which each question is printed first in one language and then in the second language, it is good practice to use two different fonts for each language throughout the questionnaire (Plateck, Pierre-Pierre, and Stevens 1985).[41]

Symbols

Symbols such as circles, arrows, boxes, triangles, and asterisks, as well as different colors or shades are excellent visual tools and should be used

---

[41] Alternatively, the questionnaire could be printed double-sided with each side having the same questions but in different languages. When more than two languages are used, it is advisable to use separate forms for each language.

not only to guide the interviewer and respondent throughout the form, but also to facilitate the work of supervisors and key operators. The questionnaire can be designed in such a way that each type of answer has an associated type of symbol. So, for instance, arrows might help identify the skipping pattern, a circle might be used whenever a check mark is called for, and a box whenever numbers are called for (see previous example 3.12) (Plateck, Pierre-Pierre, and Stevens 1985).[42]

Similarly, if the questionnaire is divided into two parts, it has been proven useful to have the two parts printed on two different paper colors.

Translation

Surveys are often conducted in multiethnic and multilinguistic societies. Thus, asking the same question in countries (or regions) with different cultures, traditions, beliefs, and languages becomes even harder and the solutions are more complex.

Three major concerns are raised by comparative research. The first is whether one concept has the same meaning in different cultures. So, for instance, the concept of illegal party contribution might have different meanings in the United States and the Philippines. Second, even if the same concept has the same meaning in different cultures, it does not imply that the same indicator of that concept would apply to all of the meanings. The notion of political activity is the same in the United States and Europe, but the pattern of activities is different for each country. The third concern refers to the analytical value of the information collected. A well-translated identical indicator can still generate a nonequivalent response pattern across cultures. This happens when different response styles occur in different cultures. So, for instance, if acquiescence is more common among small companies, then appropriate controls should be introduced to avoid the fact that apparent differences across countries actually reflect differences in the strata's composition (Warwick and Lininger 1975).

The implication is that translation in the local language should not be seen as simple "transliteration" of the words. Rather it should be a transformation of the instrument to "conceptual equivalence" (Hunt, Crane, and Wahlke 1964). In other words, it is essential that the trans-

---

[42] This helps not only in the data-collection phase but also in the data-checking stage of the survey.

lation convey a consistent message in different cultures. So if we want to measure "unlawful party contribution to political parties," we cannot use the same measurement for the United States and the Philippines, because in the latter no laws forbid such contributions. A technique to ensure good translation quality is the so-called back translation as outlined in the following four steps:

Step 1. The questionnaire is first translated from language A to language B.

Step 2. The translated version is then translated back from B into A by *a different* translator.

Step 3. The two versions of the questionnaire, original and back translated, are then compared and discrepancies clarified and corrected.

Step 4. The revised translated version is translated back into A again for comparison, and this process keeps going until there are no more inconsistencies between the two versions (Warwick and Lininger 1975).

During this translation process, it is useful to treat the pre-test as an additional tool for checking the translated version of the questionnaire. A lot of the problems of designing a cross-cultural study can be addressed

> if the investigators take to the field early in the study and allow ample time and resources for pre-testing the research instrument. The day when a single questionnaire is designed in the United States or Europe and sent to 'hired hands' in other countries is hopefully over. (Warwick and Lininger 1975, 167)

This brings us to the last step of questionnaire design: pre-testing.

Pre-Test

Armchair discussions cannot replace direct contact with the population being analyzed (Warwick and Lininger 1975).

> It is all too easy to think that one can draft a perfectly worded questionnaire while sitting in an office. In fact, it is very difficult to imagine all the possible interpretations and the variety of answers respondents may give, or the different circumstances or conditions which may alter the sense of the questions. (Plateck, Pierre-Pierre, and Stevens 1985, 21)

By the time the form reaches the pre-test stage all issues of wording, style, content, layout, and language should be resolved. The pilot represents the first "live" test of the instrument, as well as the last step in the finalization of the questions. No matter how experienced the questionnaire designer is, any attempt to shortcut this step will seriously jeopardize the accuracy of the data about to be collected. Time constraints should not come at the expense of this essential last step in the design of the questionnaire (Moser and Kalton 1971).

As discussed previously in this chapter, good question design requires clarity in the terminology adopted. "Survey questions [. . .] should mean the same thing to all respondents, and they should mean the same thing to respondent as well as to the researcher" (Fowler 1992, 218). The pilot test represents the only opportunity to verify this and the data collected will ultimately reflect any poorly defined question or concept. When asked "How many *servings* of eggs do you eat in a typical day?" some 33 percent of respondents interpreted one serving as one egg and 47 percent of them interpreted one serving as two eggs. Therefore, when the meaning of "servings" was clarified, the number of respondents reporting two eggs went from 15 to 62 percent (figure 3.16).

Bassili and Scott (1996) and Fowler (1992) show that clearer questions reduce both the time to answer as well as the requests for clarifications, thus reducing the time to complete the interview (figure 3.17).

The pre-testing of a questionnaire can be conducted following three different methods: conventional, behavioral, and cognitive.

Pre-test methods

The conventional method involves a small number of interviews followed by a debriefing in which experiences are shared and problems identified.[43] The behavioral pre-test involves structured interviews monitored by an expert whose role is to identify and code problems. In the cognitive pilot, the respondent is asked to report everything that comes to his or her mind while or after answering the questions. Preliminary experimental results show that each method serves a different purpose. The behavioral and conventional methods are more appropriate for detecting problems with both the respondent and the interviewer, whereas the cognitive method assesses the analytical accuracy of the answers by evaluating the questions from the point of view of the effort required to answer. Conventional and cognitive pre-tests also perform well in identifying semantic problems.

---

[43] This methodology is efficient if the investigator designs effective debriefing questions for both the interviewer and the respondent and if he or she is able to determine which information is not relevant (Campanelli, Martin, and Rothgeb 1991).

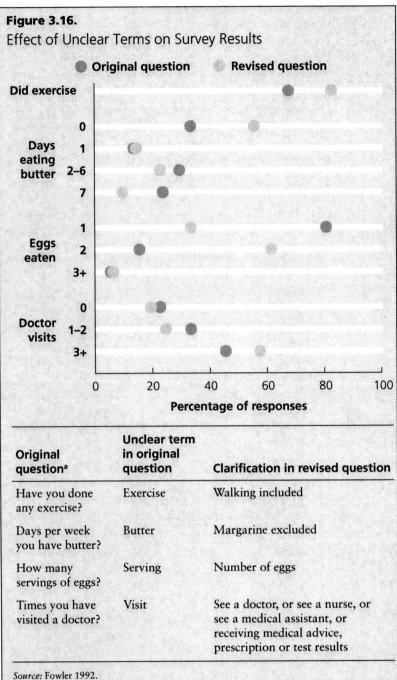

Figure 3.16.
Effect of Unclear Terms on Survey Results

Original question[a]	Unclear term in original question	Clarification in revised question
Have you done any exercise?	Exercise	Walking included
Days per week you have butter?	Butter	Margarine excluded
How many servings of eggs?	Serving	Number of eggs
Times you have visited a doctor?	Visit	See a doctor, or see a nurse, or see a medical assistant, or receiving medical advice, prescription or test results

Source: Fowler 1992.
a. Meaning of question. For exact question wording see reference.

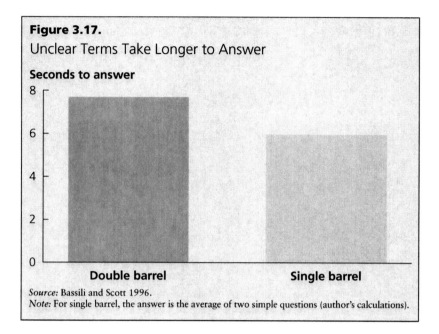

Figure 3.17.
Unclear Terms Take Longer to Answer

Seconds to answer

Double barrel | Single barrel

Source: Bassili and Scott 1996.
Note: For single barrel, the answer is the average of two simple questions (author's calculations).

In addition to these three field methods, there is a fourth method in which expert designers review the questionnaire in the office. This has proven beneficial, particularly for the identification of problems related to the analytical value of the questions (figure 3.18) (Presser and Blair 1994). Biemer and Lyberg (2003) present a useful list of coding categories that experts can use in their assessment of the questionnaire (box 3.1).

The purpose of the pre-test is threefold:

Pre-test goals

- To evaluate the adequacy of the questionnaire,[44]
- To estimate the length of the interview, and
- To determine the quality of the interviewers.

It is not easy to determine a priori the warning signs of design defects. Many different situations can occur during an interview leading to a great variety of answers to any single question. In general, too many answers at one extreme may indicate a leading question. Too many "don't know" or requests for clarifications definitely indicate vague questions, questions using uncommon words, or questions going out-

---

[44] Occasionally, the pilot can also be used to evaluate different wording of the same question. In this case, however, the survey manager must ensure that the alternative versions of the question are tested by the same interviewer on two equivalent random sample of respondents (Moser and Kalton 1971).

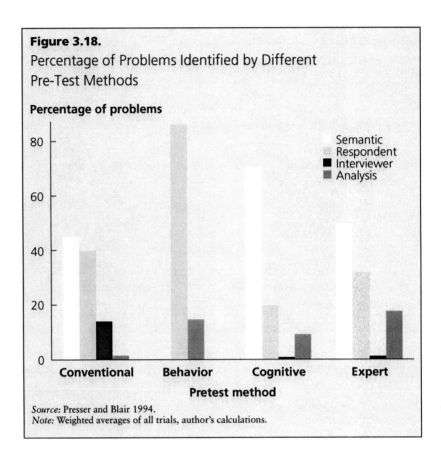

Figure 3.18.

Percentage of Problems Identified by Different Pre-Test Methods

Percentage of problems

Semantic
Respondent
Interviewer
Analysis

Pretest method

Source: Presser and Blair 1994.
Note: Weighted averages of all trials, author's calculations.

side the respondent's experience. If respondents add qualifications to their answer, the question needs to be clarified. If many refuse to answer or answer in the same way, the question must be reworded, repositioned, or cut out altogether (Moser and Kalton 1971).

Following is a checklist of concerns regarding the questionnaire that the designer should address during the pilot:[45]

- Do respondents understand what the survey is all about?
- Do they feel comfortable answering questions?
- Is the wording clear?
- Is the time reference clear to respondents?
- Are the response categories compatible with the respondent's experience?

---

[45] A systematic approach to rate questions during the pilot has been suggested by Fowler (1995, 116–124).

Box 3.1

List of Questionnaire Problems for Pre-Test Expert Review

1. PROBLEMS WITH READING: Determine whether it is difficult for the interviewers to read the question uniformly to all respondents.

   1a – WHAT TO READ: Interviewers may have difficulty determining what parts of the question are to be read.

   1b – MISSING INFORMATION: Information the interviewer needs to administer the question is not contained in the question.

   1c – HOW TO READ: Question is not fully scripted and therefore difficult to read.

2. PROBLEMS WITH INSTRUCTIONS: Look for problems with any introductions, instructions, or explanations from the respondent's point of view.

   2a – CONFLICTING OR INACCURATE INSTRUCTIONS, introductions, or explanations.

   2b – COMPLICATED INSTRUCTIONS, introductions, or explanations.

3. PROBLEMS WITH ITEM CLARITY: Identify problems related to communicating the intent or meaning of the question to the respondent.

   3a – WORDING: The question is lengthy, awkward, ungrammatical, or contains complicated syntax.

   3b – TECHNICAL TERMS are undefined, unclear, or complex.

   3c – VAGUE: The question is vague because there are multiple ways in which to interpret it or to determine what is to be included and excluded.

   3d – REFERENCE PERIODS are missing, not well specified, or are in conflict.

4. PROBLEMS WITH ASSUMPTIONS: Determine whether there are problems with assumptions made or the underlying logic.

   4a – INAPPROPRIATE ASSUMPTIONS are made about the respondent or his/her living situation.

   4b – ASSUMES CONSTANT behavior: The question inappropriately assumes a constant pattern of behavior or experience for situations that in fact vary.

   4c – DOUBLE-BARRELED question that contains multiple implicit questions.

5. PROBLEMS WITH KNOWLEDGE/MEMORY: Check whether respondents are likely to not know or have trouble remembering information.

   5a – KNOWLEDGE: The respondent is unlikely to know the answer.

   5b – An ATTITUDE that is asked about may not exist.

   5c – RECALL failure.

   5d – COMPUTATION or calculation problem.

Box 3.1 (continued)

6. PROBLEMS WITH SENSITIVITY/BIAS: Assess questions for sensitive nature or wording, and for bias.

   6a – SENSITIVE CONTENT: The question is on a topic that people will generally be uncomfortable talking about.

   6b – A SOCIALLY ACCEPTABLE response is implied.

7. PROBLEMS WITH RESPONSE CATEGORIES: Assess the adequacy of the range of responses to be recorded.

   7a – OPEN-ENDED QUESTIONS that are inappropriate or difficult.

   7b – MISMATCH between question and answer categories.

   7c – TECHNICAL TERMS are undefined, unclear, or complex

   7d – VAGUE response categories.

   7e – OVERLAPPING response categories.

   7f – MISSING response categories.

   7g – ILLOGICAL ORDER of response categories.

Source: Biemer and Lyberg 2003.

- Which items require respondents to think hard before they answer?
- What cognitive processes do they adopt to answer difficult questions?
- Which items seem to produce irritation, embarrassment, or confusion?
- Are there any items that respondents consider comical?
- Does the style of the question generate bias?
- Are the answers we get what we really want for the purpose of the study?
- Is there enough variability in the answers received?
- Are there local expressions that should be incorporated into the items to avoid ambiguity?
- Is the questionnaire too long?
- In the eye of the respondent, have any other important issues been overlooked in the questionnaire?

Many of those issues are hard to judge so it is important for experienced staff with a profound understanding of the analytical purpose of each question to participate in the pre-test. Take for instance the following question:

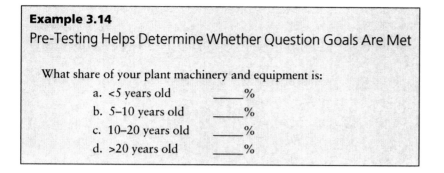

Example 3.14

Pre-Testing Helps Determine Whether Question Goals Are Met

What share of your plant machinery and equipment is:

    a. <5 years old   ____%

    b. 5–10 years old   ____%

    c. 10–20 years old ____%

    d. >20 years old   ____%

The goal of this question was to get an estimate of capital vintage in the establishment and relate it to both technological progress and productivity improvement. For this question to be of analytical value, the answer should be based on the market value of the machinery, not on its book value. Unfortunately a cognitive evaluation of this question during a pre-test has shown that the answers provided were based on the physical number of the machinery. Even when the question was reworded to clearly indicate that the market value of machinery should have been referenced, the respondents had so much difficulty answering it that they would purely guess an answer.

The pilot is also an excellent opportunity to test both the convenience of the form and the ability of interviewers.[46] Some of the questions that the survey manger should consider addressing during the pilot to assess the convenience of the instrument are as follows:

- Is the questionnaire easy to administer?
- Do filters and skip patterns work properly?
- Are instructions clear?[47]
- Are transitions from question to question smooth?

Similarly, some of the issues relevant to assess the interviewer's ability are as follows:

- How does he or she read the questions?
- How does he or she behave in difficult situations?

---

[46] Although it is not feasible to have all potential interviewers participate in the pre-test, the survey manager's experience with the pre-test can serve as a first step in establishing an expectation on the average level of interviewers. This will help him or her better tailor the training.

[47] A useful technique to test the usefulness of instructions, paraphrasing, is suggested by Gower (1993). "Respondents are asked to repeat the question in their own words, or to explain the meaning of terms and concepts [. . .] used."

- How does he or she handle questionnaire instructions?
- How does he or she explain concepts not clear to the respondent?
- How does he or she probe and record answers?

The size of the pre-test is more a matter of convenience and availability than the result of a random selection process. Generally it should be carried out in 15 to 25 establishments. Although firms of different sizes should be included in the test, the selection of respondents is more purposive than random. It is not necessary to visit establishments in different locations or industries unless there are reasons to believe that regional or sectoral differences in the interpretation of questions might exist.

Because it is difficult for one individual to carry out a good interview and observe and take notes on how to improve the instrument, it is good practice for the survey manager or an expert to accompany the interviewer during the pre-test. The expert will then observe the interviewer's behavior and the respondent's reactions, and will perform a cognitive assessment of the most challenging questions. To better perform these tasks, it is advisable to focus only on a subset of the questions on each pre-test and to apply what has been learned in previous pilots to subsequent interviews. With all the information gathered during the pre-test the questionnaire is then finalized.[48]

---

[48] At this stage, the form is almost ready to be administered. A few useful comments and modifications could come up during the training, especially if the instrument is translated into the local language.

Chapter 4
A Practical Approach to Sampling

If proper sampling procedures are followed, in a matter of days, an opinion poll conducted on approximately 1,000 individuals can be reasonably taken as a measure of public opinion for a population as large as China's. This is the power of sampling, its ability to approximate from a small group the characteristics of the whole population within a know margin of error.

Different methods of respondents' selection can be employed when conducting a survey, that is, interviewing experts, the typical respondent, or a group of respondents. Because only part of the population is sampled, the estimated parameters are subject to a sampling error. Sampling error is a measure of "how closely we can reproduce from a sample the results that would be obtained if we should take a complete count or census" (Hansen, Hurwitz, and Madow 1953, 10).

The ability to estimate and reduce this error depends on how the sample is selected. If the researcher knows what chances each population member has to be included in the sample, he can use statistical theory to estimate the properties of the survey statistics. On the contrary, when the selection of respondents is based on personal judgment, it is not possible to have an objective measure of the reliability of the sample results (Kalton 1983). This is not to say that there is no room for subjective judgment in probability sampling. Rather, subjective judgment plays an important role in sample design as long as the final selection of the sample elements is left to a random process (Hansen, Hurwitz, and Madow 1953).

Volumes have been written on probability sampling. Hence, far from being a discussion on sampling techniques, what follows is a short review of how to determine the sample size using four of the most commonly used sampling procedures: simple random sampling (SRS), stratified random sampling, systematic sampling, and probability proportional to size (PPS) sampling. Particular attention is dedicated to how to deal with

The major strength of probability sampling is that the probability selection mechanism permits the development of statistical theory to examine the properties of sample estimators. [...] The weakness of all nonprobability methods is that no such theoretical development is possible; as a consequence, nonprobability samples can be assessed only by subjective valuation.

—Graham Kalton,
Introduction to Survey Sampling

frame problems and how to perform weight adjustments. Finally, a practical case of stratified random sampling of manufacturing establishments is presented.[1]

Determining the Sample Size in Simple Random Sampling

The simplest form of probability sampling is SRS. With this method, every possible sample of equal size—as well as each individual element[2] in the population (see box 4.1)—has the same non-zero probability of being selected: the *epsem* (equal probability of selection) design.[3]

The sample size in SRS depends on three factors:

- The population size
- The variability of the parameter we wish to estimate
- The desired level of precision and confidence we wish to reach.

If we are interested in estimating the population mean of the parameter $\bar{Y}$ with precision e_0 and confidence α, the minimum sample size is then determined by the following formula:

$$n = \frac{z_{\frac{\alpha}{2}}^2 S^2}{e_0^2 + z_{\frac{\alpha}{2}}^2 \dfrac{S^2}{N}}$$

Similarly, if we are interested in estimating the population proportion $\bar{P}$ for a given characteristic with precision e_0 and confidence α, the minimum sample size is calculated as follows:

$$n = \frac{z_{\frac{\alpha}{2}}^2 P(1 - P)}{e_0^2 + z_{\frac{\alpha}{2}}^2 \dfrac{P(1 - P)}{N}}$$

where:

N = population size
n = sample size
S^2 = population variance of Y (assumed to be known)

---

[1] I am grateful to Dr. Mohammed Yusuf from Survey and Research Systems (Dhaka, Bangladesh) for comments and suggestions on this chapter.
[2] Given the peculiarities of business activities, an important problem in business surveys is the identification of the sample element (see box 4.1).
[3] As commonly done in the literature, we refer here to SRS without replacement.

Box 4.1

The Sampling Unit in Business Surveys

Contrary to household surveys in which the identification of the sampling unit is easier (that is, husband, wife, and so on), in surveys of business activities this task is complicated by the fact that there is an array of business forms, from small family-owned stores to large international corporations. So, when designing a sample of formal manufacturing activities, what is the best unit of analysis? Is it the establishment, the factory, the plant, the company, the enterprise, or the firm? Theoretical motivations related to the purpose of the study and the desired level of homogeneity, as well as practical considerations on the availability and accuracy of the data, will dictate the answer.

  While this identification is not an issue for small entities, large businesses often include different legal structures, operational structures, and ownership structures. They produce different goods, in different locations, at different scales. The resulting heterogeneity in the structure of each sampling unit makes it impossible to have an internationally recognized standardization. Nonetheless, from a theoretical point of view, two types of statistical units are generally identified. One corresponds to the level where financial decisions are made and the other corresponds to the level where production decisions are taken. If the primary interest of the researcher is the behavior related to resource allocation, then the former level is the appropriate unit of investigation (the *firm* in box figure 4.1.1).

Box Figure 4.1.1.

Unit of Analysis in a Business Survey

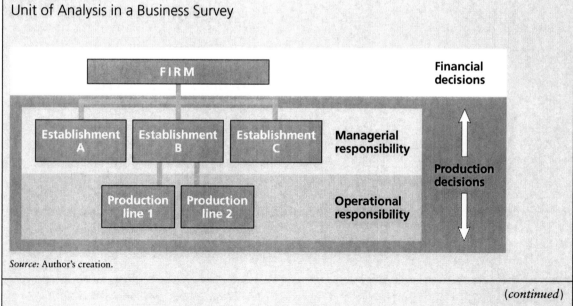

Source: Author's creation.

(*continued*)

Box 4.1 (continued)

When, on the contrary, decisions on the purchase of factors of production are of analytical interest, then the latter level of analysis should be adopted. Furthermore, within this level, two sublevels can be identified. The level at which managerial decisions are made regarding the whole production process and the level of single product operation. When the object of analysis is the overall managerial responsibility, then the *establishment* is the appropriate level of investigation. If the technological characteristics of a single production process are of interest, then the individual *production line* is the appropriate unit of reference (Nijhowne 1995).

From a practical point of view, while it is relatively easy to acquire firm data to analyze financial decisions, it is much harder to collect information on individual product lines. Although records are kept to support management decisions, it is quite unlikely to find the same level of detail at all levels of production lines in any business unit. The only way to gather these data is for the researcher to reconstruct them from aggregate values, a process that results in an inevitable loss of accuracy (Colledge 1995).

P = population proportion of Y (assumed to be known)

e_0 = desired level of precision

α = desired level of confidence (that is, for instance, 95%)

$z_{\alpha/2}$ = z distribution corresponding to α level of confidence[4]

With SRS, the population mean and population proportion as well as the corresponding variances are estimated as follows:

Parameter Estimated	Sample Mean	Sample Variance
Population Mean		
$\bar{Y} = \dfrac{\sum_{i=1}^{N} y_i}{N}$	$\bar{y} = \dfrac{\sum_{i=1}^{N} y_i}{n}$	$\mathrm{var}(\bar{y}) = \dfrac{(1-f)}{n} s^2$
Population Proportion[5]		
$\bar{P} = \dfrac{\sum_{i=1}^{N} y_i}{n}$	$\bar{p} = \dfrac{\sum_{i=1}^{n} y_i}{n}$	$\mathrm{var}(\bar{p}) = \dfrac{(1-f)}{n-1} p(1-p)$

---

[4] See appendix 4 for values of the $z_{\alpha/2}$ corresponding to different levels of confidence.

[5] Where $y_i = 1$ or $y_i = 0$ if the ith element has the desired characteristic or not, respectively.

where the variance of the sample elements is given by the following:

$$s^2 = \frac{1}{n-1}\sum_{i=1}^{n}(y_i - \bar{y})^2$$

and $f = \frac{n}{N}$ is the sampling fraction and, in SRS, the probability of inclusion.

Finally, the weight of each element is as follows:

$$\omega_i = f^{-1} = \frac{N}{n}$$

An example of SRS is presented in Box 4.2.

Determining the Sample Size in Stratified Sampling

The efficiency of the sample design can be improved by exploiting any available information on the population under study. In particular, when some population characteristics related to the variable estimated are known, this information can be used to divide the whole population into groups or strata, each sampled separately.[6] This process of stratification increases the efficiency of the design the greater the homogeneity of the elements belonging to the same group. This homogeneity, however, must refer to the characteristic that is being estimated, not to the variable used to identify the strata (Hansen, Hurwitz, and Madow 1953).

In stratified sampling, three different methods can be followed (Kish 1965; Sukhatme, Sukhatme, and Sukhatme 1984).

Method 1. Equal Allocation

The sample size is allocated equally among strata:

$$n_h = \frac{n_o}{H}$$

where:

H = number of strata
h = stratum, with $h = 1,2,3, \ldots h \ldots H$
n_h = stratum sample size
n_o = desired sample size

---

[6] See the *Productivity and Investment Climate Surveys (PICS): Implementation Manual* (World Bank 2003, 18–22) for information about how to identify strata in Investment Climate Surveys.

Box 4.2

Advising a Mayor

Suppose you are an advisor to a mayor. An opinion poll conducted by a prominent newspaper of 400 residents shows that 54 percent of residents are in favor of a new development program. Because elections are approaching and the mayor wishes to run for reelection, would you advise him to support the project in his political campaign?

The mean result from the poll (54%) is not sufficient to ensure that the majority of residents support this project. We need to determine the implied level of confidence and precision of the poll results. Basically, we need to work backward from the equation used to determine the sample size with proportions under SRS, calculating the implied error e_0 for a given α.

$$n = \frac{z_{\frac{\alpha}{2}}^2 P(1-P)}{e_0^2 + z_{\frac{\alpha}{2}}^2 \frac{P(1-P)}{N}}$$

Because we want to be certain of our results, we can assume that the level of confidence is 95 percent. The implied error is then given by the following:

$$e = \sqrt{\frac{(N-n) \times \left[z_{\frac{\alpha}{2}}^2 \times P \times (1-P) \right]}{n \times N}}$$

Assuming the population of resident voters is 650,000, the implied error is 6.4 percent. This means that we cannot be sure that the majority of the residents support this project, because the true proportion of the residents in favor of the project falls between 49.1 percent and 58.9 percent.

Suppose the mayor wants to know whether he should put this project on his reelection campaign. He asks you to conduct an opinion poll to determine the true proportion of the city population for or against it. How would you arrive at the answer?

We need three pieces of information to determine the sample size. First, we need the target population, which we know is 650,000 resident voters. Second, we need the level of error and desired confidence. Because the major wants to be reasonably certain, we set the error at +/- 3 percent, and the level of confidence at 95 percent. Finally, we need the variance of the true proportion. To be on the safe side, we can assume that the residents are equally split between supporters and opponents. This implies the maximum variance possible. In other words, we assume the worst possible scenario. This implies that we will select the highest sample size for the desired level of precision and confidence.

Box 4.2 (continued)

The required sample size is then given by the equation on proportions. That is

$$n = \frac{z_{\%2}^2 \times P \times (1 - P)}{e_0^2 + z_{\%2}^2 \times \dfrac{P \times (1 - P)}{N}} = \frac{1.96^2 \times 0.5 \times (1 - 0.5)}{0.03^2 + 1.96^2 \times \dfrac{0.5 \times (1 - 0.5)}{650000}} = \frac{3.8416 \times 0.25}{0.009 + 3.8416 \times \dfrac{0.25}{650000}} = 1065$$

Hence, you need to conduct a survey of 1,065 residents to be able to determine with 95 percent confidence what they think about this project within a 3 percent margin of error. If the survey results show that at least 54 percent of respondents are in favor of the project, we can be sure that most residents are in favor of the project and we can advise the major to support it during his campaign.

Method 2. Proportionate Allocation

The sample size is allocated proportionally to the size of each stratum:

$$n_h = n_o \frac{N_h}{N}$$

where:

N_h population size of the hth stratum and $\sum_{h=1}^{H} N_h = N$

Method 3. Optimum Allocation

The sample size is allocated among strata to reach the desired precision at the minimum cost or to reach the maximum precision for a given cost. In this case, depending on the level of precision desired or amount of resource available, four different cases can be envisaged:

Case 1. Given a desired sample size, n_o, and assuming that the unit cost across strata is the same,[7] the optimum allocation n_h across strata is determined by the following formula:

$$n_h = n_o \frac{W_h S_h}{\sum_{h=1}^{H} W_h S_h}$$

---

[7] Cost per unit in the hth stratum c_h is constant across strata:

$$C = \sum_{h=1}^{H} c_h n_h = c \sum_{h=1}^{H} n_h = cn.$$

known as "Neyman" allocation, where:

$$W_h = \frac{N_h}{N} \text{ stratum weight}$$

$$S_h^2 = \frac{1}{N_h - 1} \sum_{i=1}^{N_h} (y_{ih} - \bar{y}_h)^2 \text{ stratum variance}$$

Case 2. Given the desired level of precision, e_o, and assuming that the unit cost across strata is the same, the optimum sample size for each stratum is determined by the following formula:

$$n_h = \frac{W_h S_h \sum_{h=1}^{H} W_h S_h}{V_0 + \frac{1}{N} \sum_{h=1}^{H} W_h S_h^2}$$

and the total minimum sample size required is given by:

$$n_{\min} = \frac{\left(\sum_{h=1}^{H} W_h S_h \right)^2}{V_0 + \frac{1}{N} \sum_{h=1}^{H} W_h S_h^2}$$

where:

$$V_0 = \left(\frac{e_o}{z_{\alpha/2}} \right)^2$$

Case 3. Given the amount of resources available to conduct the survey, C_o, and assuming that the unit cost across strata is variable,[8] the optimum allocation of each n_h is determined by the following formula:

$$n_h = \frac{C_o \frac{W_h S_h}{\sqrt{c_h}}}{\sum_{h=1}^{H} W_h S_h \sqrt{c_h}}$$

---

[8] Cost per unit in the hth stratum c_h is different across strata:

$$C = \sum_{h=1}^{H} c_h n_h$$

and the total sample size is as follows:

$$n = \frac{C_o \sum_{h=1}^{H} \frac{W_h S_h}{\sqrt{c_h}}}{\sum_{h=1}^{H} W_h S_h \sqrt{c_h}}$$

Case 4. Given the desired level of precision, e_o, and assuming that the unit cost across strata is variable, the required sample size in each stratum is determined by the following formula:

$$n_h = \frac{W_h S_h}{\sqrt{c_h}} \cdot \frac{\sum W_h S_h \sqrt{c_h}}{V_o + \frac{1}{N} \sum_{h=1}^{H} W_h S_h^2}$$

and the total minimum sample size required is as follows:

$$n_{min} = \frac{\sum_{h=1}^{H} \frac{W_h S_h}{\sqrt{c_h}} \cdot \sum_{h=1}^{H} W_h S_h \sqrt{c_h}}{V_o + \frac{1}{N} \sum W_h S_h^2}.$$

With stratification, the mean and variance are estimated as follows:

Parameter Estimated	Sample Mean	Sample Variance
Population mean	$\bar{y} = \sum_{h=1}^{H} W_h \bar{y}_h$	$var(\bar{y}) = \sum_{h=1}^{H} W_h^2 \, var(\bar{y}_h)$
Population proportion	$(\bar{p}) = \sum_{h=1}^{H} W_h \bar{p}_h$	$var(\bar{p}) = \sum_{h=1}^{H} W_h^2 var(\bar{p}_h)$

where the exact formula for the variance depends on how the elements within the strata are sampled. If SRS is used within each stratum, then the variance formula becomes (1) for the sample mean:

$$var(\bar{y}) = \sum_{h=1}^{H} W_h^2 \left(\frac{1-f_h}{n_h} \right) s_h^2$$

where:

$$s_h^2 = \frac{1}{n_h - 1} \sum_{i=1}^{n_h} (y_{ih} - \bar{y}_h)^2.$$

or (2) for the sample proportion:

$$\mathrm{var}(\bar{p}) = \sum W_h^2 \left(\frac{1-f_h}{n_h - 1} \right) p_h (1 - p_h)$$

where:

$$p_h = \sum_{i=1}^{n_h} \frac{y_{ih}}{n_h}, \text{ and } y = 1 \text{ or } y = 0 \text{ if the sample unit has the characteristic}$$

of interest or not.

In stratified sampling, the probability of inclusion depends on the allocation method adopted:

Method 1. In Equal Allocation

$$f_h = \frac{n/H}{N_h}$$

Method 2. In Proportionate Allocation

$$f_h = \frac{n}{N}$$

Method 3. In Optimum Allocation

$$f_h = \frac{n_h}{N_h}$$

and the weights are calculated as usual as $\omega = f^{-1}$.

How to Carry Out Systematic Sampling

Systematic sampling consists of selecting units at fixed intervals throughout the frame (or stratum) after a random start. Given a population size, N, and a desired sample size, n, systematic sampling consists of (1) determining the sample interval $k = \frac{N}{n}$; (2) selecting a random number (RN) from 1 to k[9]; and (3) choosing all possible elements belonging to positions RN, $RN + k$, $RN + 2k$, ..., $RN + (n-1)k$.

[9] A table of random numbers is reproduced in appendix 5. This table can be used from any point in any direction (vertically, horizontally, diagonally) to get the series of random numbers needed.

Conceptually, with systematic sampling, we subdivide the population in an $n \times k$ matrix:

	1	2	3	...	k
1	y_1	y_2	y_3	...	y_k
2	y_{k+1}	y_{k+2}	y_{k+3}	...	y_{2k}
...	...	...	...	...	...
...	...	...	...	...	...
n	$y_{(n-1)k+1}$	$y_{(n-1)k+2}$	$y_{(n-1)k+3}$	...	y_{nk}

and then select the sample corresponding to the column number equal to the drawn RN.

Steps in Systematic Sampling

Suppose we have the following population frame:

Obs.	1	2	3	4	5	6	7	8	9
Y	5	9	12	10	7	5	9	11	10

Step 1. Given $N = 9$ and $n = 3$, determine $k = \dfrac{N}{n} = \dfrac{9}{3} = 3$.

Step 2. Divide the observations in the population in a $n \times k$ matrix.

$$n \begin{cases} \overbrace{\begin{bmatrix} 1 & 2 & 3 \\ 4 & 5 & 6 \\ 7 & 8 & 9 \end{bmatrix}}^{k} \end{cases}$$

Step 3. Select a RN between 1 and $k = 3$, suppose $RN = 2 = k$.

Step 4. Select the sample corresponding to column two and include population elements in position 2, 5, and 8, hence obtaining the sample.

obs	Y
2	9
5	7
8	11

The order in which units (elements) are listed is critical in systematic sampling. If the population includes homogeneous elements, the sampler should position homogeneous units across rows (not columns) in the $n \times k$ matrix described before. This creates strata composed of n rows, and systematic sampling will be equivalent to a proportional stratified sampling. One can also observe that forming the $n \times k$ matrix is equivalent to dividing the population into k clusters represented by the columns of the matrix. Hence, while listing the elements in the population, a sampler should attempt to distribute each patch or type of homogeneous units as far as possible uniformly among the clusters, that is, the columns of the matrix.

It is possible that the population size, N, is not an exact multiple of n, so that $N = n \times k + r$ where r is less than k. There are two possible ways to handle the situation. First, select r sample units at random from the population and drop them before creating the $n \times k$ matrix and then proceed from step 3 onward. Second, a more precise method would be to form the matrix with all $n \times k + r$ units so that r columns within the $n \times k$ matrix would have $n + 1$ units, while the remaining $n - r$ columns would have n units. Next, select one column at random, as in step 3, and proceed onward as usual. A similar procedure can be used in situations in which $N = n \times k - r$. The step described is equivalent to considering the list of $N = n \times k + r$ or $N = n \times k - r$ units as circular and after a random number (RN) is selected elements in position RN, 2 RN, 3 RN, and so on are selected achieving a sample of n, $n + 1$ or $n - 1$ units.[10]

In systematic sampling, the mean is calculated as follows:

$$\bar{y} = \frac{\sum_{i=1}^{n} y_i}{n}$$

because it is an *epsem* design.

Estimating the variance in systematic sampling poses challenging problems. In practice, assuming the order of elements is random,[11] the variance is computed as follows:

$$\mathrm{var}(\bar{y}) = \frac{(1 - f)}{n} s^2$$

where s^2 is the variance as calculated in SRS.

The variance in stratified systematic sampling is computed as follows:

$$\mathrm{var}(\bar{y}) = \frac{(1 - f)}{n} \sum_{h=1}^{H} W_h s_h^2$$

---

[10] Kish (1965) presents a number of other methods to deal with this problem. We refrain from addressing them here because, in general, one additional observation in a sample of an Investment Climate Survey presents no implementation problem.

[11] Kish (1965) presents alternative formulas when the SRS requirement is not met.

The probability of inclusion for each element is as follows:

$$f = \frac{1}{k}$$

and the weight is:

$w = f^{-1} = k$ and $w_h = f_h^{-1} = k_h$ in stratified SRS.

How to Carry Out the Probability Proportional to Size Selection Method

The PPS selection method is used when we follow a two-stage sampling procedure and are faced with clusters of unequal size, and if we wish to have control over the total sample size, n, and the number of clusters included in the sample while keeping an *epsem* design. With PPS, each element in the frame will be selected with a PPS of the cluster to which it belongs.

Steps in Sample Design

Step 1. Given a population, N, choose the desired sample size n.

Step 2. Choose either the number of clusters a to include in the sample or the number of cluster elements b to include in the sample, where $n = a \times b$.

Step 3. Draw a RN from 1 to N with replacement.

Step 4. Select the cluster that has the cumulative sum that first exceeds the RN.

Step 5. Sample b elements in that cluster using SRS, systematic sampling, stratified sampling, or cluster sampling.

Step 6. Repeat steps 3 to 5 a times.[12]

Because PPS is an *epsem* design, the mean is estimated as follows:

$$\bar{y} = \frac{\sum_{i=1}^{n} y_i}{n}$$

---

[12] Note that the same cluster can be selected multiple times because the RN drawing is with replacement. So, if a cluster is selected k times, $k \times b$ elements will be drawn from that cluster.

While the variance is calculated as follows:

$$\operatorname{var}(\bar{y}) = \frac{1-f}{a} s_a^2$$

where:

$$s_a^2 = \frac{1}{a-1} \sum_{j=1}^{a} \left(\bar{y}_j - \bar{y}\right)^2$$

$$y_j = \frac{\sum_{\beta=1}^{b} y_{j\beta}}{b} \quad \text{(cluster sample mean)}.$$

The probability of inclusion is given by the following:

$$f = \frac{aB_\alpha}{N} \frac{b}{B_\alpha}$$

where:

B_α = cluster size
 a = number of cluster included in sample
 b = number of cluster elements included in the sample.

Finally the weight is as follows:

$$w = f^{-1} = \frac{NB_\alpha}{aB_\alpha b}.$$

An alternative method[13] consists of selecting clusters with PPS *without replacement* and then sample elements are drawn within selected clusters at random (SRS). This procedure preserves the characteristics of *epsem* design and it is implemented in the following steps.

Steps in Sample Design

Step 1. Given a population, N, choose the desired sample size *n*.

Step 2. Choose the number of clusters *a* to be included in the sample and the number of elements *b* to be included in the sample clusters, where $n = a \times b$.

---

[13] I owe the inclusion of this method to Dr. Yusuf.

Step 3. Let i designate a cluster in the population, with a total of A clusters in the population. Furthermore, let j indicate a sample element within a cluster with a total of B_i units or elements in the ith cluster. Thus, $\sum_i^A B_i = N$.

Step 4. List the clusters and cumulated clusters' sizes B_i as follows:

$B_1 = C_1$

$B_1 + B_2 = C_1 + B_2 = C_2$

$B_1 + B_2 + B_3 = C_2 + B_3 = C_3$, etc. and

$B_1 + B_2 + B_3 + \ldots + B_A = C_3 + \ldots + B_A = C_A$

Step 5. Compute interval of selection $I = \dfrac{N}{a}$ where a is the number of clusters to be selected.

Step 6. Select an RN with $0 < RN \leq I$.

Step 7. Systematically select a clusters with cumulated C_i ($i = 1, 2, \ldots$ a) containing the selection vector elements RN, RN+I, RN+2I, $\ldots$ RN+ $(a - 1)I$.

Step 8. Select b sample elements in each selected cluster using SRS, systematic sampling, stratified sampling, or cluster sampling.

Note that a cluster may be selected more than once only if its size is larger than the interval of selection I. The procedure, however, retains *epsem* characteristics of the sample. A refined standard practice is to select the clusters with sizes larger than the interval of selection I automat ically (that is, with probability 1) and attach weight $w = 1x\dfrac{b}{B_i}$ to the sample elements selected from such clusters.

If a selected cluster has less than b sample elements, say l, all elements of the cluster are selected and the remainder $(b - l)$ elements are selected from the adjacent (serially/geographically) cluster. PPS selection (without replacement) is an *epsem* selection with weight w for all sample elements given by the following:

$$w = \frac{N}{n}.$$

The estimate of the population mean is as follows:

$$\bar{y} = \frac{\sum_{t=1}^{n} y_t}{n}.$$

The estimate of the variance of the sample mean $\bar{y}$ is given by the following:

$$\text{var}(\bar{y}) = \frac{(1-f)}{a} s_a^2$$

where:

$$s_a^2 = \frac{1}{(a-1)} \sum_{i=1}^{a} (\bar{y}_i - \bar{y})^2$$

$$\bar{y}_i = \frac{\sum_{i=1}^{b} y_{ij}}{b} \quad \text{(cluster sample mean)}.$$

How to Deal with Population Frame Problems

The accuracy of any sampling procedure rests not only on the correct application of the relevant theoretical model, but also, and critically, on the accuracy of the frame. The perfect frame in which each unit is listed exhaustively and uniquely and in which no foreign elements appear is a rare event. Often frames are riddled with problems. Identifying and correcting them remains an important part of sampling.

Frame problems are important because they affect the underlying probability of inclusion of the sample units, thus tainting the original sample design and original weights. Hence, the weights assigned to each element at the design stage must be recalibrated at the estimation stage if frame problems occur.[14] Kish (1965) identifies four categories of problems that can be attributed to faulty frames:

Problem 1. Noncoverage

Some population elements might not be included in the list. This can happen because frames are inadequate or incomplete (Kalton 1983). In business surveys, it is often the case in developing nations that frames are out of date, thus failing to include all elements of the target population.

---

[14] In addition to frame problems, survey nonresponse has an added impact on the weights; this needs to be taken into account when analyzing the data. The literature has developed a number of different procedures to adjust weights for both *unit nonresponse* and *item nonresponse*. While a discussion on adjustments for unit nonresponse is presented in the next section, methodologies to handle item nonresponse go beyond the scope of these notes.

Solutions at the Design Stage

Solution 1. *Redefine the target population* to exclude the missing elements. This solution is acceptable only when the excluded group is a very small proportion of the target population (Kalton 1983).

Solution 2. *Add supplementary frames* in which the missing elements are included. This solution is preferable to solution 1 although it might generate another problem, duplication. This problem however is less pervasive and can be easily handled (see below) (Kalton 1983).

Solution 3. *Adopt a linking procedure* to attach missing elements to existing elements in a clear, practical, and unique manner. Hence, when the existing element is drawn, all linked elements are also selected. This solution has the same drawbacks as a cluster sampling (Kish 1965).

Solution at the Estimation Stage

Solution 1. *Poststratification* uses stratification weights after the completion of the survey. This method allows the adjustments of weights in a way more respondent to the actual population (table 4.1) Poststratification weight adjustment is particularly useful in the event of an outdated frame list. Hence, for example, if an establishment listed as small at the design stage is (after the survey) discovered to belong to a different size category, it is essential to adjust the weights accordingly with a procedure similar to poststratification.

Table 4.1
Weight Adjustments for Noncoverage

	Design			Poststratification		
Strata	Population N	Sample n_h	Design Weight $w=p^{-1}$	Final Population N_{ps}	Adjustment Factor $w_{ps}=N_{ps}/N_h$	Weight Adjusted $w_{jps}=w*w_{ps}$
A	5,000	250	20	?	1.4	28
B	15,000	500	30	?	1.4	42
Total	20,000			28,000		

Source: Author's calculations.

Problem 2. Duplicates

Sometimes, especially when the frame is constructed as the combination of different frames, some elements may appear more than once. This has an impact on the probability of inclusion and thus needs to be taken into account.

Solutions at the Design Stage

Solution 1. *Adopt a unique identification method.* That is first determine a precise order for each separate listing (the first most important, the second, and so on). Then for each element in the first list eliminate duplicates appearing in the subsequent lists (Kish 1965).

Solution 2. *Adjust the sample of subsequent lists.* Draw an independent sample from each list. Then check and eliminate in the sample of any subsequent lists the elements that appear in the full previous lists (Kish 1965).

Solution at the Estimation Stage

Solution 1. *Use weight adjustment.* Reestimate the weights of the duplicate listing to account for their higher probability of inclusion. If, for instance, two independent samples A and B are drawn from two lists with probability f_a and f_b, all A sample elements that appear also in the B list should have a weight $f = f_a \times f_b$ (Kish 1965).[15]

Problem 3. Blanks or Foreign Elements

Blanks are frame elements without corresponding population elements, while foreign elements are units that belong to the frame but are outside the scope of the survey (Kalton 1983). In business surveys, this might be a company that went out of business but is still listed in the frame, or it could be a company that is operating in an industry outside the research interest.

Solutions at the Design Stage

Solution 1. *Ignore the selected element.* The implication of this is that the total sample at the end of the survey will be lower than the desired size. As a consequence, if it is possible to estimate the proportion γ of blanks and foreign elements in the frame, the sample size must be adjusted as follows:

---

[15] And, similarly, all B sample elements that appear in the A list.

$$n' = \frac{n}{(1-\gamma)}.$$

One common mistake in this case is to replace the blank or foreign element with the element next to it. This practice should be avoided because it is nonrandom and assigns a higher probability of inclusion to the elements next to the blanks and foreign (Kalton 1983).

Solution 2. *Conduct a two-stage selection.* In the first stage, a screening interview is conducted to determine whether the sampled elements exist and meet the objective of the study. Then a second selection is performed to determine a subsample of eligible elements. This approach is appropriate when only a small fraction of the population is of interest (Kalton 1983).

Problem 4. Clustering

Sometimes a listing of elements might include some clusters. In business surveys, this happens when a frame of establishments also includes firms (groups of establishments).

Solutions at the Design Stage

Solution 1. *Take all elements in the cluster.* This solution has the advantage of being easily applicable. With this approach, each cluster element will have a probability of inclusion equal to the probability of selection of the cluster itself. Hence, no reweighting is necessary. This method presents two disadvantages:

- It generates higher variance the larger is the cluster and the higher is the intraclass correlation.
- It could generate response contamination if units in the same cluster are influenced by the other element's responses. This is particularly true for attitude questions.

Solution 2. *Take only one element in the cluster.* This subsampling procedure eliminates the above disadvantages, but carries its own drawbacks. First, it is harder to implement, and second, it changes the probability of selection of the elements and thus requires reweighting. The first drawback relates to which rule should be followed in the selection of the single cluster element. To avoid selection bias, it is important for a random procedure be adopted. Kalton (1983) argues that it is unrealistic to rely exclusively on the interviewer's ability and willingness to

Table 4.2
Kish's Selection Grid

Number of Establishments in Cluster	If Questionnaire Contains Table							
	A	B	C	D	E	F	G	H
	Then Select the Establishment in Position							
1	1	1	1	1	1	1	1	1
2	1	1	1	1	2	2	2	2
3	1	1	1	2	2	3	3	3
4	1	1	2	2	3	3	4	4
Share of questionnaires containing each table	17%	8%	8%	17%	17%	8%	8%	17%

Source: Kish 1965.

apply a random process (that is, a table of random numbers). He or she might inadvertently misapply this method and select the respondent on the basis of his or her availability instead, without the researcher being able to check the procedure adopted. To avoid this bias, a widely used method is the Kish selection grid (table 4.2). This is an objective and checkable procedure to select one respondent in a cluster while keeping equal probability of selection among the cluster's elements. With this method, all eligible establishments in the cluster are first ordered on the basis of some clear, precise, and objective measure (such as total sales, number of employees, and so on). In each questionnaire a table is printed instructing the interviewer to select the respondent corresponding to a specific position in the ordered list. In this way, the interviewer has no control over the selection process. The randomness is introduced by the fact that different tables are printed on different questionnaires, each assigning a different probability of selection and giving an overall equal probability of selection for all elements (Kalton 1983).[16] So, for instance, if the interviewer has a form with table C printed on it, when he or she encounters a cluster with four eligible respondents, he or she will select the second element in the ordered list (table 4.2).

---

[16] As an alternative method, instead of printing the grid on each questionnaire, it can be printed on a number of letters given at random to interviewers.

The adoption of this procedure changes the probability of inclusion of the cluster elements. Hence, at the estimation stage, the weights must be recalibrated. The probability of inclusion of element i is dependent not only on the probability of selection of the cluster but also on the total number of elements in the cluster. So the new probability is as follows:

$$f = f_c \times f_a = \frac{n}{N} \times \frac{1}{A}$$

where:

f_c = probability of selecting the cluster
f_a = probability of selecting one unit a in the cluster of A elements.

The weight of ath element is thus:

$$\omega = f^{-1} = \frac{NA}{n}.$$

Impact of Mergers, Acquisitions, and Separations on Sampling Weights

In business surveys, frame problems are particularly frequent because establishments continuously change industry, form, and structure making the maintenance of an up-to-date listing extremely difficult. Hence, the sample designer must be particularly careful in identifying and handling missing, blanks, duplicates, or clusters. In fact, what appears to be a nonexisting establishment, in reality, could be a new establishment (or firm). The fact that establishments merge or split might give the false appearance of blanks and duplicates. If not properly handled, these phenomena might taint the underlying weights assigned at the design stage.

Three general scenarios can happen: *mergers, acquisitions,* and *separations*. In mergers and acquisitions two establishments,[17] A and B, form a new establishment, C. Hence, A and B no longer exist and the new establishment C incorporates the assets and liabilities of both A and B. In these situations, depending on how up to date the frame is,

---

[17] In this discussion, we assume the establishment to be the unit of analysis as defined in box 4.1.

Table 4.3

Frame Accuracy and Sampling Weights: The Case of Mergers, Acquisitions, and Separations in Establishment Surveys

In the Event of: Phenomenon	The Frame Includes:	The Sample Designer Can:		Unit Weight Adjustments
Merger	A or B	Select C		$w_a=w_b=w_c=N_h/n_h$
	A and B	Select C		$w_c=N_h/2n_h$
	A and C or B and C	Either treat A=blank (or B=blank[a])		n.a.
		or select C		$w_c=N_h/2n_h$
Acquisition	A and B and C	Either treat A=blank and B=blank[a]		n.a.
		or select C		$w_c=N_h/3n_h$
Separations	A	Treat A as a cluster:	Select one of 2	$w_i=2N_h/n_h$[c]
			Select all 2	$w_i=N_h/n_h$
	A and B	Either treat A=blank[b]		n.a.
		or treat A as a cluster	Select one of 2	$w_i\begin{cases}2N_h/n_h \text{ for } i\neq B \text{ or}\\ 2N_h/3n_h \text{ for } i=B\end{cases}$
			Select all 2	$w_i\begin{cases}N_h/n_h \text{ for } i\neq B\\ N_h/2n_h \text{ for } i=B\end{cases}$
	A and C	Same as in example above, with C=B		n.a.
	A and B and C	Either treat A=blank[a] or treat A as cluster	Select one of 2	$w_i=2N_h/3n_h$
			Select all 2	$w_i=N_h/2n_h$

Source: Author's creation.

Note: Assuming a stratified simple random sampling of size n_h in a population of N_h with corresponding weights $w=N_h/n_h$.

a. This is preferable.

b. This alternative is less desirable, because it implies C having a zero probability of selection.

c. If the cluster has three elements, then $w_i=3N_h/n_h$.

n.a. = not applicable.

different selection criteria should be adopted (see table 4.3). If the frame contains only one of the two original establishments, A or B, the new establishment C can be included in the sample (linking methodology) without any weight adjustments. On the contrary, if a combination of any of the two original establishments is in the frame—A and

B, A and C, or B and C—then different selection criteria can be adopted, having a different impact on the unit weight. Thus if both A and B are present in the listing, then C (the new establishment) must be selected and the unit weight of C must be modified to $\frac{N_h}{2n_h}$, because C had twice the probability of selection:[18]

$$f_C = f_A + f_B = \frac{n_h}{N_h} + \frac{n_h}{N_h} = \frac{2n_h}{N_h}$$

where f_C is the probability of selection of C.

If A and C or B and C are included in the frame, then the designer has two alternatives. One is to consider A (or B respectively) as blank. This is acceptable because C is present itself in the list and hence has a non-zero probability of selection, while A (or B) no longer exist and can be considered as frame problems (blank). No weight adjustment is necessary in this case. Alternatively, although A or B is randomly selected, the designer can choose to include C (the new establishment) in the sample (linking methodology discussed above). In this case, however, we need to adjust the sampling weight for C because it has twice the probability of selection. Thus, the weight for C becomes $\omega_C = \frac{N_h}{2n_h}$ as discussed above. The decision on the approach to follow must be made *before* the sample is drawn. In fact, in our last example, if C is randomly drawn and either A or B are also in the frame, the weight of C will depend on whether we consider A (or B) as blank, irrespective of whether they are actually drawn. For simplicity of calculation, it is recommended to consider A or B as blanks. In this scenario in fact C will have the same weight as all other elements in the stratum and no weight adjustment is needed.

The last case within mergers and acquisitions is when all three elements, A, B, and C, are in the frame. Once again, the same logic applies. If we adopt (a priori) the policy of considering A and B as blanks, no adjustment is necessary. If C is selected, then it is part of the sample, while if A and/or B are drawn, they are dropped. Alternatively, if A and/or B are selected and we link them to C (hence C is included in the sample although not directly selected), then we need to adjust the ω_C because C

---

[18] Recall that the weight is the inverse of the probability of selection.

now has three times the probability of selection compared with other elements in its stratum. Therefore $\omega_C = \dfrac{N_h}{3n}$ because

$$f_C = f_A + f_B + f_C = \frac{n_h}{N_h} + \frac{n_h}{N_h} + \frac{n_h}{N_h} = \frac{3n_h}{N_h}.$$

Separations present more complicated scenarios. The first is when only A (the old establishment) is in the frame. This is the typical case of cluster and, as such, we have two options. We can either include all the members of the cluster (that is, B and C) in our sample or include only one of them. In the first case, no weight adjustment is necessary. In the second, we need to adjust the weight because the probability of selection of each member of the cluster is not equal to the probability of selection of the cluster itself. Hence, the probability of selection of the element included in the sample, either B or C, will be equal to the probability that the cluster is selected multiplied by the probability that the element is drawn given that the cluster is selected:

$$f_i = f_A \times f_{i/A} = \frac{n_h}{N_h} \times \frac{1}{2} = \frac{n_h}{2N_h}$$

where i = B or C.[19]

Similarly, when A and B are present in the frame, we have two options. We can consider A as a blank and disregard it. This is not preferable because it would imply a zero probability of selection for C. Alternatively, we can treat A as a cluster and, again, we have two choices—either to include all elements of the cluster or just one. In both cases, however, we need to adjust the unit weights. If we select all elements of the cluster, the weight of C remains the same as all other elements of the stratum and no adjustment is needed. When we estimate the weight of B, however, we need to consider the fact that B has twice the chances of being selected— once if drawn directly and once if A is drawn. Hence, the weight of B is

---

[19] Note that throughout this section we assume a cluster of two elements. If more elements are in the cluster, the value of the probability of selection will change accordingly. Hence, if three elements are in the cluster, the probability is $f_i = f_A \times f_{i/A} = \dfrac{n_h}{N_h} \times \dfrac{1}{3} = \dfrac{n_h}{3N_h}.$

the inverse of the sum of the probability of A (the cluster) being selected and the probability of B itself being selected is:

$$f_B = f_A + f_B = \frac{n_b}{N_b} + \frac{n_b}{N_b} = \frac{2n_b}{N_b}.$$

Conversely, if we select only one of the elements of the cluster, then the weight of the chosen element must be adjusted accordingly. If this chosen cluster element is C, then the weight is $\omega_C = \frac{2N_b}{n_b}$ because its probability of selection is as follows:

$$f_C = f_A \times f_{C/A} = \frac{n_b}{N_b} \times \frac{1}{2} = \frac{n_b}{2N_b}.$$

If, however, the element drawn is B, then the unit weight of B is $\omega_B = \frac{2N_b}{3n_b}$ because its probability of selection will depend on both A being drawn and B itself being drawn:

$$f_B = f_A \times f_{B/A} + f_B = \frac{n_b}{N_b} \times \frac{1}{2} + \frac{n_b}{N_b} = \frac{3n_b}{2N_b}.$$

Finally, if all three elements A, B, and C are in the frame, we have two options. We can treat A as a blank or treat A as a cluster. The first option is preferable because it will not taint the weights of the other elements and does not involve any weight adjustments. The second option has two alternatives: we can select just one element of the cluster or all of them. If we chose only one, its weight will be estimated as the inverse of the following:

$$f_i = f_A \times f_{i/A} + f_i = \frac{n_b}{N_b} \times \frac{1}{2} + \frac{n_b}{N_b} = \frac{3n_b}{2N_b}.$$

If we chose all elements of the cluster, then the weight of each of them is simply the inverse of the following:

$$f_i = f_A + f_i = \frac{n_b}{N_b} + \frac{n_b}{N_b} = \frac{2n_b}{N_b}$$

for i = B or C.

Weight Adjustments and Poststratification

While it is not necessary to use weighted results with SRS and other *epsem* methods, when stratified random sampling is adopted, results must be weighted if population parameters need to be estimated (box 4.3). In this case, sampling weights estimated at the design stage (called design weights) must be corrected to compensate for unit nonresponse and frame problems. Both of these phenomena can have a significant impact on the final sampling weights and must to be taken into account at the end of the fieldwork.

Suppose the sampling strategy in a business survey is a stratified SRS with proportional allocation. The strata are determined using sector (garments and textiles), size (small, medium, and large), and location (north and south). Furthermore, as part of the sample design, some strata were collapsed and large establishments were selected with certainty. The sample structure and the estimated weights are summarized in table 4.4. The design weights are estimated as the inverse of the probability of selection:

$$\omega_h = f_h^{-1} = \left(\frac{n_h}{N_h}\right)^{-1} = \frac{N_h}{n_h}.$$

After the data collection is completed, the design weights need to be adjusted before the analysis can commence. The true weights (w) are obtained by multiplying the design weights (w_{DES}) by an adjustment factor for unit nonresponse (w_{RES}) and an adjustment factor for frame problems (w_{FP}):

$$w = w_{DES} * w_{NR} * w_{FP}.$$

The unit nonresponse adjustment factor is calculated by estimating the proportion of the total sample that participated to the survey. Hence,

$$w_{NR} = \frac{n_h}{n_h^r}.$$

where:

n_h^r = number of respondents who participated in the survey and belong to stratum h[20]

n_h = number of sampled elements in stratum h at the design stage

---

[20] Note that this number includes all respondents to the survey, even those who are sampled in a different stratum than h (because if inaccurate classification) but belong to h.

Box 4.3

Why it is Important to Use Weights with Stratified Sampling

Suppose the car company you work for wants to issue a warranty on transmissions. You are asked to estimate the cost of such a warranty. To do so, you need to estimate at what mileage, on average, cars require transmission repair. Assume you have the list of car owners shown in box table 4.3.1, and your budget allows you to sample nine elements. The true value, unknown to you and that you need to estimate, is 60,120 miles.

Box Table 4.3.1

List of Car Owners

Car ID	Repair Mileage (unknown)	Location	Car ID	Repair Mileage (unknown)	Location
1	85,900	Rural	11	31,500	Urban
2	99,500	Rural	12	48,600	Urban
3	82,100	Rural	13	45,500	Urban
4	70,000	Rural	14	38,500	Urban
5	74,100	Rural	15	49,000	Urban
6	77,000	Rural	16	42,000	Urban
7	68,500	Rural	17	45,500	Urban
8	94,500	Rural	18	35,000	Urban
9	69,700	Rural	19	42,000	Urban
10	65,200	Rural	20	38,500	Urban
		Average	60,120		

Source: Author's creation.

The first choice at your disposal is to follow a simple random sampling (SRS) methodology. From the nine samples, you obtain an average value of 56,767 miles.

Nonetheless you have reason to believe from previous discussions with mechanics that transmissions require repair earlier if the car is driven in rural areas than if it is driven in urban locations. Luckily your list includes this information. You decide to sample the nine elements using stratified random sampling. Because you suspect that in rural areas the variance of the parameter you want to estimate (repair mileage) is twice as high as in urban locations, you decide to sample more cars in rural stratum (6) than in the urban stratum (3), as described in box table 4.3.2.

(continued)

Box 4.3 (continued)

Box Table 4.3.2
Results Using Simple Random Sampling and Stratified Sampling

Simple Random Sampling		Stratified Random Sampling			
Car ID	Repair Mileage	Stratum	Car ID	Repair Mileage	Weight
3	82,100	Rural	1	85,900	1.67
4	70,000		3	82,100	1.67
6	77,000		4	70,000	1.67
10	65,200		5	74,100	1.67
12	48,600		8	94,500	1.67
13	45,500		10	65,200	1.67
16	42,000	Urban	14	38,500	3.33
19	42,000		15	49,000	3.33
20	38,500		20	38,500	3.33
Average		Simple average		Weighted average	
56,767		66,422		60,317	

Source: Author's creation.

With stratification, you can still estimate the mileage repair value by simple average over all nine observations. The value obtained is 66,422, which is even less accurate than the value obtained using SRS. Hence, while using the simple average with stratification improves the estimate of the parameter within each stratum, it biases its estimate of the whole population. To obtain a more accurate estimate than SRS, we must use the weights. If we do that we obtain a value of 60,317, which is closer to the true population than SRS (box table 4.3.2).

Estimating the adjustment factor for frame problems is more complex. As mentioned earlier, four main categories of frame problems might occur: noncoverage, duplicates, blanks or foreign elements, and clustering. While blanks and foreign elements are dealt with at the design stage, clustering and duplicates have an impact on the weights of the individual sampling unit.[21] Noncoverage, on the contrary, is a source of bias for the

---

[21] The implications for weight adjustment have already been discussed in the text as well as in table 4.3, so we are not including them again in this example.

Table 4.4

Sample Design: Stratified Sample Random Sampling

Stratum	Sector	Stratification Criteria Size	Location	Stratum Size N^0_h	Sample Size n^0_h	Replacements R_h	Total Sample $n_h=n^0_h+R_h$	Probability of Selection ps	Design Weight $w=ps^{-1}$
A	Garments	Small	North	1,000	76	24	100	0.10000	10.00
B	Garments	Small	South	2,000	164	36	200	0.10000	10.00
C	Garments	Medium	North	2,000	182	18	200	0.10000	10.00
D	Garments	Medium	South	600	82	13	95	0.15833	6.32
E	Garments	Large	North	200	200	0	200	1.00000	1.00
F	Garments	Large	South	180	180	0	180	1.00000	1.00
G	Textiles	Small & Med.	North	2,200	81	46	127	0.05773	17.32
H	Textiles	Small & Med.	South	1,800	95	25	120	0.06667	15.00
I	Textiles	Large	North	300	300	0	300	1.00000	1.00
K	Textiles	Large	South	220	220	0	220	1.00000	1.00

Source: Author's creation.

whole stratum. Two main noncoverage problems can take place: inaccurate coverage or incomplete coverage. Inaccurate coverage arises when an establishment is listed in the frame but no longer exists. Incomplete coverage occurs when the frame is not updated and some establishments that should be listed in a specific stratum are instead listed in another stratum, with both strata included in the sample stratification. The adjustment factor for frame problems (w_{FP}) depends on both of these factors, and its estimation is not trivial. The fact that an establishment cannot be located does not necessarily mean that it went out of business. It is possible, for example, that it moved to a different location within the study area, in which cases it should be included in the weight adjustments. The fieldwork can provide extremely useful information for their estimation.

This step (the estimation of the adjustment factor from frame problems) requires the estimation of three parameters: (1) the proportion of units p_h^{out} that are present in each stratum h but should not be because (a) they do not exist or exist outside the target population, n_h^{oos},[22] or (b) they belong to other strata in the sample, $n_h^{in} \Rightarrow i$; (2) the proportion of units that belong to h but are found in any of the other strata $i \neq h$ of our target population, $p_i^{in} \Rightarrow h$; and (3) the net rate of growth of each stratum since last update, g_h. After these three values are determined, the adjustment factor for frame problems is estimated as follows:

$$w_{FP} = \frac{N_h^{PS}}{N_h}$$

where:

$$N_h^{PS} = N_h \times (1 + g_h - p_h^{out}) + p_{i \Rightarrow h}^{in} \sum_{i \neq h} N_i$$

$$p_h^{out} = \frac{n_h^{oos} + n_{h \Rightarrow i}^{in}}{n_h} = \frac{n_h^{oos}}{n_h} + \frac{n_{h \Rightarrow i}^{in}}{n_h} = p_h^{oos} + p_{h \Rightarrow i}^{in}$$

$$p_{i \Rightarrow h}^{in} = \frac{\sum_{i \neq h} n_{i \Rightarrow h}^{in}}{\sum_{i \neq h} n_i}.$$

While g_h must be estimated on the basis of prior knowledge,[23] and the estimation of p_h^{out} is pretty straightforward, $p_i^{in} \Rightarrow h$ is complicated

---

[22] That is, they do not belong to any of the strata in our sample.
[23] Because we are interested in the net growth rate of the stratum, an analysis of the dynamics of the population under study over the past few years might provide useful information.

by the fact that units belonging to one stratum can appear in any other strata surveyed. This requires an accurate recording of what happens during the fieldwork to properly reclassify the units and obtain correct weights.[24]

As an illustration of this methodology, let us assume for simplicity *Example* that we have only the first three strata of table 4.4. After the fieldwork is completed, records indicate that (in stratum A) 85 establishments participated, 5 refused, and 10 were inaccurately classified (4 out of scope and 6 belonging to other strata in the sample). Furthermore, because of frame inaccuracy, 60 establishments belong to stratum A, but they have been sampled in strata B and C as shown in table 4.5. Let us also assume a similar pattern for strata B and C, so that at the end of the fieldwork the results are as shown in table 4.6.

After this is done, the final weights can be estimated as described above. Hence, for stratum A, the final weight is estimated as follows:

$$p_A^{out} = \frac{n_A^{out}}{n_A} = \frac{4+(1+5)}{100} = 0.10$$

$$p_{i \Rightarrow A}^{in} = \frac{\sum_{i \neq A} n_{i \Rightarrow A}^{in}}{\sum_{i \neq A} n_i} = \frac{30+30}{200+200} = 0.15$$

$$N_A^{PS} = N_A \times \left(1 + g_A - p_A^{out}\right) + p_{i \Rightarrow A}^{in} \sum_{i \neq A} N_i = 1000 \times \left(1 + 0.05 - 0.10\right)$$
$$+\, 0.15 \times 2000 = 1250$$

$$w_{FP} = \frac{N_A^{PS}}{N_A} = \frac{1250}{1000} = 1.25$$

$$w_{NR} = \frac{n_b}{n_b^r} = \frac{100}{85+30+30} = 0.69$$

$$w = w_{DES} \times w_{NR} \times w_{FP} = 10 \times 0.69 \times 1.25 = 8.62$$

All other weights are shown in table 4.7.

---

[24] To this end, appendix 7 reports the minimum amount of information to collect during the fieldwork to facilitate both weight adjustment and the compilation of figure 2.3 presented at the end of chapter 2.

Table 4.5

Weight Adjustment Components for Stratum A

Stratum	Stratum Size N_h^0	Sample Size n^0	Respondents	Inaccurate		Incomplete		Share of			Growth Rate
				Refusals n^{ref}	Out of Scope n^{oos}	To Other Strata $n_{h\to i}^{in}$	From Other Strata $n_{i\to h}^{in}$	OOS p_h^{oos}	$IN_{h\to i}$ $p_{h\to i}^{in}$	$IN_{i\to h}$ $p_{i\to h}^{in}$	g_h
A	1,000	100	85	5	4	to B 1 to C 5	from B 30 from C 30	0.04	0.06	0.15	0.05
B	1,000	200				to A (30) to C					
C	1,000	200				to A (30) to B					

Source: Author's creation.

Table 4.6
Weight Adjustment Components for All Strata

Stratum	Stratum Size N_h^0	Sample Size n^0	Respondents	Refusals n^{ref}	Inaccurate Out of Scope n^{oos}	Incomplete To Other Strata $n_{h\to i}^{in}$	Incomplete From Other Strata $n_{i\to h}^{in}$	Share of OOS p_h^{oos}	Share of $IN_{h\to i}$ $p_{h\to i}^{in}$	Share of $IN_{i\to h}$ $p_{i\to h}^{in}$	Growth Rate g_h
A	1,000	100	85	5	4	to B 1, to C 5	from B 30, from C 30	0.04	0.06	0.15	0.05
B	1,000	200	145	5	10	to A 30, to C 10	from A 1, from C 0	0.05	0.20	0.003	0.08
C	1,000	200	160	10	0	to A 30, to B 0	from A 5, from C 10	0.0	0.15	0.05	0.03
						76	= 76				

Source: Author's creation.

Table 4.7

Estimation of Final Weights

Stratum	Stratum Size N^0_h	Sample Size n^0	Share of Out p^{out}_h	Share of In p^{in}_h	Growth Rate g_h	Poststratification Population N^{PS}	Design Weight w_{des}	Response Adjustment Factor w_{res}	Frame Problem Adj Factor w_{fp}	Final Weight w
A	1,000	100	0.10	0.15	0.05	1,250	10	0.69	1.25	8.621
B	1,000	200	0.25	0.003	0.08	840	5	1.37	0.84	5.753
C	1,000	200	0.15	0.05	0.03	1,030	5	1.14	1.03	5.886

Source: Author's creation.

Sampling in Practice: How to Maximize the Sample Representativeness while Minimizing the Survey Cost through the Use of Poststratification

A common challenge when designing a survey is the desire to analyze many characteristics of the population.[25] Because of budget and time constraints, it is not possible to guarantee a certain level of precision and confidence for all of these dimensions. What this practical example proposes is to address this problem through the careful choice of key strata in drawing the sample and the use of poststratification. These techniques allow for a degree of redesigning of the sample distribution, after the survey is completed, to maintain a predetermined level of precision for different dimensions of analysis within the fixed sample size.

Let us assume that we have obtained or compiled data on the population of manufacturing establishments. The frame list includes the following: (1) sector of activity, (2) location—region, and (3) size—number of employees. The population distribution is presented in table 4.8. Sampling can be designed in the following six steps.

Steps in Sampling Design

Step 1. *Determine the sampling parameters.* The size and composition of the sample will depend on three factors:

- The objective of the study,[26]
- The available budget, and
- The desired level of precision and confidence.

Let's assume that we want to compare characteristics of the Investment Climate environment across locations, as well as estimate the determinants of firm productivity across sectors. Let's further suppose that the available budget allows for a sample size of approximately 850 establishments. Finally, let's assume that we wish to reach a level of statistical significance corresponding to 90 percent confidence and 5 percent precision.[27]

---

[25] In an Investment Climate Survey, it is often of interest to analyze the business climate across location, size of firms, sector, export orientation, foreign ownership, and so on.

[26] The objective of the study will determine the size of the target population and the characteristic of analysis.

[27] The parameters we wish to estimate are proportions, thus we use the corresponding formula described in the SRS methodology.

Table 4.8

Population Distribution by Sector, Region, and Size

By Sector		By Region	
1 Apparel	1,070	Central North	490
2 Basic metals	235	Highland	250
3 Chemical & chemical products	588	Mekong River Delta	1,361
4 Electrical machinery	238	North East	661
5 Electronics	134	North West	78
6 Food & beverage	2,348	Red River Delta	3,705
7 Furniture	727	South East	5,466
8 Leather products	370	Southern Central Coastal	746
9 Machinery and equipment	400	Grand Total	12,757
10 Medical equipment	53		
11 Metal products	1,182		
12 Motor vehicles	208		
13 Nonmetallic mineral products	1,220		
14 Other transport equipment	366		
15 Paper	599	**By Size**	
16 Publishing	438	Small	9,355
17 Rubber & plastic products	766	Medium	3,086
18 Textiles	611	Large	316
19 Tobacco	24	Grand Total	12,757
20 Wood & wood products	904		
21 Other (unclassified)	276		
Grand Total	12,757		

Source: Author's calculations.

Step 2. *Divide the population in strata and estimate different sampling schemes.* Given that the characteristics of interest are location and sector, we need to stratify the population by each of them separately. Afterward, using table 4.9, we can determine the minimum sample size needed to reach the desired level of statistical significance.

In our example, let's start with a stratification by sector. Because the population includes 21 sectors, we will have 21 strata (table 4.8). Given the desired level significance, we can use table 4.9 to calculate the min-

Table 4.9

Sample Size Requirements for 90 Percent Confidence Interval

SIZE OF POPULATION

DESIRED LEVEL OF PRECISION	50	100	200	300	500	750	1,000	2,000	3,000	5,000	10,000	100,000	1,000,000
	MINIMUM SAMPLE SIZE NEEDED												
10.0%	29	41	52	57	61	64	65	67	68	69	69	70	70
7.5%	36	55	77	88	99	106	110	117	119	121	122	124	124
7.0%	37	59	83	97	111	120	125	133	136	138	140	142	142
6.5%	38	62	90	106	124	135	142	152	156	160	162	165	165
6.0%	40	66	98	118	140	154	162	177	182	186	190	193	194
5.5%	41	70	107	130	158	176	187	207	214	220	225	230	230
5.0%	42	74	116	145	179	203	218	245	255	264	271	278	279
4.0%	45	81	137	178	233	276	304	358	380	401	418	434	436
3.0%	47	89	159	216	304	381	437	558	616	671	719	769	774
2.0%	49	95	179	256	389	524	635	931	1,102	1,292	1,484	1,713	1,740
1.0%	50	99	194	288	467	677	875	1,554	2,097	2,912	4,108	6,518	6,924

Source: Author's calculations.

Note: Assumes highest level of variance within the population.

imum sample size for each stratum. Assuming for the moment that there are no budget constraints, if we aim for a sample representative of all 21 sectors, we would need a sample of 3,436 elements, out of a population of 12,575. Similarly, if our target is a sample representative of all of the regions in the country, we would need a sample of 1,526 units (table 4.10).

Unfortunately, budget constraints rarely allow such a freedom. To meet our budget constraint of approximately 850 units, we can adopt one, or a combination, of the following two strategies:

- Merge strata[28] so that we shrink the overall number of strata, or
- Eliminate strata from our population frame.

Each of these strategies has its disadvantages. While combining strata might compromise the meaningfulness of sectoral comparisons, removing strata lessens the representativeness of the sample at the national level. The best approach is probably a combination of the two. Some strata are merged while others are kept in the stratification. This approach has the advantage of allowing both national as well as sectoral analysis while keeping the sample size at a reasonable level.

The sample designer must weigh the benefits and costs of these approaches. Assuming we decide to follow the second strategy, we must decide which sectors and/or locations to keep in the target population.[29] In reaching this decision, a number of factors must be taken into account, including the following:

- *The importance of these sectors within the objective of the study.* If the purpose of the study is to estimate productivity by focusing on the most important sectors, then the least important sectors within manufacturing should be dropped.
- *The distribution of firms by other relevant dimensions* (for example, location, size, ownership, and so on). To the extent that other dimensions are of analytical interest, the sectors included in the target population should include these dimensions. More specifically, if we wish to estimate the impact of Investment Climate vari-

---

[28] The sample designer should remember that the definition of strata is dependent on its analytical purpose. Hence, strata can be combined if appropriate to the purpose of study.
[29] In our case, only sector appears to be the binding constraint. After we eliminate some of the sectors in our target population, the total population in terms of location and ownership will also decrease. Hence the corresponding sample sizes will go below or fall near the 800 mark.

Table 4.10

Stratification and Required Sample Size for 90 Percent
Confidence and 5 Percent Error

By Sector	Population	Required Sample
Apparel	1,070	221
Basic metals	235	128
Chemical & chemical products	588	189
Electrical machinery	238	128
Electronics	134	91
Food & beverage	2,348	249
Furniture	727	202
Leather products	370	159
Machinery and equipment	400	164
Medical equipment	53	45
Metal products	1,182	226
Motor vehicles	208	119
Nonmetallic mineral products	1,220	227
Other transport equipment	366	158
Paper	599	190
Publishing	438	170
Rubber & plastic products	766	204
Textiles	611	191
Tobacco	24	22
Wood & wood products	904	213
Other (unclassified)	276	139
Total	12,757	3,436
By Region	**Population**	**Required Sample**
Central North	490	178
Highland	250	132
Mekong River Delta	1,361	231
North East	661	196
North West	78	61
Red River Delta	3,705	259
South East	5,466	265
Southern Central Coastal	746	203
Total	12,757	1,526

Source: Author's calculations.

ables on firm performance in different locations, then the sectors included in the target population must be present in these locations.

- *The ability to perform international comparisons at the sectoral level.* If in the comparator countries some sectors have already been covered, then the same sectors must be included in the target population.
- *The required sample size and replacements.* Because of nonresponse and frame problems, a number of elements to draw from the population frame must be higher than the actual desired sample size.

Although it would be impractical to show all possible scenarios, let's suppose we decide to adopt employment contribution as selection criterion. As table 4.11 shows, it appears that Mekong River Delta, Red River Delta, South East, and Southern Central Coastal are the most important locations, covering close to 90 percent of employment. Similarly apparel, food and beverages, leather products, nonmetallic mineral products, and textiles are the sectors with the highest concentration of employment (close to 70%).

If we limit our target population to these four regions and five sectors, we can reestimate the minimum required sample size (table 4.12). While the stratification by location is within budget, the minimum required sample size by sector does not meet our budget constraint. Unless we can find additional funds, we need once again to trim the number of strata (or to combine some of them) until we reach a sample size within budget, while we remain satisfied with the sectoral and location coverage.

Step 3. *Reconcile and select the strata sampling strategy to implement in the field.* Suppose we have decided to keep the four most important locations, as well as four out of the five of the sectors previously identified. Our final target population is presented in table 4.13.[30] The next question is which stratification to implement in the field out of the two possible alternatives—sector or location. This choice is important because the stratification criteria implemented in the field is the only one for which we can directly control the level of statistical significance desired.[31]

---

[30] Although the employment contribution of nonmetallic products is slightly higher than textiles, the decision to keep the latter might be determined by other considerations, such as the ability to use textiles in international comparisons.

[31] The other stratification, which we will reconstruct at the end of the fieldwork (see step 6), will have a level of significance determined indirectly by the number of elements that fall in that stratification.

Table 4.11

Employment Contribution by Sector and Location

By Location		By Sector	
Central North	3%	Apparel	17%
Highland	1%	Basic metals	1%
Mekong River Delta	7%	Chemical & chemical products	3%
North East	5%	Electrical machinery	3%
North West	0%	Electronics	1%
Red River Delta	24%	Food & beverage	15%
South East	52%	Furniture	5%
Southern Central Coastal	7%	Leather products	19%
		Machinery and equipment	2%
		Medical equipment	0%
		Metal products	3%
		Motor vehicles	1%
		Nonmetallic mineral products	8%
		Other transport equipment	3%
		Paper	2%
		Publishing	1%
		Rubber & plastic products	4%
		Textiles	7%
		Tobacco	1%
		Wood & wood products	4%
		Other (unclassified)	2%

Source: Author's calculations.

If we were to implement a stratification by sector the expected sample distribution by location would be as shown in table 4.14. Because we would randomly select elements within each sector, the expected distribution of our sampled elements by location will be approximately proportional to the underlying population distribution. Consequently, because we cannot directly control the number of elements that will fall in each of the location strata, the expected levels of precision by location will slightly differ from the desired levels of 5 percent.

Table 4.12

Target Population (Four Regions and Five Sectors) and Required Sample

Sector	Region Mekong River Delta	Red River Delta	South East	Southern Central Coastal	Total	Required Sample
Apparel	45	280	650	50	1,025	219
Food & beverage	817	374	699	152	2,042	245
Leather products	13	83	256	7	359	157
Nonmetallic mineral	153	315	444	65	977	217
Textiles	28	222	270	23	543	184
Grand Total	1,056	1,274	2,319	297	4,946	1,023
Required Sample	221	229	249	144	842	total

Source: Author's calculations.

Similarly, if we were to implement stratification by location, the expected sample distribution by sector is also shown in table 4.14.

At this point, if we are satisfied with the expected levels of precision, we can proceed to the next step and implement the stratification by sector (or location). If, however, we want to increase the expected level of precision of, say, the stratification by location, we have two options:

- We can oversample some sector strata to increase the number of elements that would fall in the desired locations.

Table 4.13

Final Target Population (Four Regions and Four Sectors) and Required Sample Size

Stratification by Sector	Required Sample	Stratification by Location	Required Sample
Apparel	219	Mekong River Delta	195
Food & beverage	245	Red River Delta	197
Leather products	157	South East	219
Textiles	184	Southern Central Coastal	120

Source: Author's calculations.

Table 4.14

Expected Sample Sizes and Levels of Statistical Significance

	When Sectoral Stratification is Implemented		
	Required Sample[a]	Expected Sample Distribution	Expected Level of Precision[b]
Mekong River Delta	213	123	7.0%
Red River Delta	216	216	5.0%
South East	243	427	3.6%
Southern Central Coastal	127	40	12.0%
	When Location Stratification is Implemented		
	Required Sample[a]	Expected Sample Distribution	Expected Level of Precision[b]
Apparel	219	185	5.60%
Food & beverage	245	451	3.50%
Leather products	157	59	10%
Textiles	184	104	7.40%

Source: Author's calculations.
a. To reach 5 percent precision.
b. Keeping the 90 percent level of confidence.

- We can perform an additional stratification and directly control the number of observations in each new stratum.

In most cases, the first option is hard to implement. Because distributions are often skewed the required oversample could be high.[32] For instance, if we want to obtain more observations in Southern Central Coastal, we could oversample the sector that has the highest concentration in that location (food). This approach, however, will not guarantee the desired location sample size of 120 unless we increase the sample size for food dramatically, which would have obvious implications for our budget.[33]

---

[32] Recall that with this approach we oversample only the sector strata. Consequently, we have only an indirect control on the desired level of precision for location.
[33] To ensure a sample of 120 in the Southern Central Coastal, we need to increase the sample size of food by more than 700 percent (that is, we need to sample 1,600 elements instead of 245).

The second option is more viable. It consists in performing an additional stratification and then assigning a number of elements within each double-strata to approach a desired level of precision for both sector and location. For example, let's assume we first stratify by sector and then stratify each sector by location as shown in table 4.15. We now have 16 strata. When assigning the sample elements to each sector stratum, we can now directly control the total number of elements in each sector-location stratum. This does not violate sampling protocol as long as the final selection of each individual element within each stratum remains random. Hence, in apparel, instead of selecting randomly 219 elements (which would give us the random distribution described in table 4.15, column 7), we can now directly assign the 219 elements to each of the four locations within apparel. To approach the desired distribution within each location, our goal is to assign more observations to Mekong River Delta and Southern Central Coastal while reducing the sample size in South East.[34] The final sample distribution is shown in the final column of table 4.15.[35]

The reassignment of sample units in the second stratification is not always easy. Note that, in our case, we oversampled the second sector to get as close as possible to the desired level of precision at the location level while meeting all the other constraints. Our final sample increased to 850 elements distributed in 16 strata (final column of table 4.15). The expected level of precision for location increases now to 6.1 percent in Southern Central Coastal (down from 12 percent), 5.7 percent in Mekong River Delta, and 4 percent in South East.

A similar approach can be followed if we have other dimensions (for example, size) for which we wish to ensure a level of precision ex ante. Suppose we are concerned that large firms might be underrepresented in the final sample because of their skewed distribution. If this is the case, we can envisage two situations:

- We are satisfied with the expected level of precision of location, but we are concerned about the expected precision by size alone. Then

---

[34] Note that in Red River Delta, because the number of observations in the sector stratification is exactly equal to the expected number of observations by location, we leave the sample size as it is.

[35] Note that although we have some flexibility in reassigning observations between strata, we still have a number of constraints to meet, including the availability of replacements. In textiles, for example, even if we wish to reduce the sample size for the South-East, we cannot increase any other location because we would run out of replacements.

Table 4.15

Stratification by Sector and Location

	First Level of Stratification				Second Level of Stratification			
Strata No.	Sector	Population	Sample	Location	Population	Expected Sample Size in Case of Random Selection within the Whole Sector	Direct Imputation of Sample Size
(1)	(2)	(3)	(4)	(5)	(6)	(7)	(8)
1				Mekong River Delta	45	10	30
2	Apparel	1,025	219	Red River Delta	280	60	60
3				South East	650	139	103
4				Southern Central Coastal	50	11	26
5				Mekong River Delta	817	98	118
6	Food & beverage	2,042	245	Red River Delta	374	45	45
7				South East	699	84	68
8				Southern Central Coastal	152	18	59
9				Mekong River Delta	13	6	8
10	Leather products	359	157	Red River Delta	83	36	36
11				South East	256	112	109
12				Southern Central Coastal	7	3	4
13				Mekong River Delta	28	10	17
14	Textiles	543	184	Red River Delta	222	75	75
15				South East	270	92	78
16				Southern Central Coastal	23	8	14
			806			807	850

Source: Author's calculations.

Note: Values might not add up exactly because of rounding.

we can use size as the dimension for the second stratification, exactly as shown above.

- We are concerned about the expected level of precision of both location and size. In this case, we should first estimate the expected level of precision by sector corresponding to a double stratification location-size. If this is satisfactory, then we proceed with the location-size stratification as shown above, disregarding sector. If we cannot exclude sector from the stratification, then we need to add a third level of stratification and follow the same methodology as presented above.

Step 4. *Implement the sampling strategy.* After the sample strategy has been finalized, the actual number of elements to be drawn from the underlying population will have to be adjusted to take into account two main factors:

- The accuracy of the population frame, and
- The expected nonresponse rate.

Often the available frame lists are old and inaccurate. Furthermore, not all selected respondents will participate in the survey. For these reasons an estimated inaccuracy rate and refusal rate must be incorporated in the calculation of the final number of elements to be drawn in each stratum. Assuming an average inaccuracy rate of 5 percent and a refusal rate of 50 percent (equally distributed across strata), then the total number of elements to be drawn must be adjusted accordingly (see table 4.16).[36]

After the total number of elements has been determined, the elements must be drawn from the population frame *randomly and in one draw* (see box 4.4). The sample and replacements must be selected at the same time to ensure that each element within each stratum has the same probability of selection. During the fieldwork, the order in which the interviews are conducted is important. First, all the elements in the sample must be interviewed. Then each of the respondents that does not exist (frame problem) or refuses to participate (nonresponse) has to be substituted in the exact order in which they appear in the drawing.

---

[36] Note that in the first strata, because the estimated number of sample + replacements is slightly higher than the population, all the elements of the strata will be included in the sample. It is nevertheless important to sample them, because the order of interviewing is critical.

Table 4.16

Sample, Replacements, and Total Elements to Draw

Strata No.	First Level of Stratification		Second Level of Stratification				
	Sector	Location	Population	Population Adjusted[a]	Sample	Replacements	Total No. of Elements to Draw
1		Mekong River Delta	45	43	30	13	43
2	Apparel	Red River Delta	280	279	60	30	90
3		South East	650	649	103	52	155
4		Southern Central Coastal	50	49	26	13	39
5		Mekong River Delta	817	816	118	59	177
6	Food & beverage	Red River Delta	374	373	45	23	68
7		South East	699	698	68	34	102
8		Southern Central Coastal	152	151	59	30	89
9		Mekong River Delta	13	12	8	4	12
10	Leather products	Red River Delta	83	82	36	18	54
11		South East	256	255	109	55	164
12		Southern Central Coastal	7	6	4	2	6
13		Mekong River Delta	28	27	17	9	26
14	Textiles	Red River Delta	222	221	75	38	113
15		South East	270	269	78	39	117
16		Southern Central Coastal	23	22	14	7	21
					850	423	1,273

Source: Author's calculations.

[a] Note the adjustment is only for frame problems (inaccuracy of listing).

Box 4.4
Using SAS to Draw Samples

Modern computing technology has made it easy to perform the actual drawing of sample elements. As for other software programs, SAS has simple commands to randomly select sample elements for a variety of sample designs: simple random sampling (SRS), stratified sampling, systematic sampling, and probability proportional to size (PPS).

(1) **Simple random sampling.** Assume the population frame is stored in the file "frame" and we wish to draw an SRS of $n = 12$ elements. The commands needed in SAS are as follows:

```
proc surveyselect data=frame method=srs n=12 out=sampleSRS;
run;
```

(2) **Stratified sampling.** Suppose we have designed a stratification and the file "frame" contains a strata variable (industry). We can then perform the following:

(a) *Equal allocation* with $n = 4$ in each stratum

```
proc surveyselect data=frame method=srs n=4 out=sampleESTSRS;
strata industry;
run;
```

(b) *Proportionate allocation* with a common rate of 20 percent in each stratum

```
proc surveyselect data=frame method=srs rate=.20
seed=1953 out=samplePSTR;
strata industry;
run;
```

(c) *Disproportionate allocation* with a $n_1 = 3$, $n_2 = 5$, and $n_3 = 4$:

```
proc surveyselect data=frame method=srs n=(3,5,4) out=sampleDSTSRS;
strata industry;
run;
```

(3) **Systematic sampling.** Suppose we wish to draw a systematic sample with a sampling rate of one-quarter. In SAS, the commands to use are as follows:

```
proc surveyselect data=frame method=sys samrate=0.25 out=samplePPS;
run;
```

(4) **Probability proportional to size.** Suppose you wish to obtain a sample with PPS allocation, with $n = 9$ and 'labor' being the size variable. The SAS commands are as follows:

```
proc surveyselect data=frame method=pps n=9 out=samplePPS;
size labor;
run;
```

Hence if, say, strata 1 include 30 sample elements and 13 replacements, if respondent number 3 refuses to participate, he or she will have to be substituted with element number 31 and so on. It is now obvious how important it is to accurately estimate the inaccuracy and nonresponse rate before the drawing of the elements. After the list of drawn elements is exhausted, we cannot draw additional elements from the original population frame without changing the probability of selection of the elements, making the calculation of weights extremely difficult.

Step 5. *Estimate the weights.* After the sample size has been determined, the weights can be estimated (design weights), as shown in table 4.17.[37] At the end of the fieldwork these design weights must be adjusted as described above to obtain the final weights.

Step 6. *Perform the poststratification.* In our example, the final weights refer to the double stratification, sector-location. With respect to these two dimensions, we can make statistically significant inferences at any time without any further adjustment. However, if we wish to make statistically significant inferences with respect to dimensions not expressly included in the sample design, we need to "poststratify" the sample distribution and estimate the corresponding sample weights.

Poststratification means stratifying after the fieldwork has been completed. To poststratify we need to know the population of the dimension of interest. Let's assume that we want to poststratify our population by ownership status—foreign direct investment (FDI) and private. For each stratum, we need to identify the population and the sample corresponding to the new dimension and then estimate the weights in the usual way. Table 4.18 shows the distribution of strata (32) with the relevant information on population, sample, and weights. These new weights can now be used to make statistically significant inferences on ownership status of our target population.

---

[37] The weights are the inverse of the probability of selection (w=N/n, where N=population and n=sample within each stratum).

Table 4.17

Final Sample and Weights

Strata No.	Sector	Location	Original Population	Final Population[a]	Sample	Design Weight	Final Sample	Final Weights
1		Mekong River Delta	45	45	30	1.500	30	1.500
2	Apparel	Red River Delta	280	280	60	4.667	60	4.667
3		South East	650	650	103	6.311	103	6.311
4		Southern Central Coastal	50	50	26	1.923	26	1.923
5		Mekong River Delta	817	817	118	6.924	118	6.924
6	Food & beverage	Red River Delta	374	374	45	8.311	45	8.311
7		South East	699	699	68	10.279	68	10.279
8		Southern Central Coastal	152	152	59	2.576	59	2.576
9		Mekong River Delta	13	13	8	1.625	8	1.625
10	Leather products	Red River Delta	83	83	36	2.306	36	2.306
11		South East	256	256	109	2.349	109	2.349
12		Southern Central Coastal	7	7	4	1.750	4	1.750
13		Mekong River Delta	28	28	17	1.647	17	1.647
14	Textiles	Red River Delta	222	222	75	2.960	75	2.960
15		South East	270	270	78	3.462	78	3.462
16		Southern Central Coastal	23	23	14	1.643	14	1.643

Source: Author's calculations.

a. This adjustment must include both frame problems because of inaccuracy and expected growth rate of stratum.

Table 4.18

Poststratification by Ownership

Strata No.	Sector	Location	Sample Design			Post Strata	Poststratification		
			Final Population	Final Sample	Final Weight		Population	Sample	Weights
1		Mekong River	45	30	1.500	Private	35	25	1.400
2		Delta				FDI	10	5	2.000
3		Red River	280	60	4.667	Private	220	50	4.400
4	Apparel	Delta				FDI	60	10	6.000
5		South East	650	103	6.311	Private	510	80	6.375
6						FDI	140	23	6.087
7		Southern	50	26	1.923	Private	35	25	1.400
8		Central Coastal				FDI	15	1	15.000
9		Mekong River	817	118	6.924	Private	615	84	7.321
10		Delta				FDI	202	34	5.941
11		Red River	374	45	8.311	Private	194	39	4.974
12	Food & beverage	Delta				FDI	180	6	30.000
13		South East	699	68	10.279	Private	618	59	10.475
14						FDI	81	9	9.000
15		Southern	152	59	2.576	Private	102	25	4.080
16		Central Coastal				FDI	50	34	1.471
17		Mekong River	13	8	1.625	Private	13	8	1.625
18		Delta				FDI	0	0	—
19		Red River	83	36	2.306	Private	75	29	2.586
20	Leather products	Delta				FDI	8	7	1.143
21		South East	256	109	2.349	Private	220	57	3.860
22						FDI	36	52	0.692
23		Southern	7	4	1.750	Private	7	4	1.750
24		Central Coastal				FDI	0	0	—

(continued)

Table 4.18 (continued)
Poststratification by Ownership

| Strata No. | Sector | Location | Sample Design | | | Poststratification | | | |
			Final Population	Final Sample	Final Weight	Post Strata	Population	Sample	Weights
25		Mekong River	28	17	1.647	Private	28	17	1.647
26		Delta				FDI	0	0	—
27		Red River	222	75	2.960	Private	188	61	3.082
28		Delta				FDI	34	14	2.429
29	Textiles	South East	270	78	3.462	Private	220	66	3.333
30						FDI	50	12	4.167
31		Southern	23	14	1.643	Private	23	14	1.643
32		Central Coastal				FDI	0	0	—

Source: Author's calculations.
Note: FDI = Foreign direct investment. — = Not applicable.

Chapter 5

Respondent's Psychology and Survey Participation

It would be too simplistic to assume that the success of a survey interview rests solely on the interaction between respondent and interviewer and on the ability of the latter to recruit the former. The survey interview is the end result of many factors, visible and not, interacting well before the interviewer and the respondent meet. It is the role of the survey manager to understand these factors, analyze them, determine the most influential in each environment, and coach interviewers about how to handle them to ensure the highest level of survey participation.

Factors Affecting Participation

Three broad factors contribute to the success of any survey interview: the social environment, the survey design, and the respondent's state of mind (figure 5.1). Their interaction generates positive and negative forces toward the survey interview that will ultimately have an impact on the quantity and quality of the data collected.

Social Environment

Two sociodemographic factors present in the social environment influence survey participation: social responsibility and social cohesion. These factors characterize the environment in which the survey takes place. The sense of social responsibility felt by the manager who is approached with the request for a survey interview, as well as the perceived legitimacy of social institutions and of the survey itself, will determine his or her predisposition toward the study (Groves, Cialdini, and Couper 1992). What motivates a business person in Germany is very likely different from what motivates a business person in Ethiopia. Understanding the extent to which these factors operate will determine the appropriate strategy.

Unfortunately, only rarely do interviewer recruits receive training [. . .] in maximizing the odds of a 'yes' over all contacts. Instead, they are trained in stock descriptors of the survey leading to the first question of the interview.

—R. M. Groves, R. B. Cialdinia, and M. P. Couper, "Understanding the Decision to Participate in a Survey"

Reduc[ing] interviewing to a set of techniques is [. . .] like reducing courtship to a formula.

—Lewis A. Dexter, *Elite and Specialized Interviewing*

Figure 5.1.

Factors Affecting Survey Participation

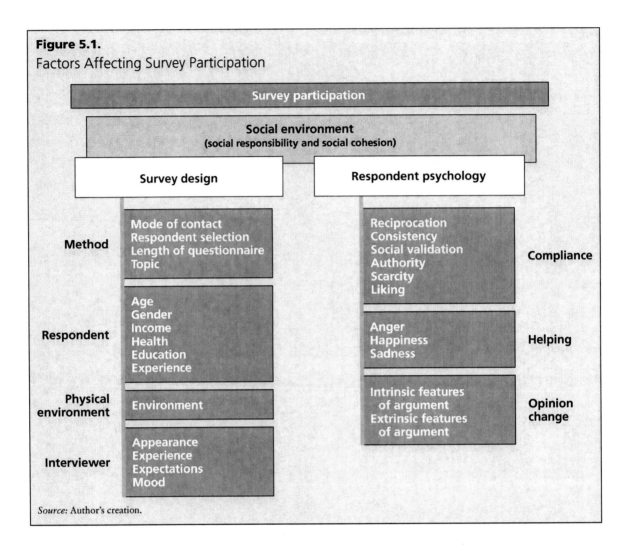

Source: Author's creation.

Survey Design

Survey design calls for a number of different choices regarding the survey methodology, the unit of investigation, and the interviewer's characteristics,[1] all of which have a different bearing on strategies to elicit

---

[1] Groves, Cialdini, and Couper (1992) also identify location as a factor. Contrary to other surveys (for example, household surveys), the physical location of the interview has little relevance in business surveys. In fact, they are generally conducted during business hours in the offices of the establishment being interviewed. Only worker surveys (occasionally conducted as part of an Investment Climate Survey) might be influenced by the location and the presence of other people.

participation. Major attributes of ***survey methodology*** that have an impact on survey participation are the mode of initial contact, the person who makes the initial contact, the length of the interview, and the topic of the survey. Different strategies have been employed by survey practitioners as a mode of initial contact to foster participation. They involve the use of advance letters, the payment of incentives, the offer of brochures or other scripts, and the timing of contact (Groves, Cialdini, and Couper 1992). It is not clear whether the use of advance letters has a positive impact on participation. Dillman, Gallegos, and Frey (1976) show that these letters improve responses, while Singer, Van Hoewyk, and Maher (2000) find no significant impact. What is evident from the literature (Goyder 1985; Heberlein and Baumgartner 1978) is that the number of times the respondent is contacted has a significant impact on his or her decision to participate. As a consequence, the use of advance letters to introduce the respondent to the upcoming business survey and to base its legitimacy should be encouraged, but it should not replace a personal visit by the interviewer. Introductory letters should be used only to provide advance notice and build the legitimacy of the study. Introductory letters should not request participation; this task should be left to a personal contact. The letter should be brief. It should make reference to the sponsors (to build legitimacy) and include contact names and phone numbers. It should also highlight the purpose of the survey (to arouse interest), while mentioning its unique characteristics and practical benefits.[2] While the letter should be addressed to the most senior executive in the company, it is unlikely, especially in large firms, that the company president will grant an interview. He or she might delegate another well-qualified executive to answer on his or her behalf (Kincaid and Bright 1957). The letter may indicate that an interviewer will follow up with a call to schedule an appointment. When scheduling the appointment, avoid expanding on the survey's description because it is more difficult to elicit participation on the phone (Atkinson 1971).

Advance Letters

Incentives

As expected, the payment of incentives does have a positive effect on participation (James and Bolstein 1992; Singer, Van Hoewyk, and Maher 1998; Singer, Van Hoewyk, and Maher 2000; Willimack,

[2] Other issues, such as confidentiality concerns, anonymity, sampling, and length are better addressed in the face-to-face visit by the interviewer. Sobal (1984) conducted an interesting review of the information disclosed in 78 survey introductions used in mailed questionnaires by members of the American Association of Opinion Research. He showed that although the majority of the introductory statements contain information on the research organization, the study director's name, and the research topic, less than half of them mentioned the sponsor and issues of confidentiality (see appendix 6).

Schuman, Pennell, and Lepkowski 1995). The impact is small—5 percent additional participation in face-to-face interviews—and has been proven effective only on the first visit (Willimack and others 1995). Although the payment of monetary incentives does not appear to bias data quality (Singer, Van Hoewyk, and Maher 2000; Willimack and others 1995), the actual payment of money poses ethical and practical problems.[3] Furthermore, the payment of incentives has been proven to be counterproductive if participation is not secured on the first visit (James and Bolstein 1990; Willimack and others 1995). In business surveys, such as the Investment Climate Surveys, it is advisable to use nonmonetary incentives, such as brochures and other scripts, which highlight the practical benefits of the survey to the individual respondent and emphasize the use of the data collected and the impact of previous studies (Gower 1993).

Timing

Finally, the timing of the interview is another factor to keep in mind when scheduling visits. Tax time, religious holidays, vacation time, and periods of economic downturn might make the interviewer's task even harder and could have a discouraging effect on the participation rate.

Contact Person

The correct identification of the person of first contact is also critical for the success of participation. It is important that the selection of the respondent be based on two criteria: the person who is eligible to answer the questions and the person who has the authority to direct other respondents to participate (Groves, Cialdini, and Couper 1992).[4]

Questionnaire Length

The length of the questionnaire is another factor occasionally presented as influencing the success of the interview, because it is taken as an indicator of the burden posed on the respondent (Groves, Cialdini, and Couper 1992). As pointed out in chapter 3, however, there is no clear empirical evidence that the survey length is a factor influencing participation. An experiment conducted on 700 respondents clearly showed that

[3] These problems relate to who should receive the incentive and how large it should be. Should all participants receive it or only those who first refuse to participate? This decision might have an impact on the sample composition (see Singer, Van Hoewyk, and Maher 2000). Is the actual payment of a monetary incentive allowed by the rules governing the funding of the study? How large should the optimal incentive be considering the socioeconomic characteristics of the respondents? All these are problems to which it is hard to find an answer, and the existing literature does not provide much help. What appears to be evident is the fact that the relationship between amount of monetary incentive and survey participation is nonlinear (figure 5.2), because after a certain threshold the incentive becomes, in the mind of the respondent, compensation for service rendered. This generates a host of additional problems for determining the appropriate fee to pay to elicit participation (Godwin 1979; James and Bolstein 1992).
[4] In an Investment Climate Survey, first the manager is approached and then the accountant, and not the other way around. This way only one person needs to be convinced.

Figure 5.2.

Survey Participation By Amount of Incentive

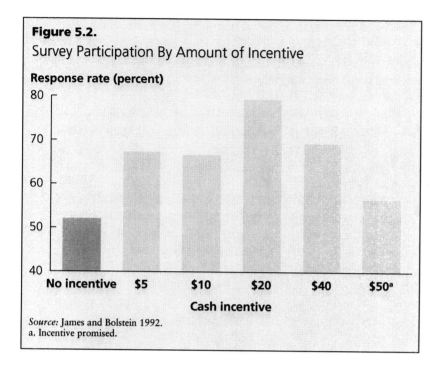

Source: James and Bolstein 1992.
a. Incentive promised.

the expected length of the interview had only a marginal and insignificant impact on participation (figure 5.3) (Sharp and Frankel 1983).

One of the most common reasons cited to justify refusal to participate is the respondent's impression that his or her time is wasted ("I am too busy," "I don't have time for this").[5] Although in a very limited number of cases time constraints are the true reason for refusals,[6] this popular justification is less related to the length of the questionnaire and more to the objective of the study. Because the arguments presented did not pique sufficient interest, the respondent replies that lack of time is the reason that he or she will not participate. The actual length of the questionnaire in itself is not truly a deterrent for survey participation, rather it is an excuse offered by a respondent who would not participate even if the questionnaire was one page long. In addition to experimental results, there is enough anecdotal evidence to support that, with the

---

[5] Another reason is not being interested (Couper 1997).
[6] This is the case in Investment Climate Surveys, because the interview does not necessarily need to take place at the moment of first contact but rather at the respondent's most convenient time.

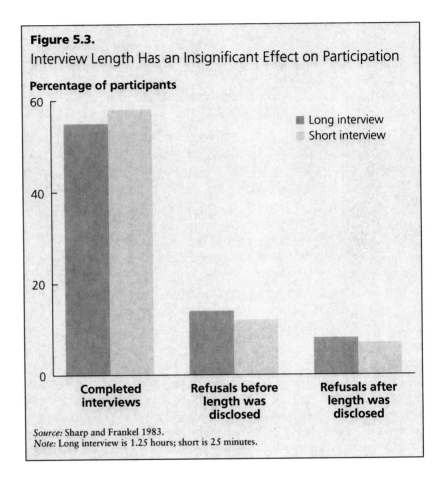

Figure 5.3.

Interview Length Has an Insignificant Effect on Participation

Percentage of participants

Source: Sharp and Frankel 1983.
Note: Long interview is 1.25 hours; short is 25 minutes.

right strategy, respondents will take part in the study regardless of its length. In Malaysia and Brazil, although the Investment Climate Survey questionnaire was particularly long, it was completed through multiple interviews. Questionnaire length is used as an excuse to avoid participation rather than as a reason for refusal. In the Philippines, one large sampled company first refused to participate, stating the length of the questionnaire as the reason for declining. Later, although the questionnaire was not modified, the company reversed its decision after a friend pleaded for their participation.[7] In general, the replacement rate of par-

_____

[7] Dexter (1970) points out in this case that, if a third party is used to convince reluctant respondents, it is important that the third party requests cooperation as a favor and refrains from going into the details of the study. This is to prevent any misinterpretation on the part of the intermediary affecting the interview.

ticipants attributed to refusal to participate is not larger than that for other reasons (for example, out of business, wrong address, out of scope, and so on).

As discussed earlier, questionnaire length affects response accuracy more than it affects survey participation. While in a few circumstances respondents decline to participate if they expect the interview to take too long, when they do participate, fatigue will hamper the accuracy of the information provided in a long interview. It is undisputed that a longer questionnaire leads to a higher risk of collecting inaccurate data and to longer completion times (Andrews 1984; Sudnam and Bradburn 1974). Experience shows that the survey instrument should not involve face-to-face interviews longer than one-and-a-half hours.[8]

The topic of the study also influences the success of the interview. The topic should be relevant to the purpose of the study, should not stimulate a sense of fear or hostility from the respondent, should not address personal issues, and should not give the sense of pursuing business secrets.[9] This last point is often raised when financial information is asked in the questionnaire. Many interviewers point out the reluctance of firms to share their true financial information, if any at all. A review of the literature by DeLameter (1982) shows no consistent evidence that the topic covered or specific sensitive questions have an influence on the decision to participate. The only effect of sensitive questions appears to be underreporting. My experience confirms DeLameter's findings. Although the specific country environment and the size of the sampled firm dictate how much financial information may be legitimately asked, if issues of confidentiality are appropriately guaranteed and the use of the information sought appropriately explained and understood, firms are more willing to share their financial data. Confidentiality assurances foster participation. However, the survey manager must be aware that these assurances have a limited effect, while the critical factor remains the trust in the integrity of the collecting agency (Singer, Mathiowetz, and Couper 1993). Furthermore, confidentiality assurances should be included only if sensitive questions are asked and should be tailored to the level of sensitivity of the questions. In fact, elaborate assurances of confidentiality might be counterproductive if used indiscriminately (Singer, Hippler, and Schwarz 1992; Singer, Von Thurn, and Miller 1995).

Topic

---

[8] Corresponding approximately to either 13 double-spaced pages, size 12 font, or 879 words.

[9] For instance, asking specific names of clients and suppliers might generate a sense of hostility and could be seen as unrelated to the purpose of the study.

A number of a *respondent's characteristics* have also been addressed in the literature as factors influencing survey participation. Age, gender, income, health status, education, geographic location, previous experience, and survey fatigue are all factors that have been considered. Although a number of these factors have been associated with survey participation (DeMaio 1980; Fowler and Mangione 1990), research evidence is mixed and the causal relationship is uncertain. More than causal factors, these characteristics determine the predisposition of respondents toward survey participation (Groves, Cialdini and Couper 1992). Psychological factors are critical components in motivating the respondent to participate. A first motive is the desire for self-expression. People often derive satisfaction from expressing their own opinion on topics of personal interests. Business people are often vocal about the problems they face in their activities, so this positive force should be taken into account by the interviewer to motivate the respondent to participate. Occasionally, feelings of altruism to help the interviewer with his or her task and the gratification from the performance of the respondent's role may represent positive forces stirring the respondent toward participation. There are, however, also negative forces in the respondent's mind that work against survey participation. Fear, apparent invasion of privacy, resentment toward the interviewer and sponsor, or threatening topics can all compromise survey participation (Warwick and Lininger 1975). It is the role of the survey manager, and even more so of the interviewer and survey firm, to understand what factors motivate or deter each respondent and how to address these factors in each circumstance. The interviewer must be aware that even positive feelings might generate bias. So, for instance, he or she must be able to understand whether a feeling of altruism might generate a courtesy bias in the respondent's behavior.

The *physical environment* in which the survey takes place also plays a role. In Investment Climate Surveys, the most important environmental factor having clear effect on the interviewing climate is the attitude of the business community toward surveys. In general, the business community is hostile to these type of studies for a number of valid reasons. The majority of managers see surveys as useless exercises that distract them from the more pressing issues of running their company without any clear positive impact on their business. This feeling is magnified if the sampled establishment is experiencing a downturn, if a number of (similar) surveys are being conducted more or less simultaneously, if the same sponsor has conducted other surveys in the recent past, or if the sponsor generates a hostile sentiment. The survey manager needs to investigate these factors while preparing for the fieldwork. Months before the interviews start, the survey manager must establish contacts with the business community to gather their support for the study and legitimate this endeavor. Here the list of potential partners depends on the particular country environment and on the selected survey firm.[10] Their role is to familiarize the associations' members and the business community, in general, with the study; foster participation; and support the implementing agency in its task. Eliciting cooperation from the business community is one of the hardest tasks, yet it is critical in fostering survey participation.

The *interviewer* remains the most important factor in motivating the respondent to participate and in ensuring the collection of quality data. As a consequence, observable characteristics and psychological factors play a fundamental role in the way he or she carries out the tasks. Brenner (1982) reports three basic sources of interviewer biases: background characteristics (such as age, education, socioeconomic status, race, religion), psychological factors (such as perceptions, attitudes, motives, expectations), and behavioral factors (such as experience, knowledge of interviewing techniques).

The interviewer's appearance and experience will have an impact on participation. Sociodemographic attributes (race, age, gender, and so on) determine the first impression the respondent will make of the interviewer at the moment of first contact, while experience (skills, confidence, and so on) will inform how the interviewer handles difficult situations and arouses the respondent's interest (Groves, Cialdini, and Couper 1992). Often students or part-time interviewers are hired to conduct a survey. While the decision to employ part-time interviewers must be weighed against the expected duration of the survey, the survey manager should use extreme caution in relying heavily on students. Their relative youth might create problems in getting answers from senior executives. Furthermore, students in particular disciplines might even be unwilling to follow a structured interviewing methodology, which requires them to ask questions exactly as written. Finally, because of holidays, classes, examinations, and so on, students tend to be less reliable in their ability to complete a project (Dexter 1970; Warwick and Lininger 1975).

Further empirical evidence shows that interviewer expectations and mood have an influence on survey participation and data accuracy. Interviewers who expect the study to be difficult show a modest but

---

[10] Potential partners are the Chambers of Commerce, industrial associations, business institutes, and so on.

consistent effect on response rate (Singer and Kohnke-Aguirre 1979).[11] It is thus important for the success of the survey not simply to train all interviewers but rather to understand the psychological forces that motivate them to participate in the survey. Many of the reasons that push the respondent to cooperate also play a role in the interviewer's decision to participate, such as intellectual curiosity and identification with broader social concerns. Other factors play an even more specific role, such as the desire to improve their skills and knowledge and career advancement. Nevertheless, there are negative forces that also could weaken the interviewer's motivation toward the survey. In addition to the obvious dissatisfaction with the level of pay and the field supervision, fatigue, fear, difficult travel conditions, and frustration in locating respondents are the most common inhibitors (Warwick and Lininger 1975). It is the survey manager's job to identify these inhibitors and take the necessary steps to correct them.

Respondent's Psychology

The third broad factor that contributes to the success of an interview is the respondent's state of mind. This is admittedly one of the most difficult factors to gauge ahead of the actual interview. A successful interviewer must possess the ability to identify in the first few minutes of interaction which factors play a leading role in the respondent's psychological predisposition toward the survey and adopt the corresponding most appropriate persuasion strategy.

Cialdini (1985) identifies six major social norms that work in any person's mind when deciding whether to yield to a request for interview: reciprocation, consistency, social proof, authority, scarcity, and liking. The rule of *reciprocation* states that any person feels obliged to return favors, gifts, invitations, and the like received by another person.[12] This feeling plays a role in survey methodology when accepting the request for interview is seen as repayment for a payment, gift, or favor. This norm is the psychological basis of offering incentives to prospective participants. Psychologists also identify an innate sense of *consistency* in people: once a person takes an uncoerced stand on an issue he or she acts in conformity with that resolution. Otherwise, he or she risks appearing illogical, irra-

---

[11] Estimated by the authors to be around 8 percent.
[12] This rule appears to be stronger than that of liking, described later. Therefore, this norm would work even if the person giving the gift is not liked by the receiver (Cialdini 1985).

tional, or unstable. This psychological norm constitutes the basis of awarding participants with certificates of commendation.[13] They generate a sense of commitment in the prospective respondent that can be used by the interviewer to elicit compliance (to show consistency).[14] The feeling of *social proof* pushes people to adopt the same beliefs and behaviors of others because they consider correct what other people think to be right. Thus, the wider the survey participation is the more likely it is that respondents who are sensitive to this particular norm will cooperate.

The sense of *authority* is yet another factor that often plays a role in the respondent's mind. People are more likely to concede to a request for an interview if it comes from a legitimate authority (in the respondent's mind). This is why it is important to have the right sponsor. The government is generally perceived as a legitimate authority and is generally more successful in gaining access.[15] *Scarcity* is another social norm that might play a role in encouraging participation. Sometimes respondents are more likely to comply with the request if they see it as a limited opportunity. This strategy assigns more value and weight to survey participation and might play a role in the decision to cooperate.

Liking is that psychological norm that pushes people to comply with requests from people who they know and like. Apart from the (obvious) physical attractiveness, other factors influence liking and thus compliance. Respondents are more willing to comply with requests from people who are similar to them, people who praise them, people who are familiar to them, and people with whom they like to be associated.

Many researchers argue that people have an innate sense of altruism that predisposes them to help others in need (*helping norm*). An appeal to this feeling of predisposition is generally used, explicitly or implicitly, to increase participation. This norm, however, is influenced by the

---

[13] This practice is not common, though, probably because it is not appreciated for its psychological impact.

[14] Any of these feelings could also work to the detriment of participation. On one occasion, I recall the respondent was not impressed by the sponsorship of the survey because he had some negative feelings against the sponsor and he decided not to cooperate to be consistent with this belief. Knowing this is still extremely valuable to the interviewer, who can appropriately focus on those aspects of the survey (including other sponsors, if available) that conform to the respondent's consistency norm.

[15] As mentioned earlier, the selection of the survey firm has a particular impact on the willingness of respondents to share information about sensitive topics. Thus, while hiring the national statistical office will make it easier to collect accounting information, a higher refusal rate can be expected for sensitive questions, such as tax evasion and informal payments to government officials.

emotional state of the respondent at the time of the request. Therefore, the respondent's mood needs to be taken into account when he or she is approached. While anger will have a detrimental impact on participation, happiness will have the opposite effect. Sadness has an ambiguous impact depending on how the cost and benefits of the survey are perceived by the respondent (Groves, Cialdini, and Couper 1992).

Finally, even the best arguments put forward by the best interviewer can fall on deaf ears if the topic is not meaningful to the respondent. Evidence shows that the best strategy to elicit *opinion change* is to fit the level of sophistication of the arguments put forward to the respondent's perceived saliency of the survey objective. If the purpose of the study is of high relevance to the respondent, a highly sophisticated introduction should be used to ensure participation.[16] If, on the contrary, the study objectives are of low personal relevance to the respondent, a more heuristic approach should be followed and the persuasion strategy should focus on extrinsic features of the study, such as the authority of the sponsor and the credibility of the implementing agency (Petty and Cacioppo 1984).

All this leads to the conclusion that "influences on the decision to participate vary over individuals" (Groves and McGonagle 2001, 252) and, therefore, there is no single opening statement or single argument that ensures the highest level of participation in all circumstances. Failed attempts to identify an optimal single script for eliciting participation have clearly demonstrated this finding (Dillman, Gallegas, and Frey 1976). On the contrary, the best persuasion strategy is tailoring, that is, "the use of different dress, physical behaviors, words, and strategies of persuasion for different sample persons" (Groves, Cialdini, and Couper 1992, 487). Empirical evidence shows the effectiveness of tailoring. Morton-Williams (1991) showed that interviewers using a prepared script got a higher refusal rate than those allowed to tailor. To achieve a higher participation rate, interviewers should adapt their initial approach to the specific situation they face, and the respondent's reaction to the initial statement should dictate their choices of subsequent strategies (Atkinson 1971; Groves and Couper 1996; Groves, Cialdini, and Couper 1992).

---

[16] The interviewer should emphasize intrinsic characteristics such as the sample representativeness, the sophistication of the analysis and its goals, and the international perspective of the study. Although the high saliency of the topic implies a lower incentive effect (Groves, Singer, and Corning, 2000), this should not push the interviewer to believe that he or she can quickly move to the interview with minimal introduction.

Training

Well-designed questionnaires and experienced interviewers are undoubtedly the two most important ingredients affecting the quality of the data collected. Yet, while the former can be easily achieved (although often overlooked), interviewers' quality is the single most difficult aspect to handle. Even the best-designed question will gather inaccurate information if the interviewer reads it, probes it, or records it incorrectly.

Age, experience, and education are the interviewers' three most important attributes in business surveys. Although age and experience are to some extent coupled, the interviewer's age is important not as much for the ability to conduct the interview (here experience plays a larger role) but rather, and critically, for the ability to secure participation. The norm of liking plays a role in the decision to participate in surveys: respondents are more prone to comply with a request when it comes from people they like. Similarity plays a role in triggering this. The more similar the person making the request, the more likely the respondent is to accept it (Cialdini 1985). In business surveys, the respondent is generally a middle-age entrepreneur; employing young interviewers, no matter how experienced, can automatically precludes this compliance norm (the larger the company, the more evident the phenomenon). Experience in the field shows that entrepreneurs, especially in larger firms, do not lend legitimacy to studies presented by young interviewers. However, in business surveys, age plays an undisputed role on yet another critical norm. Because age is the physical attribute that first appears to the respondent, even before any other norm can be appealed to, the appearance of a young interviewer has an immediate negative impact on the sense of legitimacy of the study. It has a consequent detrimental effect on the liking norm and, ultimately, on the willingness to participate.

Experience more than age has an impact on data quality. It is not surprising that inexperienced interviewers show a higher response error than young interviewers (figure 5.4) (Sudnam and Bradburn 1974). Furthermore, experience plays a critical role in securing participation—an experienced interviewer has a larger set of persuasive strategies that he or she can tailor to each interview situation (Groves and Couper 1996).

Depending on the complexity of the questions asked and definitions adopted in the form, education plays a relevant role. Fowler and Mangione (1990) have pointed out that it is an illusion to hope that interviewers will open training manuals in the course of an interview. Education will reduce the necessity to consult manuals and, conse-

Interviewer Characteristics

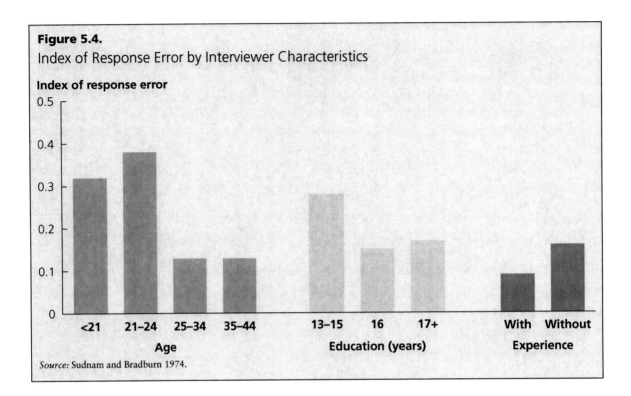

Figure 5.4.

Index of Response Error by Interviewer Characteristics

Source: Sudnam and Bradburn 1974.

quently, will improve data quantity and quality. Furthermore, because one of the interviewer's most important tasks is to probe when the respondent fails to meet the question's objective, having a clear understanding of the objective of each question will help the interviewer decide when, where, and how much probing is appropriate (Martin and Abelson 1984). Lastly, although nobody expects interviewers to be experts in every subject covered, when financial data are collected in business surveys, the practice of employing interviewers with accounting backgrounds should be encouraged.

Training   There is no doubt that training has a positive impact on both the quality of the responses recorded and on the quantity of the interviews completed. More than half a century ago researchers were testing the effect of training on data quality. The U.S. Census Bureau conducted an experiment in which the same questionnaire was administered by two separate groups of interviewers, one group receiving 5 hours of training and the second group 16 hours. On all questions, the first group of interviewers showed a consistently higher error rate (13% of nonresponse and nonacceptable answers), which was almost double the rate of the trained group.[17]

More recently, experimental research has shown that the usefulness of training is a function of the complexity of the questionnaire. While the response rate of simple questions is not statistically different between trained and untrained interviewers, the positive effect of training appears evident when the structure of the questionnaire is more complex and, thus, demands more interaction. The more the interviewer is required to give instructions, to probe, and to give explanations, the more effective is training in ensuring a higher and more accurate data collection. Billiet and Loosveldt (1988) report the results of an experiment in which trained interviewers outperformed untrained interviewers[18] in terms of reading, probing, and getting answers even on sensitive topics (figure 5.5).

Given the particular complexity of most business surveys, there is no ideal interviewer who can be employed without any training. While it is not uncommon for survey firms to promise to employ dozens of interviewers, an extremely small proportion of these interviewers would be capable of understanding and handling such a complex instrument as the Investment Climate questionnaire without appropriate preparation. This is where training conducted by an experienced survey manager with a profound understanding of the questionnaire and survey situations plays a crucial role. The selection of interviewers should be tailored to the distinct objectives of the survey. It is extremely hard to know when this match between interviewers' capabilities and survey objectives has been made, apart from warning signs that stem from poor interviewers. Recognizing that a successful interview is not just a matter of techniques but also of intuition and ability, it is possible to identify a priori some interviewer characteristics that will make a difference (Warwick and Lininger 1975). However, only after an intense training and face-to-face mock interviews will the survey manager have a better feel of the ability of prospective interviewers to handle business surveys.[19]

---

[17] Survey Research Center, University of Michigan (1951). *Field Methods in Sample Interview Surveys.* Survey Research Center, University of Michigan, Ann Arbor, Michigan. As reported in Moser and Kalton 1971, 290.

[18] In this experiment, trained interviewers received extensive training while untrained interviewers received only elementary instructions. Furthermore, to control for other independent characteristics, all interviewers were female and had a minimum of experience.

[19] The complexity of the typical Investment Climate Survey precludes the use of simpler training techniques, such as on-the-job training, in which interviewers follow a more experienced interviewer to learn the techniques, or they learn the technique by reading dedicated material. Conversely, a formal training session of up to one week should be held and conducted by the survey manager.

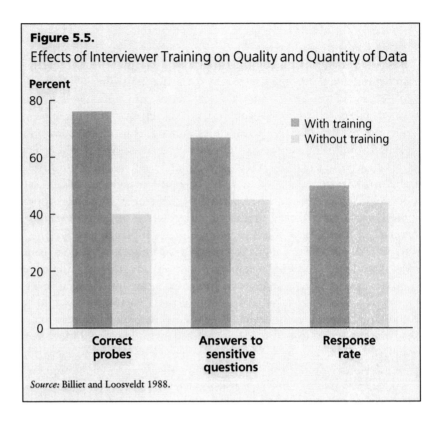

Figure 5.5.
Effects of Interviewer Training on Quality and Quantity of Data

Source: Billiet and Loosveldt 1988.

Training, therefore, should be seen by the survey manager as more than just an opportunity to present the project and explain the questions, which can and should be covered in the survey manual. Rather the survey manager should approach training as a more complex endeavor in which he or she gauges the quality of enumerators and transmits enthusiasm for the project to all involved. "If the interviewer is interested in the study, enthusiastic about his work, and likes the respondent, these feelings will usually be communicated to the respondent with positive effects on the latter's participation" (Warwick and Lininger 1975, 189). It is important that the survey manager take the time to explain the purpose of the survey, the research aim, how the questions meet the goal, and the importance of the interviewer's role in achieving survey quality. Finally, an understanding of the psychological and behavioral motivations of the different actors—interviewers and respondents—should be the seasoned survey manager's starting point for training.

Practical Training Tips

Although high refusal rates might compromise the composition of the sample,[20] the typical training session dedicates little, if any, attention to behavioral rules and suggestions about how to handle initial contacts. As in many other surveys, the most common complaint from Investment Climate Survey interviewers is the difficulty of securing participation; however, few guidelines covering this important aspect of data accuracy are addressed during training. What follows is an attempt to describe a set of behavioral rules and social skills for training prospective interviewers.

Interviewer DOs and DON'Ts

Be prepared. Any interview requires a lot of preliminary preparation. You must study the survey materials and learn the questionnaire by heart. You must become familiar with the procedures and be ready to provide information and give answers. You must be organized (Morton-Williams 1991).[21]

Be likeable. Present yourself as a friendly but professional person. Before you can sell the survey, you must sell yourself. If appropriate, make friendly comments about things you see (that is, trophies, and so on). At all times you must be polite and respectful, especially if the respondent is rude. Never be patronizing (Morton-Williams 1991).

Be positive. Use positive verbs and expressions. Show you're happy to conduct the survey and highlight the positive aspects of the survey. People are naturally predisposed to dislike people who are negative (Cialdini 1985).

Be responsive to the specific situation you're facing. If the respondent is busy, annoyed, upset, or in bad mood, apologize and offer to come back on a different date. Give the information that is requested in a form that the respondent can understand (Morton-Williams 1991).

Be neutral. Show interest and appreciation for the respondent's answers, but do not volunteer any personal information and never share opinions with him or her.[22] Personal information might influence the respondent

---

[20] This phenomenon is particularly important in business surveys. Because there are not many large companies, the refusal of even a few might jeopardize the representativeness of the sample (Kincaid and Bright 1957).

[21] The psychological norm of consistency works against the unprepared interviewer. An untrained interviewer gives the impression that what he or she is doing is not important, and thus the respondent would not participate in an unimportant event.

who is trying to please the interviewer, might exacerbate the differences between interviewer and respondent, and might establish a personal rather than professional interview style. If the respondent asks personal questions, answer by stressing your professional characteristics and experiences. Furthermore, any feedback given to the respondent must not include any evaluation or judgment on the part of the interviewer. Even simple expressions of surprise, doubt, or disbelief amount to a leading question (Atkinson 1971; Dexter 1970; Fowler and Mangione 1990).

Do not lie. Answer questions truthfully while pointing out the positive aspects of the response.

Do not threaten the respondent. Keep a polite distance. Always ask if you can enter the room or if you can sit down. Don't mention legal obligations to participate (Morton-Williams 1991).

Do not rush. If the respondent is busy, be prepared to leave and come back at a more convenient time. Don't rush the respondent into participation until you are absolutely sure he or she is on board. Similarly, if you don't feel well, either physically or psychologically, or if you are stressed, postpone the interview. There is a good chance you will have a lower response rate if you press on with the interview (Morton-Williams 1991).

Do not ignore respondent's questions and expressions of reluctance. You must be observant and vigilant. You must be ready to answer any question or concern he or she might have and handle any expressions of reluctance appropriately (Atkinson 1971; Morton-Williams 1991). In the unlikely event in which he or she asks you a detailed technical question for which you don't have an answer, you should apologize and ensure the respondent that the supervisor will contact him or her to address the concern.

Securing Participation

Initial Contact

Timing and location. The interview should be set up at a time and location that is most convenient for the respondent. Generally, this is during

---

[22] Presser, Blair, and Triplett (1992) go on to say that not only the interviewer's beliefs but also the known opinion of the sponsoring agency might influence the undecided respondent.

regular office hours at the offices of the establishment being surveyed. The interviewer should assume that the respondent is not too busy to conduct the scheduled interview and should make arrangements to return at a more convenient time only if the respondent suggests it (Warwick and Lininger 1975). Similarly, if the interview goes too long and the respondent suggests to cut it short, the interviewer should set up the next meeting before he or she leaves or, if only few questions are left, should attempt to conclude the interview.

First impression. The interviewer's sociodemographic characteristics exert a lot of psychological influence on the respondent's first impression and on his or her decision to participate. Age, sex, appearance, religious belief, and class difference might affect the communication process during the interview or even the decision to take part in the study. These sociocultural factors must be taken into account in the preparation of survey interviews. The interviewer's actual appearance is the most immediate clue of his or her background. The interviewer should dress in a simple and inconspicuous manner, reflecting the characteristics of the respondent and of the environment in which the interview takes place. The interviewer should avoid displaying aspects of personal appearance that might evoke strong reactions from the respondent and should also avoid wearing particular clothing or accessories that associate him or her to a particular social group or cause (Warwick and Lininger 1975).

Establish and maintain interaction. There is no one single right way to introduce a survey. Each interviewer should develop and practice his or her own introductory statement until it comes naturally in accordance with the following general rules:

- *Opening remarks.* The interviewer should appear relaxed and confident.[23] The interviewer should introduce himself or herself by name, explain why he or she is there, and identify the organization he or she represents. The interviewer should wear an official identification card and display his or her credentials to avoid raising suspicions about the study (Warwick and Lininger 1975). Some

---

[23] This implies that the interviewer needs to prepare and practice the introductory statement ahead of time; he or she must always keep eye contact, organize the papers and documents in advance, and speak clearly and at a normal speed. At the same time, the interviewer must observe what is happening in the surroundings, what is the reaction and the mood of the respondent. Basically he or she needs to start "tailoring" (Morton-Williams 1991).

practitioners suggest adding, when the circumstance warrants it, positive comments about things seen in the office, thus appealing to the norm of liking (Dexter 1970; Morton-Williams 1991).

- *Explaining the study.* Soon after the introductory remarks end, the interviewer should explain the purpose of the study. Interviewers should not assume that the respondent is aware of the survey even if an advance letter has been sent. At this stage, it is very important to dispel any misconceptions. The respondent might misinterpret the reason for the visit and assume that it is related to business activity. If he or she agrees to the survey under this misconception, the interviewer should not be surprised to find the respondent justifiably annoyed when he or she realizes the true purpose of the visit (Atkinson 1971).

Three factors have been proven to affect persuasion: the quantity of the arguments presented, the quality of the arguments, and the relevance of the topic to the respondent. Research on attitude change shows that the number of arguments (quantity) presented has an impact on respondent attitudes only if saliency is low (figure 5.6). Conversely, the quality of the arguments has a positive impact on respondents only if personal involvement is high (figure 5.7) When respondents show high involvement, argument

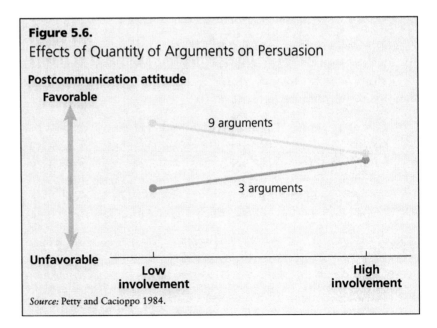

Figure 5.6.
Effects of Quantity of Arguments on Persuasion

Postcommunication attitude
Favorable

9 arguments

3 arguments

Unfavorable

Low involvement

High involvement

Source: Petty and Cacioppo 1984.

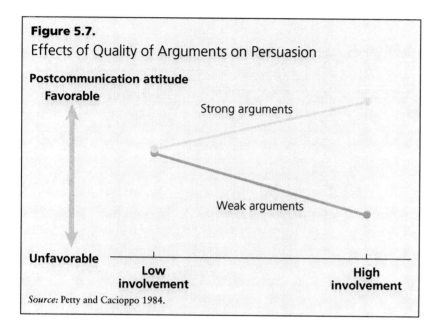

Figure 5.7.
Effects of Quality of Arguments on Persuasion

Postcommunication attitude
Favorable

Strong arguments

Weak arguments

Unfavorable

Low involvement   **High involvement**

Source: Petty and Cacioppo 1984.

quality has a much stronger effect on persuasion, while weak arguments might be counterproductive. At the same time, when saliency is low, the quantity of the arguments appears to be effective, while their quality has no significant persuasive effect (figure 5.8) (Petty and Cacioppo 1984).

These few minutes of introduction will determine the climate of the entire interview. Hence, this time is extremely important and it must be used to pique the respondent's interest and eliminate any doubt in his or her mind. Three main points should be highlighted in the interviewer's speech: (1) the purpose of the interview and the sponsoring agencies; (2) the practical benefits of participation for the individual respondent; and (3) the confidentiality of the information collected.[24] It is definitely useful to show some results from similar surveys in other countries, ideally in a short brochure, and to show clippings from local newspapers. While being careful not to reveal more details than needed, interviewers should be prepared to modify their introduction to fit the unfolding interaction with the respondent. It is a good idea to be

---

[24] Some practitioners suggest to add, and show, a confidentiality statement on the back of the ID cards. (Atkinson 1971).

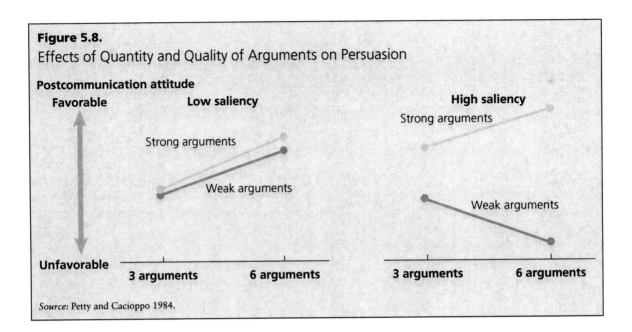

Figure 5.8.

Effects of Quantity and Quality of Arguments on Persuasion

Postcommunication attitude

Source: Petty and Cacioppo 1984.

ready to provide additional information about the sample composition, how the particular respondent has been selected, and the
analysis of the data collected. None of these topics, however,
should be discussed at length until the interviewer detects which
argument the respondent is most sensitive to. Hopefully, after this
brief introduction, the respondent will begin to engage, so that the
interviewer can determine where the respondent stands. Throughout the interaction, the interviewer should not use the words study,
research, or paper. These terms reduce the sense of usefulness of
the interview in the eye of the respondent. Typically, entrepreneurs
are not interested in research; they value practical analysis.

Tailoring. Following the introductory statement, successful interviewers
adapt their approach to the respondent's verbal and physical behavior.
Each respondent's reaction should dictate the interviewer's choice of subsequent statements and strategies. Successful tailoring requires the interviewer (1) to have a variety of cues, phrases, and descriptors at his or her
disposal to use in any situation; (2) to be able to interpret the respondent's words and behavior; and (3) to apply the appropriate techniques
in response. However, for the interviewer to successfully apply tailoring,
he or she needs to keep the conversation going without abrupt interrup-

tions or untimely requests for participation. Thus, "maintaining interaction is the means to achieve maximum benefits from tailoring, for the longer the conversation is in progress, the more cues the interviewer will be able to obtain" (Groves and Couper 1996, 68).

Dealing with Reluctance

There are three strategies that can be employed to preempt expression of reluctance to survey participation: (1) understanding the respondent's psychology and tailoring the interviewer's reaction to it; (2) highlighting the practical aspects and the benefits of participating in the survey; and (3) reassuring the respondent and acting in a nonthreatening manner. Reluctance can occur at any point of the initial contact and can be manifested not only verbally but also with specific behaviors (for example, breaking eye contact, looking over your shoulders, looking away, looking at a watch, going through documents, and so on). The successful interviewer needs to adapt and adjust his or her own strategy to the unfolding situation. Thus, he or she needs to be able to interpret what is happening and select the appropriate response. The first prerequisite of a good interviewer is to have considerable and accurate perception skills. According to Morton-Williams (1991), interviewers must be able to accomplish the following:

- Watch for signs of suspicion, fear, or reluctance;
- Observe cues;
- Listen to what the respondent says and how he or she talks;
- Tailor his or her approach to the unfolding situation;
- Address expressions of reluctance directly; and
- Be ready to change strategy.

Gauging Respondent's Psychology

As in any social interaction, the psychology of the people involved plays a critical role. Understanding and using the following basic psychological rules of compliance is a key to a successful interview:

- *Consistency norm.* If the interviewer is able to identify any of the respondent's commitments, which can be related to the survey objectives or sponsors, he or she can leverage this psychological norm to gain cooperation. For instance, if the respondent hints that he or she is involved in initiatives or associations aimed at improving the business environment, the delivery of public services, and so on, then the survey can be presented as a means to achieve this goal. The key is to determine the respondent's commitments. Once this is established, the experienced interviewer can link the respondent's commitment to the objective of the survey for the purpose of securing participation.

- *Social proof.* If the respondent asks, "Who else is involved?" this indicates that he or she is sensitive to social validation. If other people are participating, he or she will be more likely to participate as well. In this situation, the interviewer must be ready to provide information on the sample distribution as well as to explain how the size of the sample will give more weight to the results and the policy implications resulting from the survey. Two characteristics of this norm play a key role. First, this norm is triggered by uncertainty. Second, this norm can be best exploited by appealing to people similar to the respondents (Cialdini 1985). Successful interviewers need to appreciate and be ready to exploit this psychological norm.

- *Scarcity.* Because people value more opportunities when they are less available, the interviewer can appeal to this norm with such expressions as "Only a select number of entrepreneurs will take part in this survey" or "Only few days are left to complete the survey." The interviewer should emphasize not only the unique opportunity offered to the respondent to complete the survey and to have his or her opinion count and heard (Groves, Cialdini, and Couper 1992) but also the opportunity to use the sponsors of the survey as the vehicle through which his or her opinions and concerns will inform policy creation. Two factors can be employed to enhance this feeling. First, experiments show that the value of a scarce item is even greater if it is first made available and then becomes more scarce. Second, competition with others toward a scarce item makes it even more valuable (Cialdini 1985).

- *Authority.* If the respondent asks, "Who is behind this?" he or she is sensitive to the authority norm. The interviewer should honestly answer who is sponsoring the study.[25] Generally, the sponsoring institutions are mentioned in the letter of invitation and the interviewer should highlight those that most likely will foster higher participation from the individual respondent. It is not necessary to mention the funding arrangements or all agencies and institutions

---

[25] Note that identifying the appropriate psychological norm at play is not always easy. If the respondent asks, "Who is behind this?" or "Who *else* is behind this?" a different norm might be at play (authority and social proof, respectively).

involved in the study (Warwick and Lininger 1975). Appearance has also proven to play a role within this norm. Interviewers wearing their official dress (that is, Government Statistical Office staff) will elicit a sense of authority. Similarly, titles are perceived as symbols of authority and, if and when appropriate, should be mentioned to elicit participation (Cialdini 1985).

- *Liking.* Different factors have been associated with this norm: similarities in interests, background, or even dress increase the likelihood of compliance. Because everyone likes people who praise them, being complimentary can affect liking. Praise should not be detailed but rather simple and general and should always be honest, because respondents who feel manipulated will react negatively. Finally, familiarity produced by pleasurable contacts and cooperation toward a common goal are powerful causes of liking (Cialdini 1985).

Handling Practical Problems[26]

It is always possible that respondents will come up with a number of excuses and reasons to avoid participation. The interviewer should be aware of these excuses and have strategies in place to deal with them. The respondent's reply to a request for an interview could be as follows:

- *"I am too busy." "I don't have time for this."* In this case, if the respondent has a few minutes available, it might be a good idea to present the objectives of the study and engage the respondent. Before leaving, it is also advisable to leave a letter[27] explaining the study and schedule the next appointment. A second visit emphasizes the importance of the interview. If the respondent is making excuses to avoid the interview, it is possible that he or she is not interested. In this case, an alternate strategy to arouse the respondent's interest must be employed (Warwick and Lininger 1975).

---

[26] In what follows, we make more specific reference to the Investment Climate Surveys.
[27] This letter is different from the advance letter sent by mail, whose goal was to arouse the respondent's interest to persuade him or her to voluntarily participate in the survey. This cover letter, instead, should be an expanded version of the introductory letter sent to respondents ahead of the beginning of the fieldwork. It should be concise and include the following elements: (1) purpose of data collection and how survey results are likely to be of benefit to the respondent, (2) assurance of confidentiality of data collected, (3) identification of institutions and agencies involved in the data collection, (4) identification of who is responsible for the survey and who is carrying it out, and (5) the names and contacts of the survey director and other officers from the sponsoring agencies.

- *"I am not interested."* In this situation, the interviewer should maintain his or her composure and try to identify the exact reason for the rejection. If the respondent does not have any specific objection, it might be possible to convince him or her to participate by asking about a specific problem he or she is facing at work and changing his or her stance by employing the consistency norm. If the respondent has a specific objection, such as confidentiality, the interviewer should be ready and able to address the specific concern and proceed with the interview. Avoid general debates about the study (Warwick and Lininger 1975). If this strategy fails, however, and the interviewer realizes that the respondent is genuinely not interested, it is best to avoid pursuing an interview. Experiments have shown that respondents not interested in the survey, but later recruited, provide less accurate answers (Couper 1997).
- *"Do I have to do this?"* Here, as always, honesty is required. The interviewer should mention that the respondent is under no legal obligation to participate. However, he or she should stress that the respondent's participation, because of a random selection process, is important in reaching the goal of the study. The interviewer should stress the potential benefits of participation and the weight of the sponsoring institutions (Warwick and Lininger 1975). The interviewer should stress that this is a chance for the respondent to have his or her say, to make a contribution (Morton-Williams 1991), and to speak for himself or herself as well as for other entrepreneurs.
- *"How long is it going to take?"* The interviewer should stress that the actual length of the interview depends a lot on the respondent. If he or she is interested in a given topic, and is spending more time on it than other respondents, then the interview could take longer. The interviewer must honestly provide an approximate amount of time based on the estimation during the pilot.
- *"What benefit do I get?"* This is probably the most frequent objection and the interviewer should be well prepared to address it methodically. While it is unethical to promise specific benefits (such as a financial benefit) stemming from any survey, the interviewer should be ready to indicate the practical usefulness of the survey to identify problems faced by the business community and to help the government address these problems to improve the investment climate.

- *"What is this survey about?"* *"What is it for?"* First, the interviewer should reassure the respondent ("I will be happy to present you with the details"). Then the interviewer should apologize if the respondent did not receive the advance letter, should provide the respondent with a copy of the letter, and should relay the introductory statement.

- *"Why does it have to be me?"* *"I don't know enough about this."* If this response is given, the interviewer needs to put the respondent at ease. The interviewer needs to be reassuring by stressing that everyone's view is important, not only the views of the well-informed, and that no one else can replace him or her in the study (Morton-Williams 1991). The interviewer should also stress the relative weight of his or her opinion within the sample composition.

- *"Can you come another time?"* The interviewer should apologize for the bad timing and show his or her willingness to come at a more convenient time. The interviewer should schedule a new appointment before leaving. If the respondent is available after a short period of time, the interviewer might consider waiting for his or her return instead of rescheduling a new appointment.

- *"This is a very sensitive question."* The interviewer should stress the confidentiality statement and should be prepared to present in more detail the steps taken to ensure it. The interviewer should stress the anonymity of the form, that is, show that no names appear on the form and that no questions on names, addresses, or clients are included in the questionnaire. The interviewer can confidently add that no firm has ever been identified in an Investment Climate Survey. Finally, the interviewer can add that the respondent is not expected to answer all questions.

- *"What kind of questions are you going to ask?"* With this observation, the respondent shows a sense of fear for the role he or she is supposed to play. The interviewer should put him or her at ease by providing examples of questions he or she will be asked. This could be a good opportunity to begin the interview.[28]

- *"I have done it before without any benefit."* Handling situations in which the respondent questions the value of the survey is among the most difficult tasks for the interviewer. Here, rather than stress the good things about the survey, it is preferable to stress its new and practical aspects. Very likely the respondent

---

[28] Recall that the interview should start with easy questions (see chapter 3).

associates a survey to some previous negative experience. So the best strategy would be to point out what makes this survey different from the ones before. Stress the new technique employed (such as productivity analysis) and show the practical impact (newspaper articles, clippings from other countries). Make sure not to promise things the survey cannot deliver.

Similarly, the interviewer can be faced with the following situational circumstances:

- *Respondent is away.* It is feasible for the manager to miss the appointment because of force majeure. In this case, the interviewer should give a minimal explanation about the survey and schedule a new appointment in the next few days. It is recommended not to give extensive explanations or to attempt to convince people to participate other than the selected respondent. Secondhand explanations of the purpose of the survey are generally not effective in eliciting participation. Unfortunately, sometimes the manager's absence is an indication that he or she is avoiding participation. In this case, the interviewer should attempt to win the support of other senior staff (Atkinson 1971).

- *Respondent is unresponsive.* This is an attempt by the respondent to undermine the interviewer's role as a petitioner for an interview. In this situation, the interviewer might feel the need to fill the silence with additional information or, worse, with a request for interview (Morton-Williams 1991). The best strategy is to engage the respondent by asking him or her direct and obvious questions related to the purpose of the study (such as "What is the biggest problem you are facing right now?").[29]

- *Respondent is hyperresponsive.* When interviewing elites, it is quite possible that the respondent will subject the interviewer to a continuous series of questions to determine his or her level of competence and commitment. In more extreme cases, the respondent might attempt to undermine the interviewer's confidence (for example, making negative comments on the survey, being aggressive). In these circumstances, the best strategy is for the interviewer to respond positively, smile, and point out the unique features of the survey, keeping in mind that the respondent is just testing his or her

---

[29] As mentioned earlier, the greatest interviewer's asset is his or her ability to tailor. Thus, if unresponsiveness is an expression of reluctance because of the current mood, the best strategy is to apologize for the bad timing and come back at a later date.

abilities. The interviewer should provide answers to the respondent's questions, remembering that the study is backed by the sponsoring agencies. Nobody expects the interviewer to be an expert on every topic. If a question is technical, the interviewer should assure the respondent that he or she will be contacted by the central office with an answer. Paying particular attention during training will help the interviewer handle these situations (Zuckerman 1972).

- *Refusal.* In any survey, there are always respondents who wish not to be interviewed. Assessing when this is the case requires considerable judgment on the part of the interviewer. Sometimes the refusal is a veiled request for additional assurances. In other cases, it indicates a real desire not to be interviewed. In the latter circumstance, the respondent's wish must be respected and the interviewer must politely leave without any debate. This will also facilitate a second attempt by more senior staff (Warwick and Lininger 1975). Interviewers should remember that (1) the majority of respondents will be happy to participate, (2) some respondents will be a bit reluctant, (3) a few respondents will need more convincing, and (4) a tiny proportion of respondents will always refuse no matter what (Morton-Williams 1991). Evidence shows that expressions of reluctance can be overcome (figure 5.9). Interviewers should realize that they cannot reach a 100 percent success rate. Even the best interviewers receive refusals. If the interviewer has a bad day, he or she should (1) take a day off, (2) think of the pleasant interviews he or she has conducted, (3) talk to a supervisor, and (4) remember that he or she is not alone in this endeavor (Morton-Williams 1991).
- *Tandem interviewing.* It is a good practice to have two interviewers conduct the interview. This has the advantage of smoothing the interview process—with one interviewer asking questions and the other recording the answers—thus avoiding interruptions in the conversation, increasing the accuracy of the data collected, and saving the respondent's time. Conversely, the practice of having an additional respondent present during the interview should be avoided. Although it might appear that the presence of a second respondent is a source of supplementary information, in practice, this works to the detriment of the interview. According to Kincaid and Bright,

   For one thing, where the difference in ranks [is] considerable, either there [is] complete silence on the part of the subordi-

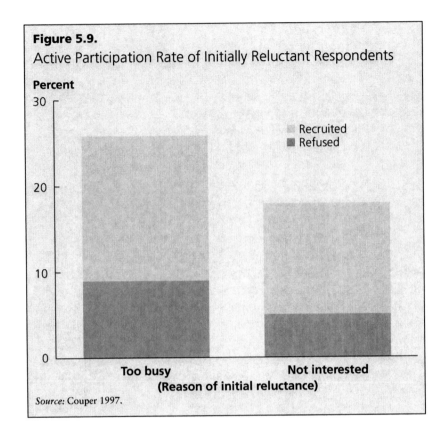

Figure 5.9.
Active Participation Rate of Initially Reluctant Respondents

Source: Couper 1997.

nate or the superior waste[s] time asking the subordinate
views on matters about which [he has] expressed himself.
[. . .] In cases where the rank of the two respondents [is]
about equal, time [is] wasted by the respondent's tendency
to end a statement by seeking confirmation from each other.
(1957, 310)

Nevertheless, if the interviewer cannot avoid having a second respondent present, he or she should be aware that the presence of a third
party will have a different impact on data quality depending on the type
of question asked. When asking factual questions, the presence of a
third party is less of a problem and occasionally could be beneficial.
However, when opinion and knowledge questions are asked, the presence of additional respondents makes the interview more complex because it becomes more difficult to avoid having the additional
respondent help or educate the selected respondent. In these circum-

stances, the presence of a third party should be handled carefully. The interviewer should record only the replies of the respondent and preempt interruptions by tactfully asking the other person to hold his or her views for the moment while expressing that he or she is interested in hearing them after the interview. It is essential in this situation to assign a specific role to the third party, otherwise he or she might adopt one that will disrupt the interview (Atkinson 1971).

- *Exaggeration.* Occasionally it is possible that the respondent might want to impress the interviewer with a false image of himself or herself. In these cases, the interviewer should clearly indicate to the respondent that he or she is not impressed by such exaggeration. The interviewer should express that anything the respondent says is fine with him or her as long as it is the respondent's honest opinion (Atkinson 1971).
- *Untrue response.* If the interviewer feels that the respondent is not answering truthfully, he or she should ask the question again using a preamble such as "Sorry, let me check, I am not sure whether I made clear what we are asking here." The tone used should give the sense that the question asked is not of any special significance and that the respondent can modify his or her answers (Atkinson 1971).
- *Masked willingness to cooperate.* If the interviewer senses from the facetiousness of the respondent's answers that the respondent is not really interested in participating, the interviewer should stress the seriousness of the task and emphasize that he or she is interested only in meaningful answers. The respondent should take his or her role seriously. However, if the respondent does not take the role seriously, the interviewer should attempt to find out why the respondent is not interested and use all his or her skills to change the respondent's mind. If everything fails, the interviewer should not continue the interview (Atkinson 1971).

A related, but less problematic issue, is the amount of interruptions considered acceptable (for example, phone calls received during the interview). In these circumstances, the interviewer should convey to the respondent that his or her undivided attention is needed and, if the respondent cannot completely avoid interruptions, he or she should tactfully attempt to reduce them to a minimum.

- *Handing out the questionnaire.* Occasionally, respondents ask to read the questions directly on a blank form during the interview. This request, although apparently simple and harmless, should be resisted. By directly reading the questionnaire, the respondent might be influenced by the presence and order of alternatives. He or she might "educate" himself or herself on the flow of answers and carefully select specific answers to avoid having to answer additional questions (Atkinson 1971). If the respondent insists on having a blank copy of the form, it is preferable to give him or her a copy of the form with only the questions (without any skipping pattern or set of alternatives).

Conducting the Interview

Interview Style

The interviewer's job is not only to communicate the questions to the respondent but also to convey the framework in which he or she formulates the answers. At the beginning of any interview, the respondent is not sure what role he or she is supposed to play. The respondent is not clear if he or she has to play a task-oriented role in which he or she is required to respond adequately and accurately, or a conversational role in which he or she tries to relate to the interviewer by conforming to the interviewer's apparent opinions or by attempting to make a good impression on the interviewer. During the brief social interaction of an interview, the style employed by the interviewer has an impact on how the respondent perceives his or her role and, consequently, this has an impact on the accuracy of the data collected.

With a formal style, the interviewer clarifies that the respondent's role is to provide accurate information without engaging in irrelevant conversation with the interviewer. With a socioemotional style, the respondent is given the impression that he or she is not called upon to provide accurate information because any answer is warmly received. This style allows the interviewer more freedom in conducting the interview but also brings a greater risk for data quality. The interviewer can, voluntarily or involuntarily, (1) communicate opinions to the respondent, (2) assume the respondent has particular opinions and thus pose the question directively, and (3) infer the respondent's answer from previous information. Thus, socioemotional style carries a higher response effect, particularly when the topic is not salient, the question is sensitive, and the set of response alternatives might generate a sense of acquiescence. Respondent's education also appears to be related to the quality of reporting. A personal style seems to be more appropriate for respondents with little education, while an impersonal approach results in more accurate data among respondents with higher education. Accordingly, in business surveys, it is advisable to follow a formal style throughout the interview even if the respondent is more oriented toward a socioemotional style (Dexter 1970; Dijkstra and van der Zouwen 1987; Martin 1984; Morton-Williams 1991).

We must recognize that the interviewer is called on to perform two distinct roles in his or her interaction with the respondent. The interviewer needs to be a neutral communicator but also a persuader. Unless the interviewer can convince the respondent to participate, there will be no opportunity to act as a neutral communicator. Therefore, during the introductory stage, when the interviewer needs to secure participation, it might be preferable to adopt a more relaxed, more social approach in which the interviewer relates to the prospective respondent's concerns and mood. It is important, however, that the interviewer appropriately communicate the change in style before the interview begins.[30] This is necessary because it is not clear whether the respondent can make this distinction himself or herself (Martin 1984).

Respondent's Role

After the introductory phase is finished and before the questioning begins, it is important to communicate to the respondent how to perform his or her role as information provider and explain the setting in which he or she will be asked to provide information. Martin (1984) identifies five different ways in which the respondent sees an interview: (1) as an intimate conversation, (2) as a citizen referendum, (3) as a form-filling exercise, (4) as a test, or (5) as a subterfuge. It is feasible to assume that each of these possible interpretations might influence the respondent's answers to some if not all of the questions. For example, a manager might personally be against corruption but have to practice it to run his or her business. It is therefore important to ensure that the respondent understands the point of view he or she needs to assume when answering the questions.

Asking the Questions

There is a lot of debate in the literature about which interviewing method provides the most accurate answers: standardized or flexible. With

---

[30] This can be easily accomplished by providing the respondent with a set of directions about how to perform his or her role.

the former, the interviewer is required to read each question exactly as it is written and leave any interpretation to the respondent. Supporters of the flexible approach argue that the standardized method undermines the validity of the answers because each respondent might have a different interpretation of the same question. Therefore, they argue, interviewers should engage the respondent with a conversational style in which they are free to use their own words to convey the same meaning of the question to each respondent. The debate on standardization is fuelled by the fact that, no matter how much people try, it is impossible to design questions that are always clear and have the same meaning for all respondents. Although a number of steps can and should be taken to reduce this risk to a minimum, it is always possible that somewhere in the questionnaire some respondent might not clearly understand a question, a concept, or a definition. When this happens, no matter what the interviewer does or does not do, there is going to be some degree of measurement error (Fowler and Mangione 1990).

The debate between standardized and flexible interviewing technique thus transforms into a debate between which measurement error—respondent or interviewer—is smaller. Obviously, the existence of such a debate demonstrates that there is no conclusive evidence on which approach is superior. There is plenty of empirical evidence showing that even a single word in a question can significantly change the pattern of answers. However, it is not possible to conclude that the validity of the data is always improved by standardization, when the respondent is unsure of the true meaning of the question he or she is answering.[31] When the respondent is so confused that he or she requests a clarification, it is reasonable to assume that a well-trained interviewer will be the best tool to reduce measurement errors.

These opposing theories have merits and the best solution is somewhere in the middle. As a general rule, the interviewer should ask the question in a natural tone exactly as it is written in the questionnaire, including all alternatives.[32] In exceptional circumstances, when the respondent cannot understand the question even after it has been read a second time, and only if the respondent asks for an explanation, the interviewer should be

---

[31] We would not be measuring the phenomenon we wish to measure, but rather the phenomenon the respondent *thinks* we want to measure. In this circumstance, the best solution would be a nonresponse. However, even this is hard to enforce given the respondent's propensity to provide any answer.

[32] To phrase the question conversationally, it is important for the interviewer to learn and even memorize part of the questionnaire (Atkinson 1971).

given greater freedom to ask the question using different words, as long as the meaning of the question remains the same and the explanation is provided nondirectively.[33] This mixed approach improves the quality of the data collected. In an experiment conducted by Schober and Conrad (1997), the authors show that the response accuracy was close with both methodologies, standardized and flexible, if the questions were easy to understand. However, the flexible approach proved much better in the event of a complex question (figure 5.10). This approach works only if two conditions are met: first, the questionnaire is properly designed for a standardized interview; and, second, the interviewers receive a comprehensive and detailed training.

The main reasons pulling an interviewer away from standardization are related to questionnaire design. If the question is hard to read, if the concept of the question is hard to grasp, or if the style of the question is not conversational, the interviewer will attempt to phrase the question using his or her own words to facilitate the respondent's job (Fowler and Mangione 1990). Interviewers move away from standardization because

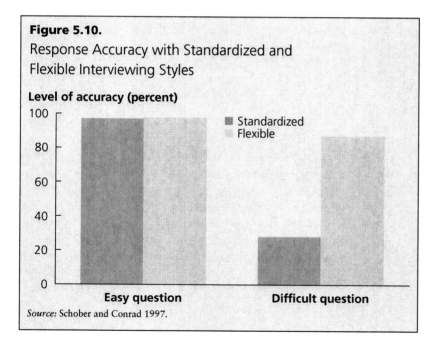

Figure 5.10.

Response Accuracy with Standardized and Flexible Interviewing Styles

Level of accuracy (percent)

■ Standardized
Flexible

Easy question   Difficult question

Source: Schober and Conrad 1997.

---

[33] See the next point on how to conduct probing.

of their genuine desire to make it easier for the respondent to answer the questions and, as a result, to get more accurate information. Similarly, given that even the most experienced interviewers often are unaware of the risks of this deviation, an appropriate training session in standardized interviewing is equally necessary. By showing the effects of question rewording on data accuracy, this session will emphasize that—when respondents provide inadequate replies—interviewers should not act directively and should not add unrelated information to the question asked. The training session should demonstrate that doing so could compromise the accuracy of the answers.

Probing

One important aspect of the interview process is how to behave when the respondent provides an inadequate answer, that is, an answer that is partial, irrelevant, inaccurate, or nonresponsive. Probing is the action of asking the respondent to provide clarifications or additional information. Understanding how to probe is among the most difficult of the interviewer's tasks for two reasons. First, it is difficult because it must be performed in a nondirective way. During an interview, it is possible for the interviewer to inadvertently rephrase a question in a way that might lead or educate the respondent.[34] Second, it is difficult because it is not always obvious when the respondent's answer requires a probe. Interviewers must be careful not to overprobe because this might annoy the respondent or make him or her feel obliged to provide an answer at any price. Conversely, bias can be introduced by failing to probe. This is more likely to occur with open-ended questions and "don't know" answers. Open-ended questions are hard to probe because the interviewer needs to assess whether the question has been answered and whether the answer is complete and accurate. Similarly, a "don't know" answer can simultaneously be a legitimate answer and a temporary response, giving the respondent more time to think about the real answer. It can even be a sign that the respondent is unsure whether the answer is what the interviewer expects (Fowler and Mangione 1990).

Although there are no rules about how much probing is appropriate and decisions are left to the interviewer's discretion, few practitioners

---

[34] "A directive probe is one that increases the likelihood of one answer over others. [. . .] any probe that can be answered with a 'yes' or 'no' is directive. In addition, any probe that lists or mentions some possible answers, but excludes others, is also directive because it increases the likelihood that the mentioned answers will be chosen" (Fowler and Mangione 1990, 40).

recognize that not all questions should be probed similarly. Atkinson (1971) identifies two styles of probing that correspond to two types of questions: factual questions and opinion or knowledge questions. In both cases, when the respondent does not understand the question on first reading, the question must be read a second time exactly as it is stated. After this second attempt, if the question is still not understood or the answer is incomplete, the interviewer is allowed greater freedom in probing factual events. The interviewer can rephrase the question using his or her own words within the terms of reference of the instructions provided during the training and in the survey materials. The interviewer can also use open nondirective expressions, as well as the "zeroing in" technique[35] to elicit more precise answers. Finally, if an accurate figure is not available, the interviewer can settle for the best estimate the respondent can provide.

On the other hand, after the second reading of an opinion or knowledge question, a more rigid probing style must be followed because, in this circumstance, it is much easier for the interviewer to lead or educate the respondent by slightly changing the wording of the question. In these circumstances, the interviewer should encourage additional information from the respondent only by using neutral expressions, such as "Can you tell me more about that?" "Can you explain a bit more what you mean with (. . .)?" "Which of these would be the closest to describe the way you feel?" or "Are there other (explanations/methods/cases)?" It is not a good idea to summarize the respondent's answer nor to wait in silence for more information. The first approach might generate bias because of the different ways that interviewers summarize, while the second approach could be misinterpreted by the respondent (figure 5.11) (Moser and Kalton 1971).

Prompting

Prompting means suggesting various answers[36] so that the meaning of the question is precisely defined and the respondent can easily provide his or her answer. Prompting is particularly useful when the question has a wide range of meanings and the researcher does not wish to use

---

[35] With this method, after the respondent provides a general idea of where the answer lies, the interviewer follows up with a nondirective question to further narrow the range of his answer (Fowler and Mangione 1990).

[36] This is the case of a question with a list of precoded answers among which the respondent has to choose one (running prompt) or provide a reply for each item (individual prompt) (Atkinson 1971).

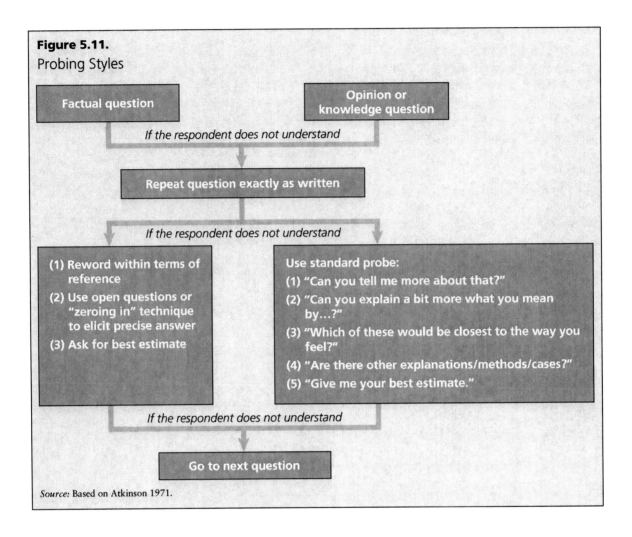

Figure 5.11.
Probing Styles

Factual question

Opinion or knowledge question

If the respondent does not understand

Repeat question exactly as written

If the respondent does not understand

(1) **Reword within terms of reference**
(2) **Use open questions or "zeroing in" technique to elicit precise answer**
(3) **Ask for best estimate**

Use standard probe:
(1) **"Can you tell me more about that?"**
(2) **"Can you explain a bit more what you mean by...?"**
(3) **"Which of these would be closest to the way you feel?"**
(4) **"Are there other explanations/methods/cases?"**
(5) **"Give me your best estimate."**

If the respondent does not understand

Go to next question

Source: Based on Atkinson 1971.

an open-ended question or when answering requires a high degree of effort on the part of the respondent. Because prompting basically amounts to suggesting answers, it should be used only when asked for in the survey form (Atkinson 1971).

Providing Instruction and Feedback

Instructions are added into the survey form to help the respondent perform the task accurately. They must be short and clear, and must be read by the interviewer before the question is asked. Instructions ask respondents to think carefully before answering, to take their time before providing an answer, or remind them that accurate and complete answers are needed.[37] Feedback is used to let the respondent know how well he or she is performing his or her job. Feedback must be nondirective and can include such expressions as "Thank you for your frankness," "We are interested in details like this," or "You answered quickly. Sometimes it is easy to forget all the details. Can you think again about it one more time?" (Kalton and Schuman 1982).

Ending the Interview

When the interview is completed, the interviewer should always thank the respondent for his or her participation. Before leaving, the interviewer should make sure that he or she has answered all of the respondent's questions. The interviewer should obtain permission to contact the respondent again to verify items if omissions or inconsistencies are discovered and require clarification (Atkinson 1971).

---

[37] If the form is self-administered, instructions must be highlighted in bold. Respondents, in fact, tend not to read instructions, or they refer to them only when they think they need help (Gower 1993).

Chapter 6

Why Data Management Is Important

Does zero really mean zero? A timely delivery of quality survey data requires accurate data management. Contrary to what many believe, planning for data entry should start immediately after the decision to implement a survey has been made. As a matter of fact, data management begins with the questionnaire design. In particular, the physical layout of the form must meet a number of data entry requirements such as the following:

- Questions should not be crowded to save space
- Check boxes and coding boxes should be located next to the relevant question
- Precoded answers should always appear alongside the relevant answers
- Open-ended questions should provide enough space for the response
- The answering pattern should be uniform, preferably from top to bottom
- "For official use" should be clearly identified for questions that need to be coded after enumeration in the field office

While designing the questionnaire, it is thus necessary for the survey manager to interact extensively with the data manager because he or she will have

[A]n especially sharp eye for flaws in the definition of units of observation, skip patterns, etc. Likewise the analysts who have helped to write the questions should help the data manager determine the appropriate range of consistency checks. (Grosh and Muñoz 1996, 127)

Furthermore, it is advisable to provide the data manager with some training.

It needs to be strongly emphasized that cleaning of [. . .] survey data is not a trivial task: it has frequently proved in practice to be the most time-consuming of all data processing tasks in surveys.

—United Nations,
*National Household Survey
Capability Programme*

in substantive aspects of the survey. This should include not only appreciation of the goals of the survey and the methodology being used but also thorough understanding of the questionnaire and the interviewing methods. This can be gained by attending the interviewer training sessions. (Rattenbury 1980, 10)

To ensure the collection of accurate data in a timely manner, four fundamental procedures must be implemented:

- Coding
- Editing
- Electronic Data Entry
- Cleaning

Coding

Coding is the process of summarizing survey answers into meaningful categories to identify patterns (Moser and Kalton 1971). Coding involves two steps: defining a coding frame and assigning corresponding values. Basically, coding frames identify the categories of answers. This task is easy when answers have a simple pattern, such as yes/no questions,[1] but it can become quite complex and cumbersome when the range of possible answers for a given question is large, for example, "How do you acquire technology innovation?" In this case, critical decisions must made about how to classify potential answers. The level of depth of the classification should reflect the analytical purpose of the question, while keeping in mind the respondent's ability to use the chosen categories. If the classification adopted is not clear to the respondent, he or she might simply refuse to answer or provide a biased response.[2] This reaction demonstrates that "the construction of the coding frames is not a task to be delegated to routine clerks; it has to be done by somebody fully in touch with the purpose of the survey and the way the results are to be used" (Moser and Kalton 1971, 417).

The assignment of numeric labels to questionnaire entries is of critical importance for the accuracy of data entry. To the largest extent possible, numeric labels should be preassigned and clearly appear next to

---

[1] While is not advantageous to indicate it for every entry on the paper questionnaire, the reader should be reminded that the coding for all questions also includes NA (not applicable), DK (don't know), and REF (refuse to answer).

[2] In this task the survey manager's experience and the outcome of the pretest might be of great help. It is also good practice to always include "Others (specify)" as a residual category.

each question to facilitate data entry. Open-ended questions should not be coded during the interview. This exercise is time-consuming and, more importantly, introduces new sources of bias in the data (United Nations 1982). It is also important that questions with answers in the same range be coded in the same way and in the same order throughout the instrument.

Of critical importance in this process is the distinction between NA (not applicable), NP (not provided), DK (don't know), and REF (refuse to answer). Experience clearly shows that data entry errors and confusion among answers can be avoided if negative three-digit numbers are used to identify the aforementioned values in the data set.

Finally, all answer alternatives should be uniquely coded. Sometimes it might seem that slight variations in answers do not need to be coded differently. Practitioners might be under the false impression that "space can be saved by combining several questions into one code. However, such false economy can result in loss of valuable information, and certainly increases the risk of making errors" (United Nations 1982, 13). A typical case in point is the distinction between NA and NP. While many agree that there is a substantial difference in the information provided by NA, DK, and REF, some practitioners believe that NA and NP basically provide the same type of information. Quite to the contrary, NA and NP provide different information and should be clearly discriminated in the assignment of codes. As figure 6.1 shows, NP indicates that a particular event does not exist, while NA implies the existence of the event, although it is not "used" by the respondent (for example, although an available bank provides loans, the respondent does not have one).

Editing

Editing is the process through which the completed questionnaire is reviewed to detect and correct errors. It is a task conducted both by the enumerator at the end of each interview and by the supervisor in the field office. Although routine in its nature,

> anyone who has ever glanced through a completed questionnaire returned from the field will be aware of the absolute necessity for careful editing. Even the best interviewers are liable to make errors, omit to ask questions or to record answers and, when the field staff is inexperienced, editing assumes a crucial role. (Moser and Kalton 1971, 411)

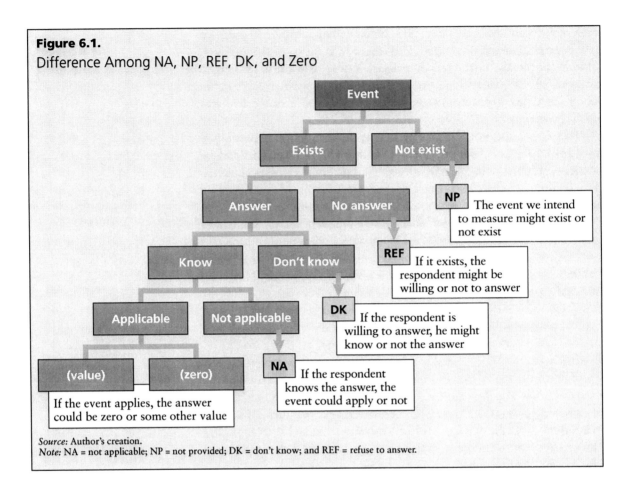

Figure 6.1.

Difference Among NA, NP, REF, DK, and Zero

Source: Author's creation.
Note: NA = not applicable; NP = not provided; DK = don't know; and REF = refuse to answer.

The process of editing consists of checking that the information collected is complete, accurate, and consistent.

Completeness implies confirming that all relevant questions have been asked and have a recorded answer. Because it is possible for the interviewer to recall an answer that he or she forgot to record during the interview, editing should be carried out soon after the end of the interview and before the next interview begins. Completeness does not mean that all questions must be asked and must have a recorded answer. As a matter of fact, it is likely that not all questions will apply to all respondents and that, even if a question is applicable, not all respondents will be able or willing to provide an answer. Therefore, the presence of blanks in the questionnaire does not necessarily imply incompleteness. There is no reason to fill in a survey with NA entries when the questions are not relevant to the particular respondent and should be skipped.

Accuracy implies checking that all recorded answers are easily identified. The tension of the interview might cause the interviewer to fail to clearly mark relevant answers or to mark more than one option. When arithmetic is needed to arrive at an answer, accuracy means checking the calculation performed in the field. Finally, checking for accuracy of open-ended questions means that each question is answered in a legible manner and that the codes assigned are correct and uniform.

Consistency implies checking that all logical relations between questions are respected. If an establishment does not import goods, an answer should not be recorded for a question asking for the major country of import, no matter where in the questionnaire this question is located. Here, a critical role is held by the skipping pattern. Staff checking for consistency must pay special attention to the existence of questions having inverted scale within the same questionnaire to ensure that the interviewer recorded the correct answer. Finally, consistency implies that the interviewers have interpreted the questions in a uniform way. Occasionally, during the editing stage, different interpretations of questions emerge, which need to be appropriately rectified (Moser and Kalton 1971).

All completed questionnaires must be edited and, even when this task is performed by the supervisor, the interviewer's assistance is crucial in understanding how to correct invalid entries. It is advisable to keep a log file of errors encountered for each interviewer because many mistakes are interviewer specific. When an incorrect entry cannot be corrected and the question is important, the interviewer should go back to the respondent for clarifications.

Electronic Data Entry

The benefits of adopting a data entry software form to obtain an electronic version of the paper data are clear to all those involved in surveys and do not need to be repeated here. What is not clear to all is the amount of time it takes to develop and test such a form. In the Living Standards and Measurement Study (LSMS)[3] experience, it usually takes "six to eight weeks for the complete preparation and testing of the data

---

[3] LSMS household surveys stands for Living Standards and Measurement Study and represents household surveys regularly conducted by the World Bank in developing countries. See http://www.worldbank.org/lsms/ for more details.

entry program" (Moser and Kalton 1971, 128). In the Investment Climate Survey experience, given that the questionnaire is shorter and the structural relationship between records is simpler than the typical LSMS, approximately four weeks should be allocated to develop and test an entry form.

The development of an entry form starts with the selection of a software package. There are a number of packages that can be used for this purpose, some of which are freeware.[4] Each package has different features and different characteristics. The decision on the most appropriate package to adopt should be based on the survey firm's current practices and available hardware, as well as the know-how in the survey country. It is not practical to adopt Microsoft Access© in a country where few people know how to use it or where the available hardware will not support it.[5]

Although the decision about which software to adopt should be left to the survey firm, the survey manager must ensure that the data entry form adopted meets the following minimum number of requirements to guarantee accurate data entry:

- *Unique identifier.* The form must require each record to have a unique identifier (ID) before any data can be entered (see box 6.1). It is good practice to use numeric values as identifiers.
- *Variable name.* The form must require each field (variable) to have a clearly defined and unique name. When variable names are well constructed, it is possible to identify the question corresponding to the variable name immediately without even looking at the questionnaire. It is good practice to have variable names start with a letter.[6]

---

[4] See footnote 7 in chapter 2.

[5] When conducting multicountry surveys, there is some debate among practitioners about whether is it preferable to develop the data entry form centrally or to decentralize this process in the field. The former alternative seems preferable for at least three reasons. First, each survey firm might already be using a different software. Second, even if this is not the case, it might be still preferable to increase the survey firm's capability by subcontracting this task to a local provider. Third, the use of a software for which there are locally trained people will be extremely useful when problems arise while using the application.

[6] A number of software programs have such a requirement.

Box 6.1

How to Assign Questionnaire IDs

Firm-Level Survey of Armenia

The questionnaire number (ID code) consists of eight digits, which represent the following:

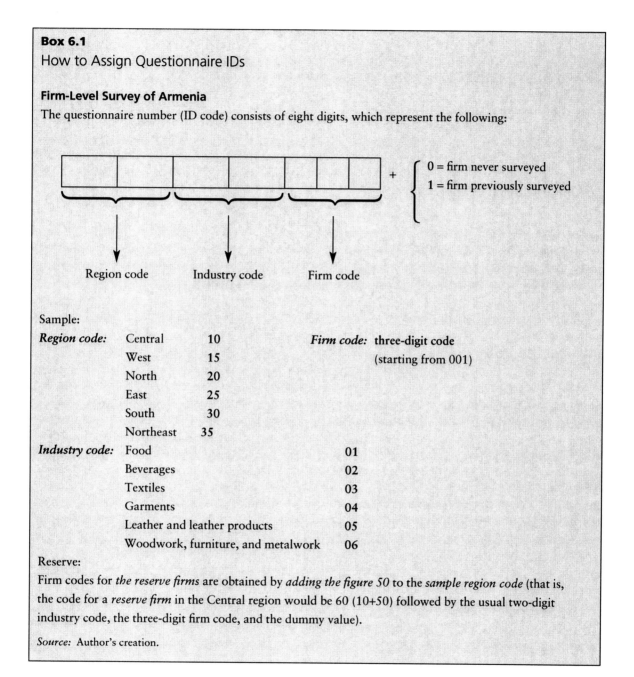

Sample:

Region code:	Central	10	*Firm code:*	three-digit code
	West	15		(starting from 001)
	North	20		
	East	25		
	South	30		
	Northeast	35		

Industry code:	Food	01
	Beverages	02
	Textiles	03
	Garments	04
	Leather and leather products	05
	Woodwork, furniture, and metalwork	06

Reserve:

Firm codes for *the reserve firms* are obtained by *adding the figure 50* to the *sample region code* (that is, the code for a *reserve firm* in the Central region would be 60 (10+50) followed by the usual two-digit industry code, the three-digit firm code, and the dummy value).

Source: Author's creation.

- *Quality control.* The form must allow each record entered to be the object of three types of automatic quality control checks:
  - *Range checks.* Every variable in the questionnaire must have a range check. For instance, when the question is a percentage, values outside the 0–100 range must be disallowed. Similarly, if the numeric value for yes is 1 and no is 2, all yes/no questions must disallow other values.[7]
  - *Logical checks.* These checks verify that the skipping patterns have been respected and that answers to interrelated questions are consistent (Grosh and Muñoz 1996). Thus, for instance, if the establishment interviewed does not have a loan, no answer should be recorded for the amount or composition of collateral. Similarly, if the establishment manufactured output in a specific year, then values for production, sales, and inventories need to be answered in a consistent manner.
  - *Reliability checks.* These checks verify that answers provided are coherent. This is the case, for example, for a multicomponent question whose sum must equal 100, or whose sum must be equal to the total provided in another question (for example, workforce composition and total workforce).
- *Data output and dictionary file.* Finally, the software used must be able to output the data in a format that is compatible with other software and, more important, that can produce a dictionary file. With the development of technology, it is easy to convert virtually any file from one format to another. However, not many software programs can produce dictionary files,[8] which are critical to making data user friendly.

Anyone who has been involved in the development of an entry form would agree that "setting up the boundaries for the range checks on some numeric variables is an art" (Grosh and Muñoz 1996, 131). While, in many cases, it is easy to identify the restrictions on each check (range, consistency, and reliability), in every questionnaire there are instances where this task becomes more laborious. Because there is no

---

[7] The form developer should keep in mind that the legal codes for NA, DK, and REF will apply to all questions, thus should be consistently allowed throughout the data entry form. Similarly, because it is impossible to check text, the use of string as answers should be reduced to the absolute minimum.

[8] A dictionary file contains the basic documentation of the variables in the data file. It specifies, for each variable, the name, its description (label), its type (string and numeric), its value range (categorical or continuous), and its record length.

universally valid rule, the checks embedded in the data entry form should (1) highlight possible erroneous values and (2) allow for the possibility of being overwritten by the supervisor after an appropriate examination of the paper copy of the questionnaire.

Another major concern to be addressed when developing a data entry form refers to the level of depth of the embedded controls. Too few checks allow incorrect entries to be accepted, while too stringent controls might stall the data entry and delivery process. Here, again, no universal rule exists given the peculiar characteristic of each questionnaire. It becomes the job of the survey manager to strike a difficult balance between these two competing choices, aided only by experience and a profound understanding of the questions' objectives.

It is good practice to test the form ahead of the start of the fieldwork to avoid unnecessary delays in data delivery. A useful approach in testing the form is the "trace sample" in which "a small sample of fictitious cases that represent a wide range of situations" is used (United Nations 1982, 54).

Finally, to minimize errors while speeding up data entry, the screen layout of the data entry form should faithfully reproduce the physical layout of the questionnaire. Each questionnaire page should correspond to each data entry screen. The data entry operator should not have to switch screens for data that appear on the same questionnaire page or vice versa.

Cleaning

After the recorded data have been reviewed by the interviewer, edited by the supervisor, and entered electronically as previously described, the data files are sent to the central office for the last but not least important step, cleaning.

Cleaning represents the set of final editing and imputation procedures used to enhance data quality and prepare data for analysis. Cleaning is an essential part of the survey operations and, at the same time, an extremely delicate process. Because editing and imputation amount to altering the actual responses recorded in the field, inaccurate cleaning can seriously compromise the validity of the data in the following ways:

- Significantly change the data collected
- Introduce errors in the final data
- Destroy evidence of poor-quality data

Nevertheless, if conducted properly, cleaning can achieve the following:

- Improve or, at the least, retain the quality of the data collected
- Make the data more user friendly for analysis
- Increase the credibility of the data collected

It is absolutely essential to use experienced staff in cleaning any data, especially when this step is completed in the absence of the completed paper questionnaire (United Nations 1982).

The methodology adopted in the Investment Climate Surveys when establishment survey data sets are cleaned follows two guiding principles:

- *The sanctity of the data collected is paramount.* Values are replaced (edited or imputed) only if an error can be detected "beyond any reasonable doubt." When in doubt, it is best to let the data users decide how to treat potential invalid entries. With this approach, we don't destroy evidence of poor data and we don't introduce errors in the data.[9]
- *Extensive imputation is not allowed.* As Fellegi and Holt (1976, 17) rightly pointed out, "one should, whenever possible, avoid 'manufacturing' data instead of collecting it." Hence, if errors occur in 5 percent or more of the reported values, no action is taken and the data are returned to the field office for additional checking and, if necessary, follow-up interviews. This is done to avoid significantly changing the data collected.

Practical Steps in Cleaning Survey Data

In practice, Investment Climate Survey data sets are cleaned in three steps:

Step 1. *Verification of structural stability.* The first set of checks refer to the structural composition of the data file(s) and its correspondence to the questionnaire. These controls are conducted to ensure that the following is accomplished:

- The data file(s) contain all the sections of the questionnaire
- Each record has a unique ID

---

[9] This principle has a clear implication for the treatment of outliers. Erroneous entries and outliers are two completely different phenomena requiring two completely different approaches. While the treatment of errors is described in these pages, outliers are numbers that fall within the possible range of values, although they are unusual in their magnitude. Being unusual, however, does not imply being wrong "beyond any reasonable doubt." As a consequence, the treatment of outliers is left to the data users' discretion and justification.

- The IDs used correspond to the selected sample
- Each variable has a unique label
- Each label in the data corresponds to the labels in the paper questionnaire
- All variables in the data set appear in the questionnaire and vice versa
- The preassigned codes are entered correctly, including preassigned string variables
- Unique codes are used for not applicable (NA), don't know (DK), refuse to answer (REF), and not provided (NP)
- The dictionary file is available
- The coding frame is available

Particular attention must be paid to two values: NA and 0 (zero). Occasionally, 0 is used both as a numeric value and as NA (in violation of what was described previously and illustrated in figure 6.1). The accurate discrimination between these two entries is not a trivial task and, if this problem is not detected and corrected early, it can have serious consequences on the quality of the final data (figure 6.2).[10]

Step 2. *Identification of invalid entries.* The second step is intended to detect invalid entries through a set of rules similar, although more stringent, to the ones used in the development of the data entry form. A data point can be invalid for two reasons: either because the value itself is erroneous (that is, out of range), or because, even when correct, the internal consistency with another question is invalid (that is, an establishment that classifies itself as an exporter while reporting 0 percent of output as exports). Therefore, there are two levels of controls that need to be put in place: a first level referring to each question taken individually and a second level referring to consistency across questions.[11]

Step 3. *Editing and imputation.* Finally those entries deemed invalid are "corrected" through editing or imputation or by simply flagging

---

[10] It is feasible, although not common, to have a zero acquisition cost for a generator when public agencies provide grants to facilitate the development of particular industries or locations. Such is the case with the United Nations Development Programme project for "Revitalization of microhydro electric generator in Sirnarasa village" in Indonesia, available at http://www.undp.org/sgp/cty/ASIA_PACIFIC/INDONESIA/pfs272.htm.

[11] Because it is possible that internal consistency checks involve questions located in separate sections of the questionnaire, the data checkers must have a thorough understanding of the structure of the questionnaire (see example 6.3).

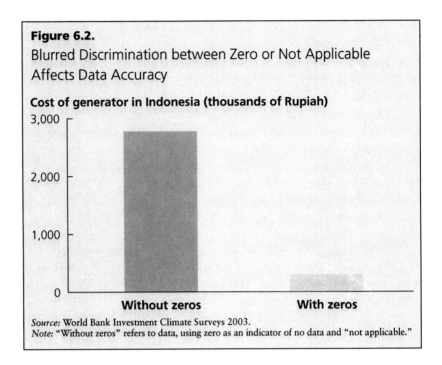

Figure 6.2.
Blurred Discrimination between Zero or Not Applicable Affects Data Accuracy

Cost of generator in Indonesia (thousands of Rupiah)

Source: World Bank Investment Climate Surveys 2003.
Note: "Without zeros" refers to data, using zero as an indicator of no data and "not applicable."

them and requesting the assistance of the field office. The correction of invalid entries takes place in three stages:

- *Quantification of erroneous entries.* A frequency distribution of the invalid entries is generated, and if the pattern of erroneous values suggests problems at the data entry stage,[12] no action is taken other than referring back the problem to the field office for clarification and amendment.
- *Correction of typographical errors.* If the inspection of erroneous data clearly (that is, beyond any reasonable doubt) highlights typographical errors, they are promptly edited. By scrutinizing interlinked questions, typographical errors can more easily be detected.
- *Reconciliation of internally consistent errors.* The final and by far the most difficult stage in the cleaning process is the investigation of internal inconsistencies among individually correct questions. Because situational and methodological factors often contribute to these inconsistencies, it becomes extremely challenging to

[12] This is the case when the 5 percent rule is violated, or when a common error is detected in percentage questions (that is, entering both 0.02 and 2 percent in the same question).

establish a general rule for data consistency checks. Because of the endless possible combinations of response artifacts affecting response consistency (see example 6.1 which shows how one apparently simple question can be answered inconsistently in 25 different ways), and because of the multiplicity of interpretation that a question can elicit in the field, scrutiny of the answers to a survey question often reveals a much more subtle and difficult set of interpretations than originally supposed. "Changes in wording that might seems trivial at first glance may prove on further analysis to imply subtle and significant changes in meaning" (Martin and Abelson 1984, 287). Consequently, *the resolution of internal inconsistencies can only be achieved through a detailed investigation of the distribution of correct and incorrect answers together with the construct of the relevant questions and the survey methodology adopted,* making this task complex and time-consuming. While up to this step cleaning simply involved the identification of the consequences of response artifacts by means of statistical processes, this final step of data cleaning involves the application of cognitive models aimed at identifying the causes of these errors. Hence, data cleaners performing this task must be aware of all potential response artifacts (social desirability bias, order effect, position effect, sensitive bias, recall bias, and so on) because they all have an impact on internal consistency.

That said, when situational and methodological factors cannot be used to explain the apparent inconsistency among questions, the cleaning strategy in Investment Climate Surveys is based on the probability of error estimated on the level of difficulty of the interlinked questions. Because answering easier questions requires lower cognitive effort than answering difficult ones, when the choice must be made between two individually correct but, when cross-checked, inconsistent answers to questions of different levels of difficulty, holding methodological and situational factors constant, the answer to the most difficult question (that is, the more specific question) is assumed to be more reliable. So, for example, if the respondent answers no to the question "Do you use any software?" but provides the answer "Netsoft XW version 5.3, release 4" to the subsequent question "Which software do you use?" after ascertaining the existence of Netsoft XW version 5.3, release 4 in the survey country, we can assume the more specific question to be correct. In applying this principle, each question is rated according to the cognitive effort it requires to be answered. As a general rule, easier questions are assumed to be yes/no questions, other binomial precoded questions (for example, male/female), and opinion questions (for example, poor/good). Higher cognitive effort is expected when the respondent is asked to provide percentages, choose among a list of alternatives, or indicate a length of time. Finally, the most difficult questions are those for which the respondent has to fill in values (that is, accounting questions), recall events in the past, or reply to sensitive questions[13] (figure 6.3; also see example 6.3).

Contrary to what many believe, *cleaning data sets does not necessarily entail the removal of all invalid and inconsistent values*. In fact, apart from instances in which it is not possible to do so, there are circumstances when it is not desirable to eliminate inconsistencies. The

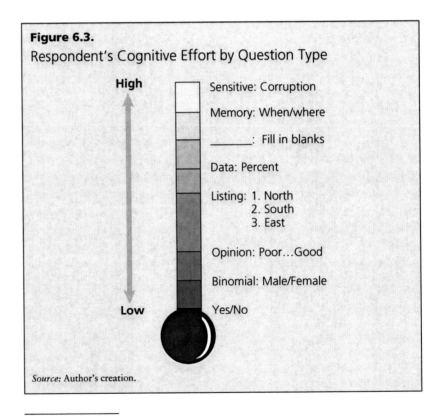

Figure 6.3.
Respondent's Cognitive Effort by Question Type

High

Low

Sensitive: Corruption

Memory: When/where

_____: Fill in blanks

Data: Percent

Listing: 1. North
2. South
3. East

Opinion: Poor…Good

Binomial: Male/Female

Yes/No

Source: Author's creation.

---

[13] This is a relative rating scale subject to methodological factors related to questionnaire design. Hence, a yes/no question referring to a sensitive topic (Do you pay bribes?) would not fit this classification.

ability of the data cleaner to correct invalid entries depends, to a large extent, on how well the questionnaire has been designed, how accurately the data are recorded, and how far back in time the survey has been completed (see example 6.4). No amount of cleaning can correct badly designed questionnaires and substitute for proper data entry forms short of fabricating answers. Cleaning might also require going back to the survey firm and to the completed paper questionnaire.[14]

Furthermore, there are circumstances in which cleaning inconsistencies among questions would not only be inappropriate but would actually result in diluting data accuracy. Few practitioners recognize that *not all inconsistencies are flaws in the data.* On the contrary, there is a particular set of inconsistencies that is a useful source of information for the data analyst and, hence, should be kept in the original data set. These are the inconsistencies involving attitude questions. Managers that rate corruption as a very severe problem, while reporting that they pay a lower amount of bribes than those rating corruption as just severe, are not necessarily behaving inconsistently because a host of factors might trigger this attitude-behavior. One possible explanation of this apparent attitude-behavior inconsistency is the fact that managers perceiving corruption as most pervasive are more reluctant to pay bribes. When attitude questions are part of the inconsistency, it becomes impossible for any data cleaner to assess the direction of the inconsistency and to properly clean it, because in addition to the usual situational and methodological factors, psychological mechanisms play a critical role in the way respondents provide answers. Because no data cleaner has access to the respondent's state of mind at the time of the interview, no cleaning technique can be reasonably applied.

Practical Examples in Cleaning Internal Inconsistencies

Following are a number of actual examples, which are presented to familiarize the reader with the cleaning procedure applied in Investment Climate Surveys. For simplicity, we assume that NA, REF, and DK have already been analyzed and replaced with blanks. As mentioned earlier, the reader should remember that, to safeguard the integrity of the data, the methodology highlighted in the following pages is applied only if inconsistencies do not exceed 5 percent of the reported answers.

---

[14] It is important that cleaning starts before the fieldwork is completed.

Figure 6.4.

Ostensibly Innocuous Questions Can Produce Inconsistent Answers

Q.6. How many additional plants/factories are under [KG]'s control? _____ (number)

   [A plant or factory is defined as a manufacturing facility that is geographically distinct from other facilities. A production line does not, by itself constitute a plant or factory.]

Q7. How many are located:

    1. In your metropolitan area: _____ (number)

    2. In this district (other than in Q.7.1):   _____ (number)

    3. In this country(other than in Q.7.1 and Q.7.2): _____ (number)

    4. In other countries: _____ (number)

Example 6.1. Multiplicity of inconsistent answers.

Example 6.1. refers to the two questions shown in figure 6.4.

The expectation is that the value reported on question 6 (Q6) will be equal to the sum of the components of question 7 (Q7): $Q6 = \sum_{i=1}^{4} Q7i$.

Table 6.1 shows the distribution of consistent and inconsistent answers. While the values on the diagonal represent consistent answers (95 percent of cases), a small proportion of answers are inconsistent. So, for instance, there are eight establishments answering 0 to Q6 and 1 to Q7. A further investigation shows that inconsistent answers are reported in 25 different ways (table 6.2). So, for instance, three establishments answer inconsistently by reporting 0 to Q6 and 1 to Q7.1 (see row a), while five respondents answer inconsistently by reporting 1 to Q7.2 (see row b).

In resolving these inconsistencies, two factors played a role. First, the question's design: Q6 clearly asks for "additional" plants/factories, while Q7 does not, enabling the data cleaner to better resolve cases in which the difference between the two answers is 1.[15] Second, an analysis of the pattern of inconsistencies by interviewer revealed that the distribution of inconsistent answers was not equally distributed among all interviewers. On the contrary, few interviewers consistently misinterpreted Q7 by including in its answer the establishment where the interview took place. These considerations enabled the data cleaner to eliminate all inconsistencies.

---

[15] This is an example of methodological factors influencing data cleaning.

Table 6.1

Distribution of Consistent and Inconsistent Answers

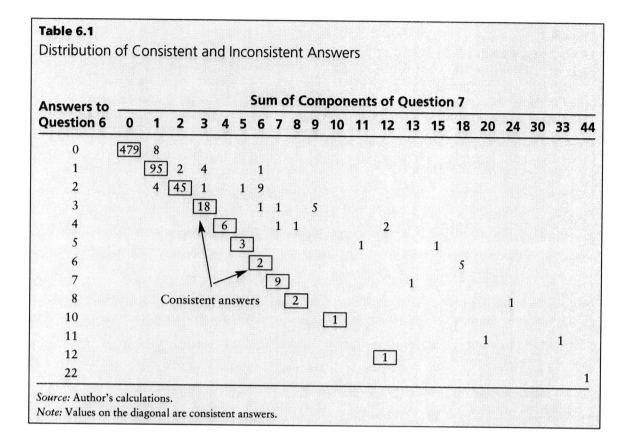

Answers to Question 6	Sum of Components of Question 7																				
	0	1	2	3	4	5	6	7	8	9	10	11	12	13	15	18	20	24	30	33	44
0	479	8																			
1		95	2	4			1														
2		4	45	1		1	9														
3				18			1	1		5											
4					6			1	1				2								
5						3					1			1							
6							2									5					
7								9						1							
8									2								1				
10											1										
11																	1	1			
12													1								
22																					1

Consistent answers

Source: Author's calculations.

Note: Values on the diagonal are consistent answers.

In the cleaning process of this question, some inconsistencies are admittedly easier to tackle than others. Thus, it was easier to determine the following:

- In the majority of cases, when the difference between Q6 and Q7 was only 1, the respondents excluded the establishment where the interview took place from Q6 but not Q7. This is, in part, supported by the fact that while Q6 specifically indicates "additional" plants/factories in its wording, Q7 does not, giving the impression that it refers to all plants/factories. This consideration helped resolve inconsistencies in rows a, b, c, d, g, and n.
- In a number of instances, it was also evident that the respondent (and the interviewer) did not pay attention to the exclusive nature of each component of Q7 (that is, establishments included in Q7.1 should not be included in Q7.2). This consideration

Table 6.2

Multiplicity of Inconsistent Answers

Answer to Question 6	Sum of Components of Question 7	Individul Answers to				Number of Cases	
		Q7.1	Q7.2	Q7.3	Q7.4		
0	1	1				3	(a)
			1			5	(b)
1	2	1		1		1	(c)
		1	1			1	(d)
	3	1	1	1		4	(e)
	6	2	2	2		1	(f)
2	1		1			1	(g)
		1				3	(h)
	3	1		2		1	(i)
	5	1	2	2		1	(j)
	6	2	2	2		9	(k)
3	6	1	2	3		1	(l)
	7	1	3	3		1	(m)
	9	3	3	3		5	(n)
	7	1	3	3		1	(o)
4	8	1	3	4		1	(p)
	12	4	4	4		2	(q)
5	11	1	5	5		1	(r)
	15	5	5	5		1	(s)
6	18	6	6	6		5	(t)
7	13	3	3	7		1	(u)
8	24	8	8	8		1	(v)
11	20	10		10		1	(w)
	33	11	11	11		1	(y)
22	44	20	2	22		1	(z)

Source: Author's calculations.

enabled the solution of inconsistencies in rows e, i, j, k, l, m, n, p, q, r, s, t, u, v, and y.

- Although row f clearly shows the same inconsistent behavior as seen in the second bullet, even correcting this error would not eliminate the inconsistency because Q6=1 and Q7=2. Given that Q6 specifically asks for additional plants/factories, while Q7 does not, it appears more likely that the respondent did include the establishment where the interview took place in Q7; thus, Q7 was changed from 2 to 1.
- In row w, it was impossible to detect any direction of inconsistency because the respondent seems to answer some question consistently and others inconsistently. Given the cross-consistency/inconsistency within the same respondent, no cleaning was possible.

Example 6.2. Questionnaire structure complexity.

Example 6.2 shows that a complex questionnaire structure makes it difficult not only for the interviewer to properly conduct the interview (by accurately following the skipping pattern), but also for the data cleaner to untangle the inconsistency of answers. The actual questions are presented in figure 6.5.

Q16 is a filter question asking whether the firm has ever applied for a bank loan. If the respondent chooses yes, he is asked Q17–Q27; if no, the interviewer will go directly to Q28. Meanwhile, Q29–Q31 are based on the assumption that the respondent's latest loan application was rejected, thus implying that he or she has already answered yes to Q16. In other words, Q17–Q27 and Q29–Q31 are linked to yes in Q16, while Q28 is linked to no in Q16. The questionnaire structure for this example is shown in figure 6.6.

The survey data show that the skipping pattern's complexity takes a toll on respondents. As a result, the following inconsistencies appear in the data:

- Some respondents replied no to Q16, while answering some of the questions in Q17–Q27 (five cases) or in Q29–Q31 (three cases) (see figure 6.7).
- Other establishments replied yes to Q16 but still responded to Q28 (20 cases) (see figure 6.8).
- Other respondents did not answer Q16 but answered Q17–Q27/ Q29–Q31 (seven cases) and Q28 (three cases) (figure 6.9).

When attempting to clean these inconsistencies, the questionnaire design must be taken into account, particularly the presence or absence of

Figure 6.5.

Question Flows

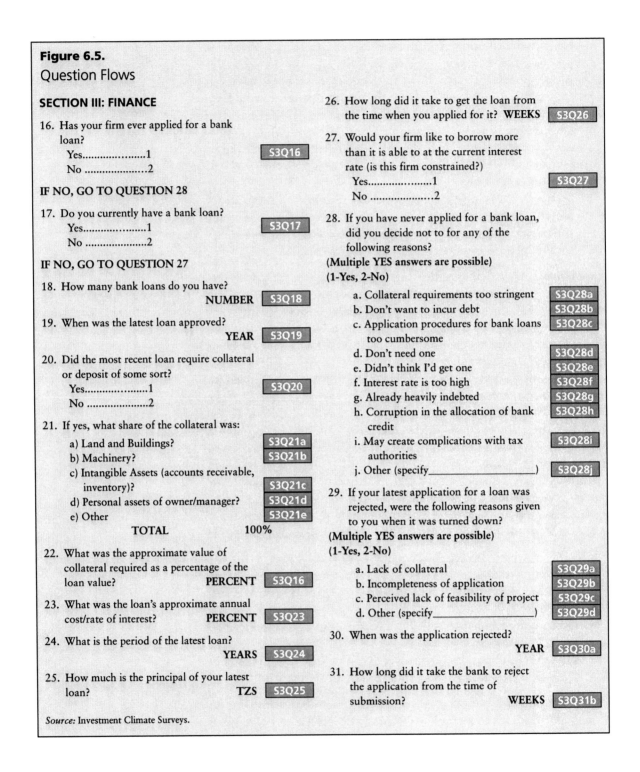

SECTION III: FINANCE

16. Has your firm ever applied for a bank loan?
    Yes....................1   S3Q16
    No 2

IF NO, GO TO QUESTION 28

17. Do you currently have a bank loan?
    Yes....................1   S3Q17
    No 2

IF NO, GO TO QUESTION 27

18. How many bank loans do you have?
    NUMBER   S3Q18

19. When was the latest loan approved?
    YEAR   S3Q19

20. Did the most recent loan require collateral or deposit of some sort?
    Yes....................1   S3Q20
    No 2

21. If yes, what share of the collateral was:
    a) Land and Buildings?   S3Q21a
    b) Machinery?   S3Q21b
    c) Intangible Assets (accounts receivable, inventory)?   S3Q21c
    d) Personal assets of owner/manager?   S3Q21d
    e) Other   S3Q21e
    TOTAL   100%

22. What was the approximate value of collateral required as a percentage of the loan value?   PERCENT   S3Q16

23. What was the loan's approximate annual cost/rate of interest?   PERCENT   S3Q23

24. What is the period of the latest loan?   YEARS   S3Q24

25. How much is the principal of your latest loan?   TZS   S3Q25

26. How long did it take to get the loan from the time when you applied for it? WEEKS   S3Q26

27. Would your firm like to borrow more than it is able to at the current interest rate (is this firm constrained?)
    Yes....................1   S3Q27
    No 2

28. If you have never applied for a bank loan, did you decide not to for any of the following reasons?
    (Multiple YES answers are possible)
    (1-Yes, 2-No)
    a. Collateral requirements too stringent   S3Q28a
    b. Don't want to incur debt   S3Q28b
    c. Application procedures for bank loans too cumbersome   S3Q28c
    d. Don't need one   S3Q28d
    e. Didn't think I'd get one   S3Q28e
    f. Interest rate is too high   S3Q28f
    g. Already heavily indebted   S3Q28g
    h. Corruption in the allocation of bank credit   S3Q28h
    i. May create complications with tax authorities   S3Q28i
    j. Other (specify_____)   S3Q28j

29. If your latest application for a loan was rejected, were the following reasons given to you when it was turned down?
    (Multiple YES answers are possible)
    (1-Yes, 2-No)
    a. Lack of collateral   S3Q29a
    b. Incompleteness of application   S3Q29b
    c. Perceived lack of feasibility of project   S3Q29c
    d. Other (specify_____)   S3Q29d

30. When was the application rejected?   YEAR   S3Q30a

31. How long did it take the bank to reject the application from the time of submission?   WEEKS   S3Q31b

Source: Investment Climate Surveys.

Figure 6.6.
Question Structure

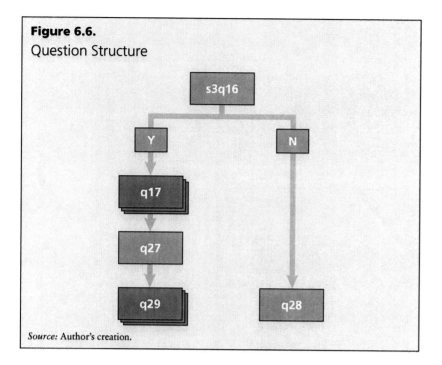

Source: Author's creation.

Figure 6.7.
Inconsistent Answers (1)

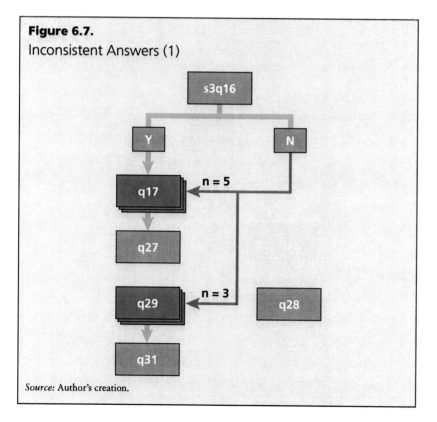

Source: Author's creation.

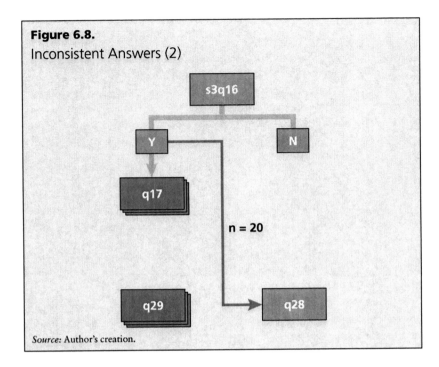

Figure 6.8.
Inconsistent Answers (2)

Source: Author's creation.

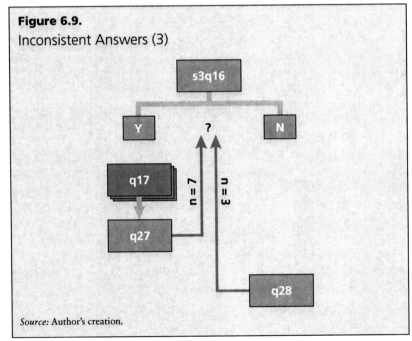

Figure 6.9.
Inconsistent Answers (3)

Source: Author's creation.

skipping patterns as well as the complexity of the question flow. The cleaning strategy in this case was as follows:

- When Q16 is missing, yes was imputed if any one question in Q18–Q26 was answered. Q27 was not included in the consistency check, because it is not *clearly* linked to Q16 (the desire of a firm to borrow more has nothing to do with the loans it has or has ever had). Furthermore, yes was also imputed in Q16 when Q17 was answered with yes (but not when Q17 had an answer of no) (three changes).
- Q16 was imputed with yes when respondents did not answer Q28 but answered some of the questions in Q17–Q27/Q29–Q31 (one change).
- Because a skipping pattern between Q17–Q27 and Q29–Q31 was missing, the inconsistencies could not be resolved when respondents answered both Q17–Q27/Q29–Q31 and Q28. As a consequence, these inconsistencies were retained.

Example 6.3. Cross-check inconsistencies with remote questions.

Example 6.3 illustrates how the data cleaner may have to resort to questions located in different parts of the questionnaire to resolve inconsistent answers. This case refers to questions intended to establish the export orientation of the establishment (figure 6.10).

Question III.4 (q304) asks whether the establishment exports (yes/no). Q.III.5 (q305) is a filter question asking whether it exported directly or not. Q.III.6 (q306) and Q.III.7 (q307) ask more detailed information on exporting. The questionnaire structure is presented in figure 6.11.

If the respondent answers no to Q.III.4, then he or she should skip to Q.III.8, whereas if the answer is yes, then Q.III.5–7 should also be answered. However, 136 inconsistent cases emerged from the data where respondents answered no to Q.III.4 but answered at least one question in Q.III.5–7 (figure 6.12).

In an attempt to solve some of these inconsistencies, other questions on export orientation were used as cross-checks. See figure 6.13 for a list of questions.

All inconsistencies were resolved as follows (see figure 6.14):

- The 4 observations answering Q.III.6 were changed to yes in Q.III.4.
- The 10 observations reporting yes in Q.III.5 were changed to yes in Q.III.4.
- The 1 observation answering Q.III.6 was changed to yes in Q.III5.

Figure 6.10.

Questions on Export

III.4 Were any of the products of this establishment exported last year? q304 *Codes: Yes=1, No=2*

(If answer for question III.4 is NO, then go to question III. 8)

III.5 If yes, did you export directly last year? q305 *Codes: Yes=1, No=2*

III.6 If you export, what was the year when your business first exported? q306 Year

III.7 If "yes" to question number III.4, please answer the following with respect to customer to which you made your largest exports last year.

   a) What percent of your total exports did you ship to this customer last year? q307a %
   b) For how many years have you done business with this customer? q307b
   c) Where is this customer based? q307c
   Codes: 1=North America, 2=European Union, 3=Other European, 4=Middle East, 5=Central Asia, 6=South Asia, 7=Other Asia, 8=Other

III.8 Would you rather sell in an export market than in a domestic market? q308 *Codes: Yes=1, No=2*

Source: Investment Climate Surveys.

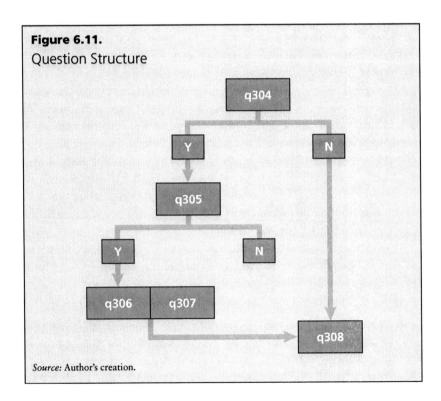

Figure 6.11.

Question Structure

Source: Author's creation.

Figure 6.12.

Question Inconsistencies

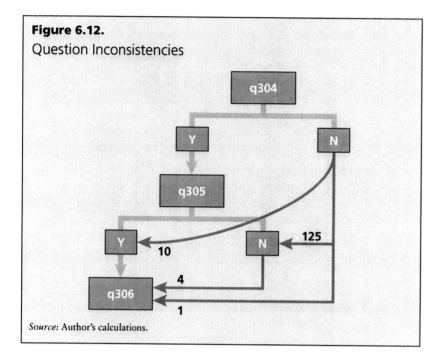

Source: Author's calculations.

Figure 6.13.

Remote Questions Used for Cross-Checks

X. 7. What percent of annual sales has been sold to

	2001	2000
a. other divisions of your company....	qx06a1 %	qx06a2 %
b. other companies domestically........	qx06b1 %	qx06b2 %
c. abroad (exports).............................	qx06c1 %	qx06c2 %
Total	100%	100%

X. 8. What percent of your plant's sales revenue was from exports during the fiscal year of ...? *(NA for non-exporters)*

	2001	2000	1999
Direct Export....................................	qx08a1 %	qx08a2 %	qx08a3 %
Indirect Export (through distributor)	qx08b1 %	qx08b2 %	qx08b3 %
	100%	100%	100%

Source: Investment Climate Surveys.

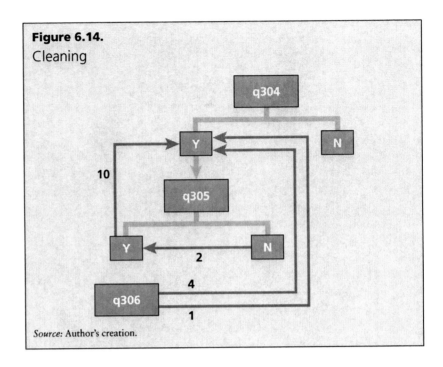

Figure 6.14.
Cleaning

Source: Author's creation.

- The 125 no responses in Q.III.5 were dropped because this was simply an erroneous data entry (the presence of an explicit filter allowed us to make this change).

Example 6.4. Limitations of cleaning.

Example 6.4 demonstrates the role and limitations of data cleaning. This actual case is an instructive example because it shows the importance of (1) the design of the question, (2) the existence of accurate data entry software, (3) the limitations faced by the data cleaner, and (4) the detrimental impact on data quality of using one entry with multiple meanings.

In a survey conducted in Asia, the same question was asked in two different parts of the form, to two different respondents, in two different formats (one with a filter and one without a filter). The actual questions are shown in figure 6.15.

Being an objective question for which both respondents are presumed to have information, we would expect that in all instances when XV.11=yes the corresponding answers for XV.12 and VI.11 would be positive. Similarly, all respondents that replied no to XV.11 should have reported only NA to XV.12 and VI.11.

Figure 6.15.

Questions Asked to Different Respondents

Respondent A

VI.11. What percent of your workforce is unionized? ___%

Respondent B

XV.11. Are any of your employees members of a trade union? Yes / No

XV.12. What percentage of your plant's employees belong to a trade union? ___%

Source: Investment Climate Surveys.

The actual response pattern is presented in figure 6.16. The data clearly show some inconsistencies with respect to XV.11 and XV.12 and XV.11 and VI.11.

Before looking at this specific questions, a general problem often recurring in this data set was identified: the interchangeable use of 0 (zeros)

Figure 6.16.

Distribution of Answers to Questions XV.11 (Q15.11), XV.12 (Q15.12), and VI.11 (Q6.11) before Cleaning

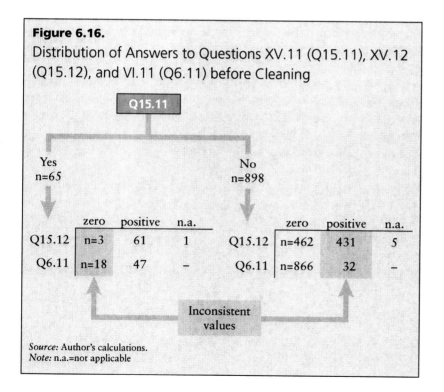

Source: Author's calculations.
Note: n.a.=not applicable

and NA. As mentioned earlier, this makes the cleaning process (as well as the analysis) extremely difficult and often impossible.

Regarding the consistency between XV.11 and XV.12, thanks to proper question design, we were able to distinguish and drop zeros in XV.12 when XV.11 was no and were replaced with NA. We did this because answering no to XV.11 implies skipping XV.12.

The next step was to identify inconsistent answers across questions. As figure 6.17 shows, of all the respondents reporting not having unionized workers (XV.11=no) an unusually high number (n=431) did report a positive percentage of unionized workers (XV.12>0). A close examination of XV.12, when XV.11=no, revealed that almost all answers were 2. Given that throughout the form 2 was used as a numeric code for no, there was the suspicion that, for some unknown reason, 2 really meant no (a value that would have been consistent with the linked question). This suspicion was confirmed by the field survey manager. Thus, the final decision to replace 2 with NA was taken. Although everyone involved in the cleaning agreed that the 2s really meant no, there was always the possibility that some of the 2s could really mean that 2 percent of the workforce was unionized. In an at-

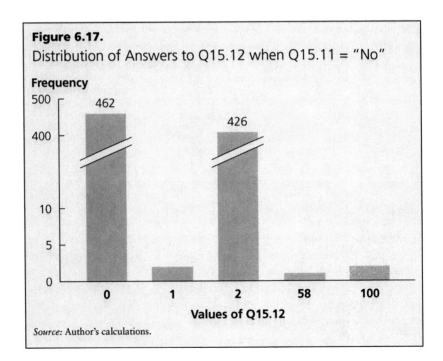

Figure 6.17.
Distribution of Answers to Q15.12 when Q15.11 = "No"

Source: Author's calculations.

tempt to save some of these values, VI.11 was used to validate XV.12. Consequently, the decision was taken to keep 2 in XV.12 when 2 also appeared in VI.11. Nonetheless, in all instances in which XV.12 was 2, VI.11 was missing. This fact further confirmed our presumption that 2 really meant no.

After dropping all 2s, three observations still showed inconsistency between XV.12 and VI.11. Because the percentage of inconsistent questions was below the 5 percent mark, the usual cleaning methodology was applied with no being replaced by yes in VI.11 in the three instances in which XV.12 had a positive legal value.

Three observations showed another inconsistency, because the respondent answered yes to XV.11 but then reported 0 percent in XV.12. In this case, the cleaning should have been straightforward had we not had too many zeros throughout the form. Because a percentage question is given priority over a simple yes/no question, the standard practice would have been to replace no with yes in XV.11. In this specific case, however, because zeros were used throughout the form to indicate NA, it was not clear whether these three zeros really meant zero (and thus were inconsistent) or NA (and thus were legal values). This demonstrates the importance of making a clear distinction between zeros and NA to clean the data. Again VI.11 was used as a source of validation. Because the corresponding values of VI.11 were also NA, and the changes accounted for less than 5 percent of the observations, the final decision was taken to interpret the zeros as NA.

At the end of the first round of cleaning, inconsistencies between XV.11 and XV.12 were eliminated as shown in figure 6.18.

Inconsistencies, however, were still present between XV.11 and VI.11. Although these two questions were asked to two different respondents in two different parts of the form, because the question was objective in nature and general in value, we would expect consistency among answers. Unfortunately, this was not the case for 5 percent of the answers. In 18 cases, the manager reported not having unionized workers (VI.11=0 percent), while the accountant reported having them in XV.11. Similarly, 32 managers reported having unionized workers in VI.11, while the accountant (or human resources manager) reported not having them in XV.11.

Previously, with XV.11 and XV.12, we could cross-check the questions to clean inconsistencies; however, in this case, it was much harder to be reasonably sure to perform any cleaning. Although we were aware

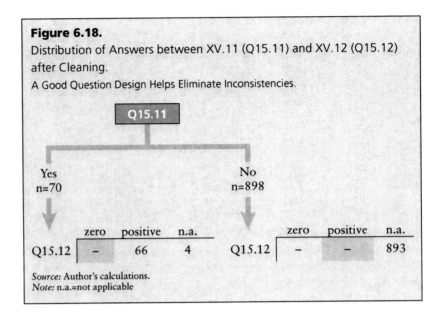

Figure 6.18.
Distribution of Answers between XV.11 (Q15.11) and XV.12 (Q15.12) after Cleaning.
A Good Question Design Helps Eliminate Inconsistencies.

	zero	positive	n.a.		zero	positive	n.a.
Q15.12	–	66	4	Q15.12	–	–	893

Source: Author's calculations.
Note: n.a.=not applicable

of the fact that a high percentage of answers were coded as zeros, while meaning missing, it was impossible to distinguish which case was which. Because two different answers were coded with the same value, any cleaning effort was impossible. The absence of a well-structured question not only makes the collection of accurate answers difficult, but also makes the cleaning of inconsistencies impossible. Hence, we were unable to correct any of the inconsistencies among VI.11, XV.11, and XV.12.

At the end of the cleaning process, the number of inconsistent values was reduced, but not all of the inconsistencies could be reasonably eliminated (figure 6.19). It is left to the analyst to make the final decision about how to deal with the existing inconsistencies.

Figure 6.19.

Distribution of Answers Among XV.11 (Q15.11), XV.12 (Q15.12), and VI.11 (Q6.11) after Cleaning.

Some inconsistencies still remain because of incorrect questionnaire design and different respondents.

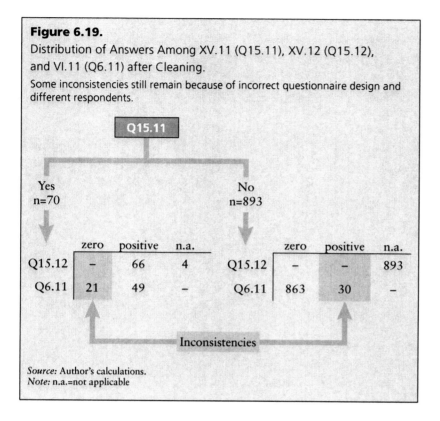

Source: Author's calculations.
Note: n.a.=not applicable

References

Andrews, F. M. 1984. "Construct Validity and Error Components of Survey Measures: A Structural Modeling Approach." *Public Opinion Quarterly* 48 (2): 409–42.

Atkinson, Jean. 1971. *Handbook For Interviewers.* Office of Population Census and Surveys, Social Survey Division. Her Majesty's Stationery Office. London.

Auriat, Nadia. 1993. "My Wife Knows Best: A Comparison of Event Dating Accuracy Between the Wife, the Husband, the Couple, and the Belgium Population Register." *Public Opinion Quarterly* 57 (2): 165–90.

Bassili, J. N., and B. S. Scott. 1996. " Response Latency as a Signal to Question Problems in Survey Research." *Public Opinion Quarterly* 60 (3): 390–99.

Benton, J. Edwin, and John L. Daly. 1991. "A Question Order Effect in a Local Government Survey." *Public Opinion Quarterly* 55 (4): 640–42.

Biemer, Paul P., and Lars E. Lyberg. 2003. *Introduction to Survey Quality.* New Jersey: John Wiley & Sons.

Billiet, J., and G. Loosveldt. 1988. "Improvements of the Quality of Responses to Factual Survey Questions by Interviewer Training." *Public Opinion Quarterly* 52: 190–211.

Bishop, George F., Robert W. Oldendick, and Alfred J. Tuchfarber. 1983. "Effects of Filter Questions in Public Opinion Surveys." *Public Opinion Quarterly* 47 (4): 528–546.

Bishop, George F., Robert W. Oldendick, Alfred J. Tuchfarber, and Stephen E. Bennett. 1980. "Pseudo-Opinions on Public Affairs." *Public Opinion Quarterly* 44 (2): 198–209.

Bishop, George F., Alfred J. Tuchfarber, and Robert W. Oldendick. 1986. "Opinions on Fictitious Issues: The Pressure to Answer Survey Questions." *Public Opinion Quarterly* 50 (2): 240–50.

Blair, E., and S. Burton. 1987. "Cognitive Processes Used by Survey Respondents to Answer Behavioral Frequency Questions." *The Journal of Consumer Research* 14 (2): 280–88.

Bogen, K. 1996. "The Effect of Questionnaire Length on Response Rates—A Review of the Literature." U.S. Bureau of Census, Washington, DC.

Bradburn, N. M., L. J. Rips, and S. K. Shevell. 1987. "Answering Auto-biographical Questions: The Impact of Memory and Inference on Surveys." *Science* 236: 157–61.

Brenner, Michael. 1982. "Response-effects of 'Role-restricted' Characteristics of the Interviewer." In *Response Behavior in the Survey-interview,* ed. W. Dijkstra and J. van der Zouwen, 131–65. New York: Academic Press Inc.

Browne, M. N., and S. M. Keeley. 2001. *Asking the Right Questions.* Upper Saddle River, NJ: Prentice-Hall, Inc.

Burton, S., and E. Blair. 1991. "Task Conditions, Response Formulation Processes, and Response Accuracy for Behavioral Frequency Questions in Surveys" *Public Opinion Quarterly* 55 (1): 50–79.

Campanelli, Pamela C., Elisabeth A. Martin, and Jennifer M. Rothgeb. 1991. "The Use of Respondent and Interviewer Debriefing Studies as a Way to Study Response Errors in Survey Data." *The Statistician* 40 (3), Special Issue: Survey Design, Methodology and Analysis (2): 253–64.

Cantril, Hadley S., and S. Wilks. 1940. "Problems and Techniques: Experiments in the Wording of Questions." *Public Opinion Quarterly* 4 (2): 330–338.

Cialdini, Robert. 1985. *Influence: Science and Practice.* Glenview, IL: Scott, Foresman and Company.

Colledge, Michael. 1995. "Frames and Business Registers: an Overview." In *Business Survey Methods,* ed. Brenda Cox, David Binder, Nanjamma Chinnappa, Andres Christianson, Michael Colledge, and Phillip Kott. New York: John Wiley & Sons.

Converse, Jean M., and Stanley Presser. 1986. *Survey Questions: Handcrafting the Standardized Questionnaire.* Sage University Papers, Series on Quantitative Applications in the Social Sciences, Series no. 07-063. Sage Publications, Newbury Park, CA.

Couper, M. 1997. "Survey Introductions and Data Quality." *Public Opinion Quarterly* 61 (2): 317–38.

Cox, E. P. 1980. "The Optimal Number of Response Alternatives for a Scale: a Review." *Journal of Marketing Research* 17(November): 407–22.

Crespi, Irving, and Dwight Morris. 1984. "Question Order Effect and the Measurement of Candidate Preference in the 1982 Connecticut Elections." *Public Opinion Quarterly* 48 (3): 578–91.

Delaine, Ghislaine, and others. 1991. "The Social Dimensions of Adjustment Integrated Survey: A Survey to Measure Poverty and Understand the Effects of Policy Change on Households." SDA Working Paper, no. 14. Social Dimensions of Adjustment Program, World Bank, Washington, DC.

DeLameter, John. 1982. "Response-Effects of Question Content." In *Response Behavior in the Survey-interview,* ed. W. Dijkstra and J. van der Zouwen, 13–48. New York: Academic Press Inc.

DeMaio, T. 1980. "Refusals: Who, Where and Why." *Public Opinion Quarterly* 44 (2): 223–33.

Dexter, Lewis Anthony. 1970. *Elite and Specialized Interviewing.* Evanston, IL: Northwestern University Press.

Dijkstra, W., and J. van der Zouwen. 1987. "Styles of Interviewing and the Social Context of the Survey-Interview." In *Social Information Processing and Survey Methodology,* ed. H. Hippler, N. Schwarz, and S. Sudman, 200–11. New York: Springer-Verlag.

Dillman, D. A., J. G. Gallegos, and J. H. Frey. 1976. "Reducing Refusal Rates in Telephone Interviews." *Public Opinion Quarterly* 40 (1): 66–78.

Duncan, O. D., B. Fishhoff, and C. Turner. 1984. "Introduction." In *Surveying Subjective Phenomena,* ed. Charles F. Turner and Elizabeth Martin, vol. 1, 1–21. New York: Russell Sage Foundation.

Economist, The. 2003. "The World This Week." November 8–14, 8.

———. 2004. "Democracy's Low-Level Equilibrium." August 14, 2004, 35–36.

Fellegi, I. P., and D. Holt. 1976. "A Systematic Approach to Automatic Edit and Imputation." *Journal of the American Statistical Association* 71 (353): 17–35.

Finn, R. H. 1972. "Effects of Some Variations in Rating Scale Characteristics on the Means and Reliabilities of Ratings." *Educational and Psychological Measurement* 32: 255–65.

Foddy, William. 1993. *Constructing Questions for Interviews and Questionnaires.* Cambridge, UK: Cambridge University Press.

Fowler, F. J. 1992. "How Unclear Terms Affect Survey Data." *Public Opinion Quarterly* 56 (2): 218–31.

———. 1995. *Improving Survey Questions: Design and Evaluation.* Applied Social Research Methods Series, vol. 38. Thousand Oaks, CA: Sage Publications.

Fowler, F. J., and T. W. Mangione. 1990. *Standardized Survey Interviewing.* Applied Social Research Methods Series, vol. 18. Newbury Park, CA: Sage Publications.

Gallagher, Daniel J., and G. Rodney Thompson. 1981. "A Readability Analysis of Selected Introductory Economics Textbooks." *Journal of Economic Education* 12 (2): 60–63.

Gaskell, G. D., Daniel B. Wright, and Colm A. O'Muircheartaigh. 2000. "Telescoping of Landmark Events: Implications for Survey Research." *Public Opinion Quarterly* 64 (1): 77–89.

Godwin, R. K. 1979. "The Consequences of Large Monetary Incentives in Mail Surveys of Elites." *Public Opinion Quarterly* 43 (3): 378–87.

Gower, Allen. 1993. "Questionnaire Design for Establishment Surveys." In *Proceedings of the International Conference on Establishment Surveys.* American Statistical Association, Buffalo, New York, June 27–30.

Goyder, J. 1985. "Face-to-Face Interviews and Mailed Questionnaires: The Net Difference in Response Rate." *Public Opinion Quarterly* 49: 234–52.

Grosh, Margaret E., and Juan Muñoz. 1996. *A Manual for Planning and Implementing the Living Standard Measurement Study Survey.* Working Paper, no. 126. World Bank, Washington, DC.

Groves, R. M., R. B. Cialdini, and M. P. Couper. 1992. "Understanding the Decision to Participate in a Survey." *Public Opinion Quarterly* 56: 475–95.

Groves, R. M., and M. P. Couper. 1996. "Contact-Level Influences on Cooperation in Face-to-Face Surveys." *Journal of Official Statistics* 12 (1): 63–83.

Groves, R. M., and K. A. McGonagle. 2001. "A Theory-Guided Interviewer Training Protocol Regarding Survey participation." *Journal of Official Statistics* 17 (2): 249–65.

Groves, R. M., E. Singer, and A. Corning. 2000. "Leverage-Saliency Theory of Survey Participation." *Public Opinion Quarterly* 64 (3): 299–308.

Hansen, M., W. Hurwitz, and W. Madow. 1953. *Sample Survey Methods and Theory,* vol. 1. New York: John Wiley and Sons.

Heberlein, T. A., and R. Baumgartner. 1978. "Factors Affecting Response Rates to Mailed Questionnaires: A Quantitative Analysis of the Published Literature." *American Sociological Review* 43 (4): 447–62.

Hippler, Hans-J., and Norbert Schwarz. 1986. "Not Forbidding Isn't Allowing: The Cognitive Basis of the Forbid-Allow Asymmetry." *Public Opinion Quarterly* 50 (1): 87–96.

Homan, S., M. Hewitt, and J. Linder. 1994. "The Development and Validation of a Formula for Measuring Single-Sentence Test Item Readability." *Journal of Educational Measurement* 31: 349–58.

Hunt, William H., Wilder W. Crane, and John C. Wahlke. 1964. "Interviewing Political Elites in Cross-Cultural Comparative Research." *The American Journal of Sociology* 70 (1): 59–68.

James, J., and R. Bolstein. 1990. "The Effect of Monetary Incentives and Follow-Up Mailings on the Response Rate and Response Quality in Mail Surveys." *Public Opinion Quarterly* 54 (3): 346–61.

———. 1992. "Large Monetary Incentives and Their Effect on Mail Survey Response Rates." *Public Opinion Quarterly* 56 (4): 442–53.

Kalton, G. 1983. *Introduction to Survey Sampling.* Newbury Park, CA: Sage Publications.

Kalton, G., and H. Schuman. 1982. "The Effect of the Question on Survey Responses: A Review." *Journal of the Royal Statistical Society. Series A (General)* 145 (1): 42–73.

Keogh, Erica. 2003. "Developing a Framework for Budgeting for Household Surveys in Developing Countries." Chapter 14 in *Household Surveys in Developing and Transition Countries: Design, Implementation and Analysis,* ed. United Nations Statistics Division. Available online at http://unstats.un.org/unsd/HHsurveys/part1_new.htm.

Kincaid, Harry, and Margaret Bright. 1957. "Interviewing the Business Elite." *The American Journal of Sociology* 63 (3): 301–11.

Kish, Leslie. 1965. *Survey Sampling.* New York: John Wiley & Sons.

Krosnick, J. A., and D. F. Alwin. 1987. "An Evaluation of a Cognitive Theory of Response-Order Effects in Survey Measurement." *Public Opinion Quarterly* 51 (2): 201–19.

Leigh, J. H., and C. R. Martin. 1987. "Don't Know Item Nonresponse in a Telephone Survey: Effects of Question Form and Respondent Characteristics." *Journal of Marketing Research* 24: 418–24.

Loftus, E. F., and G. Zanni. 1975. "Eyewitness Testimony: The Influence of the Wording of a Question." *Bulletin of the Psychonomic Society* 5 (1): 86–88.

Martin, E. 1984. "The Role of the Respondent." In *Surveying Subjective Phenomena,* ed. Charles F. Turner and E. Martin, vol. 1, 257–78. New York: Russell Sage Foundation.

Martin, E., and R. Abelson. 1984. "The Question-and-Answer Process." In *Surveying Subjective Phenomena,* ed. Charles F. Turner and Elizabeth Martin, vol. 1, 279–301. New York: Russell Sage Foundation.

McAllister, Ian, and Martin P. Wattenberg. 1995. "Measuring Levels of Party Identification: Does Question Order Matter?" *Public Opinion Quarterly* 59 (2): 259–68.

McClendon, McKee J., and David J. O'Brien. 1988. "Question-Order Effects on the Determinants of Subjective Well-Being." *Public Opinion Quarterly* 52 (3): 351–64.

McConnell, Campbell. 1983. "Readability: Blind Faith in Numbers?" *Journal of Economic Education* 14 (1): 65–71.

Miller, G. A. 1956. "The Magical Number Seven, Plus or Minus Two: Some Limits on Our capacity for Processing Information." *The Psychological Review* 63: 81–97.

Morton-Williams, Jean. 1991. "Obtaining Co-Operation in Surveys: The Development of a Social Skills Approach to Interviewer Training in Introducing Surveys." Working Paper, no. 3. Joint Centre for Survey Methods, London.

Moser, C. A., and G. Kalton. 1971. *Survey Methods in Social Investigation.* London: Heinemann Educational Book Limited.

Narayan, S., and J. A. Krosnick. 1996. "Education Moderates Some Response Effects in Attitude Measurement." *Public Opinion Quarterly* 60 (1): 58–88.

Nijhowne, Shaila. 1995. "Defining and Classifying Statistical Units." In *Business Survey Methods,* ed. Brenda Cox, David Binder, Nanjamma Chinnappa, Andres Christianson, Michael Colledge, and Phillip Kott. New York: John Wiley & Sons.

Payne, S. L. B. 1951. *The Art of Asking Questions.* Studies in Public Opinion, no. 3. Princeton: Princeton University Press.

Peterson, Robert A. 2000. *Constructing Effective Questionnaires.* Thousand Oaks, CA: Sage Publications.

Peterson, Robert A., and Roger Kerin. 1980. "Household Income Data Reports in Mail Surveys." *Journal of Business Research* 8: 301–13.

Petty, R. E., and J. T. Cacioppo. 1984. "The Effects of Involvement on Response to Argument Quantity and Quality: Central and Peripheral Routes to Persuasion." *Journal of Personality and Social Psychology* 46 (1): 69–81.

Plateck, R., F. K. Pierre-Pierre, and P. Stevens. 1985. *Development and Design of Survey Questionnaires.* Statistics Canada. Census and Household Survey Methods Division. Ottawa.

Presser, S., and J. Blair. 1994. "Survey Pretesting: Do Different Methods Produce Different Results?" *Public Opinion Quarterly* 24: 73–104.

Presser, S., J. Blair, and T. Triplett. 1992. "Survey Sponsorship, Response Rate, and Response Effects." *Social Science Quarterly* 73 (3): 699–702.

Presser, S., and S. Zhao. 1992. "Attributed of Questions and Interviewers as Correlates of Interviewing Performance." *Public Opinion Quarterly* 56 (2): 236–40.

Project Management Institute, Inc. 2000. *A Guide to the Project Management Body of Knowledge (PMBOK Guide).* Newtown Square, PA: PMI.

Rasinski, Kenneth A. 1989. "The Effect of Question Wording on Public Support for Government Spending." *Public Opinion Quarterly* 53 (3): 388–95.

Rattenbury, Judith. 1980. "Survey Data Processing: Expectations and Reality." Mimeo. Paper presented at the World Fertility Survey Conference, London, July 7–11.

Rea, Louis M., and Richard A. Parker. 1997. *Designing and Conducting Survey Research: A Comprehensive Guide.* San Francisco: Jossey-Bass.

Schober, M. F., and F. G. Conrad. 1997. "Does Conversational Interviewing Reduce Survey Measurement Error?" *Public Opinion Quarterly* 61: 576–602.

Schuman, H., and S. Presser. 1981. *Questions and Answers in Attitude Surveys.* New York: Academic Press.

———. 1979. "The Open and Closed Question." *American Sociological Review* 44 (5): 692–712.

Schwarz, N., H. Hippler, B. Duetsch, and F. Strack. 1985. "Response Scales: Effects of Category Range on Reported Behavior and Comparative Judgments." *Public Opinion Quarterly* 49 (3): 388–95.

Schwarz, N., B. Knauper, H. Hippler, E. Noelle-Neumann, and L. Clark. 1991. "Rating Scales." *Public Opinion Quarterly* 55 (5): 570–82.

Scipione, Paul A. 1995. "The Value of Words: Numerical Perceptions Associated with Descriptive Words and Phrases in Marketing Reports." *Journal of Advertising Research* 35: 36–43.

Sharp, L. M., and J. Frankel. 1983. "Respondent Burden: A Test of Some Common Assumptions." *Public Opinion Quarterly* 47 (1): 36–53.

Sigelman, Lee. 1981. "Question-Order Effects on Presidential Popularity." *Public Opinion Quarterly* 45 (2): 199–207.

Singer, E., H. Hippler, and N. Schwarz. 1992. "Confidentiality Assurances in Surveys: Reassurance or Threat?" *International Journal of Public Opinion Research* 4 (3): 256–68.

Singer, E., and L. Kohnke-Aguirre. 1979. "Interviewer Expectation Effects: A Replication and Extension." *Public Opinion Quarterly* 43 (2): 245–60.

Singer, E., N. A. Mathiowetz, and M. P. Couper. 1993. "The Impact of Privacy and Confidentiality Concerns on Survey Participation." *Public Opinion Quarterly* 57 (4): 465–82.

Singer, E., J. Van Hoewyk, and M. Maher. 1998. "Does the Payment of Incentives Create Expectation Effects?" *Public Opinion Quarterly* 62 (2): 152–64.

Singer, E., J. Van Hoewyk, and M. Maher. 2000. "Experiments with Incentives in Telephone Surveys" *Public Opinion Quarterly* 64 (2): 171–88.

Singer, E., D. R. Von Thurn, E. R. Miller. 1995. "Confidentiality Assurances and Response: A Quantitative Review of the Experimental Literature." *Public Opinion Quarterly* 59 (1): 66–77.

Smith, T. M. 1984. "Nonattitudes: A Review and Evaluation." In *Surveying Subjective Phenomena,* ed. Charles F. Turner and Elizabeth Martin, vol. 2, 215–55. New York: Russell Sage Foundation.

Sobal, J. 1984. "The Content of Survey Introductions and the Provision of Informed Consent." *Public Opinion Quarterly* 48 (4): 788–93.

Stevens, Kevin T., Kathleen C. Stevens, and William P. Stevens. 1992. "Measuring the Readability of Business Writing: The Cloze Procedure Versus Readability Formulas." *The Journal of Business Communication* 29 (4): 367–82.

Sudnam, S., and N. M. Bradburn. 1974. *Response Effects in Surveys: a Review and Synthesis.* Chicago: Aldine Publishing Company.

Sudnam, S., N. M. Bradburn, and N. Schwarz. 1996. *Thinking About Answers: The Application of Cognitive Processes to Survey Methodology.* San Francisco: Jossey-Bass.

Sukhatme, P. V., B. V. Sukhatme, and S. Sukhatme. 1984. *Sampling Theory of Surveys with Applications,* 3rd ed. Ames, IA: Iowa State University Press.

Tourangeau, Roger, and Tom W. Smith. 1996. "Asking Sensitive Questions: the Impact of Data Collection Mode, Question Format, and Question Context." *Public Opinion Quarterly* 60 (2): 275–304.

United Nations. 1982. *National Household Survey Capability Programme—Survey data processing: A Review of Issues and Procedures.* New York: United Nations, Department of Technical Cooperation for Development and Statistical Office.

Warwick, D. P., and C. A. Lininger. 1975. *The Sample Survey: Theory and Practice.* New York: McGraw-Hill.

Weeks, Michael F. 2003. "An Introduction to Survey Management." A two-day short course sponsored by the Joint Program in Survey Methodology. Presented at The Inn and Conference Center, Adelphi, Maryland, December 8–9.

Wildt, A. R., and M. B. Mazis. 1978. "Determinants of Scale Response: Label Versus Position." *Journal of Marketing Research* 15: 261–67.

Willimack, D., H. Schuman, B. Pennell, and J. Lepkowski. 1995. "Effects of a Prepaid Nonmonetary Incentive on Response Rates and Response Quality in a Face-to-Face Survey." *Public Opinion Quarterly* 59 (1): 78–92.

World Bank, Private Sector Investment Climate Unit. 2003. *Productivity and Investment Climate Surveys (PICS): Implementation Manual.* Washington, DC: World Bank.

Zuckerman, H. 1972. "Interviewing an Ultra-Elite." *Public Opinion Quarterly* 36 (2): 159–75.

Appendix 1

Perception Questions in the Investment Climate Survey Core Questionnaire

Q18.   Please tell us if any of the following issues are a problem for the operation and growth of your business. If an issue poses a problem, please judge its severity as an obstacle on a four-point scale where:

0 = No obstacle 1 = Minor obstacle 2 = Moderate obstacle
3 = Major obstacle 4 = Very severe obstacle

	No Problem		Degree of Obstacle		
A. Telecommunications	0	1	2	3	4
B. Electricity	0	1	2	3	4
C. Transportation	0	1	2	3	4
D. Access to Land	0	1	2	3	4
E. Tax Rates	0	1	2	3	4
F. Tax Administration	0	1	2	3	4
G. Customs and Trade Regulations	0	1	2	3	4
H. Labor Regulations	0	1	2	3	4
I. Skills and Education of Available Workers	0	1	2	3	4
J. Business Licensing and Operating Permits	0	1	2	3	4
K. Access to Financing (e.g., collateral)	0	1	2	3	4
L. Cost of Financing (e.g., interest rates)	0	1	2	3	4
M. Economic and Regulatory Policy Uncertainty	0	1	2	3	4
N. Macroeconomic Instability (inflation, exchange rate)	0	1	2	3	4
O. Corruption	0	1	2	3	4
P. Crime, Theft, and Disorder	0	1	2	3	4
Q. Anticompetitive or Informal Practices	0	1	2	3	4
R. Legal System/Conflict Resolution	0	1	2	3	4

Appendix 2

Objective Questions Used for Parametric Estimation of Survey Firm Fixed Effect

Corruption

39. We've heard that establishments are sometimes required to make gifts or informal payments to public officials to "get things done" with regard to customs, taxes, licenses, regulations, services, etc. On average, what percent of annual sales value would such expenses cost a typical firm like yours? _____ %

43. When establishments in your industry do business with the government, how much of the contract value is typically expected in gifts or informal payments to secure the contract? _____ %

41. Recognizing the difficulties many enterprises face in fully complying with taxes and regulations, what percentage of total sales would you estimate the typical establishment in your area of activity reports for tax purposes? _____ %

Red Tape

38. In a typical week, what percentage of senior management's time is spent in dealing with requirements imposed by government regulations (e.g., taxes, customs, labor regulations, licensing, and registration), including dealings with officials, completing forms, etc.? _____ %

42. On average, how many **days last year** were spent in inspections and mandatory meetings with officials of each of the following agencies in the context of regulation of your business? And what were the costs associated with these interactions?

    (a) Tax inspectorate: total days spent in inspections, required meetings with officials.

36. (a) If you import, what was the average and the longest number of days in the last year that it took from the time your goods arrived in their point of entry (e.g., port, airport) until the time you could claim them from customs?

_____ days on average   NA (we don't import)

36. (b) If you export, what was the average and the longest number of days in the last year that it took from the time your goods arrived in their point of exit (e.g., port, airport) until the time they clear customs?

_____ days on average   NA (we don't export)

37. If you could change the number of regular full-time workers you currently employ without any restrictions (i.e., without seeking permission, making severance payments, etc.), what would be your optimal level of employment as a percent of your existing workforce? _____ %

(Note: 90% implies you would reduce your workforce by 10%, 110% means you want to expand by 10%.)

Infrastructure

19. During how many days last year did your establishment experience the following service interruptions, how long did they last, and what percent of your total sales value was lost last year due to:

	Days	Value (% sales)	
(a) power outages or surges from the public grid?	_____	____	NA
(b) insufficient water supply?	_____	____	NA
(c) unavailable mainline telephone service?	_____	____	NA

22. What percentage of the value of your average cargo consignment is lost while in transit because of breakage, theft, or spoilage? _____ % of consignment value

The full core questionnaire is available at http://www.ifc.org/ifcext/economics.nsf/Content/IC-SurveyMethodology.

Appendix 3

Parametric Results of Survey Firm Fixed Effects on Objective Questions

The results presented in this appendix are based on data from the Investment Climate Surveys from the following countries: Albania 2002, Algeria2002, Armenia2002, Azerbaijan2002, Bangladesh2002, Belarus2002, Bosnia Herzegovina2002, Bulgaria2002, Bulgaria2004, Cambodia2003, China2002, Croatia2002, Czech2002, Ecuador2003, Egypt2004, El Salvador2003, Eritrea2002, Estonia2002, FYROM 2002, Georgia2002, Guatemala2003, Honduras2003, Hungary2002, Indonesia2003, Kazakhstan2002, Kenya2003, Kosovo2003, Kyrgyzstan 2002, Kyrgyzstan2003, Latvia2002, Lithuania2002, Lithuania2004, Moldova2002, Moldova2003, Montenegro2003, Nicaragua2003, Pakistan2002, Philippines2003, Poland2002, Poland2003, Romania 2002, Russia2002, Serbia2001, Serbia2003, Slovakia2002, Slovenia 2002, South Africa2003, Sri Lanka2004, Tajikistan2002, Tajikistan 2003, Tanzania2003, Turkey2002, Uganda2003, Ukraine2002, Uzbekistan2002, Uzbekistan2003, Vietnam2005, Yugoslavia2002, Zambia2002.

See appendix 2 for the list of questions.

These data are available online at http://iresearch.worldbank.org/ics/jsp/index.jsp.

Table A3.1

Survey Firm Fixed Effect on "Unofficial Payments to Get Things Done"

	Unofficial Payments to Get Things Done (% annual sales)				
Government Agency	−1.579	−1.811	−1.869	−1.858	−1.854
	(12.77)**	(13.84)**	(14.19)**	(14.02)**	(13.90)**
Private Int'l. Survey Firm	−0.214	−0.176	−0.214	−0.221	−0.204
	(1.74)	(1.42)	(1.73)	(1.79)	(1.65)
Europe & Central Asia	−1.703	−2.076	−2.094	−2.164	−2.177
	(10.19)**	(11.77)**	(11.83)**	(12.15)**	(12.19)**
Latin America & Caribbean	2.560	2.216	2.188	2.072	2.075
	(13.12)**	(10.93)**	(10.76)**	(10.10)**	(10.12)**
Middle East & North Africa	5.112	4.976	5.015	4.883	4.879
	(21.54)**	(20.87)**	(20.97)**	(20.45)**	(20.42)**
South Asia	−0.666	−0.903	−0.851	−0.836	−0.870
	(5.60)**	(7.31)**	(6.85)**	(6.74)**	(6.91)**
Sub-Saharan Africa	−2.222	−2.524	−2.627	−2.570	−2.643
	(13.36)**	(14.47)**	(14.93)**	(14.53)**	(14.88)**
Foreign Firm		−0.324			−0.102
		(3.31)**			(0.99)
Exporter			−0.391		−0.124
			(4.79)**		(1.40)
Small				0.162	0.177
				(1.75)	(1.90)
Medium				−0.561	−0.519
				(4.66)**	(4.26)**
Large				−0.375	−0.325
				(3.00)**	(2.54)*
Very large				−0.774	−0.704
				(6.93)**	(5.93)**
Constant	3.398	3.781	3.864	4.005	4.019
	(27.49)**	(27.74)**	(28.07)**	(26.17)**	(26.17)**
Observations	15153	14951	14790	14774	14635
R-squared	0.09	0.10	0.10	0.10	0.10

Note: Absolute value of t statistics in parentheses.

*significant at 5 percent; **significant at 1 percent.

All independent variables are dummies. Private local survey company is the omitted category.

Table A3.2

Survey Firm Fixed Effect on "Gifts Expected as Percent Value of Government Contracts"

	Gifts Expected as Percent Value of Government Contracts				
Government Agency	−3.059	−3.025	−3.063	−3.115	−3.109
	(14.41)**	(12.66)**	(12.85)**	(12.81)**	(12.78)**
Private Int'l. Survey Firm	−0.009	0.047	0.023	−0.021	0.029
	(0.04)	(0.22)	(0.11)	(0.10)	(0.14)
Europe & Central Asia	−2.523	−2.572	−2.533	−2.510	−2.538
	(8.93)**	(8.36)**	(8.27)**	(8.16)**	(8.25)**
Latin America & Caribbean	2.221	2.196	2.232	2.043	2.025
	(9.90)**	(8.62)**	(8.79)**	(7.92)**	(7.85)**
Middle East & North Africa	−0.406	−0.491	−0.428	−0.670	−0.722
	(2.28)*	(2.72)**	(2.37)*	(3.69)**	(3.95)**
South Asia	−0.364	−0.408	−0.244	−0.202	−0.227
	(1.63)	(1.69)	(1.01)	(0.82)	(0.91)
Sub-Saharan Africa	−1.790	−1.772	−1.770	−1.866	−1.912
	(6.97)**	(6.24)**	(6.22)**	(6.50)**	(6.63)**
Foreign Firm		−0.470			−0.305
		(3.63)**			(2.26)*
Exporter			−0.488		−0.262
			(4.55)**		(2.23)*
Small				0.968	0.994
				(8.06)**	(8.25)**
Medium				0.469	0.566
				(2.98)**	(3.54)**
Large				0.318	0.450
				(1.98)*	(2.74)**
Very large				−0.288	−0.098
				(1.93)	(0.62)
Constant	4.326	4.391	4.402	3.954	3.979
	(21.79)**	(18.88)**	(18.97)**	(16.10)**	(16.19)**
Observations	15578	15371	15263	15124	15041
R-squared	0.11	0.11	0.12	0.12	0.12

Note: Absolute value of t statistics in parentheses.
*significant at 5 percent; **significant at 1 percent.
All independent variables are dummies. Private local survey company is the omitted category.

Table A3.3
Firm Survey Fixed Effect on "Estimated Percent of Total Sales Declared for Tax Purposes"

	Estimated Percent of Total Sales Declared for Tax Purposes				
Government Agency	−25.712	−16.960	−17.415	−17.868	−17.854
	(18.58)**	(11.09)**	(11.38)**	(11.31)**	(11.27)**
Private Int'l. Survey Firm	−0.830	−0.870	−0.714	−0.790	−0.813
	(0.76)	(0.80)	(0.65)	(0.73)	(0.74)
Europe & Central Asia	10.342	19.375	19.273	18.927	19.087
	(7.04)**	(11.99)**	(11.99)**	(11.68)**	(11.72)**
Latin America & Caribbean	6.084	15.110	15.100	13.903	14.100
	(5.01)**	(10.87)**	(10.93)**	(9.73)**	(9.81)**
Middle East & North Africa	27.113	27.396	27.685	26.763	26.831
	(19.88)**	(20.12)**	(20.32)**	(19.30)**	(19.27)**
South Asia	51.922	52.122	53.023	52.463	52.661
	(18.80)**	(18.98)**	(19.31)**	(18.45)**	(18.50)**
Sub-Saharan Africa	2.983	11.591	11.939	11.464	11.273
	(1.88)	(6.78)**	(6.96)**	(6.59)**	(6.43)**
Foreign Firm		0.490			1.510
		(0.50)			(1.44)
Exporter			−1.820		−1.252
			(2.33)*		(1.44)
Small				3.409	3.488
				(4.58)**	(4.66)**
Medium				2.877	2.943
				(2.76)**	(2.78)**
Large				1.511	1.677
				(1.32)	(1.43)
Very large				−3.040	−2.836
				(2.67)**	(2.32)*
Constant	47.290	38.240	38.518	37.325	37.138
	(42.92)**	(29.44)**	(29.90)**	(27.74)**	(27.46)**
Observations	7840	7694	7653	7402	7375
R-squared	0.16	0.17	0.17	0.18	0.18

Note: Absolute value of t statistics in parentheses.
*significant at 5 percent; **significant at 1 percent.
All independent variables are dummies. Private local survey company is the omitted category.

Table A3.4

Firm Survey Fixed Effects on "Percent of Senior Management's Time Dealing With Government"

	Percent of Senior Management's Time Dealing With Government Regulations				
Government Agency	0.667	−1.072	−1.087	−0.667	−0.709
	(2.88)**	(3.98)**	(4.01)**	(2.40)*	(2.53)*
Private Int'l. Survey Firm	−6.294	−6.378	−6.290	−6.215	−6.256
	(19.06)**	(19.17)**	(18.99)**	(19.08)**	(19.18)**
Europe & Central Asia	1.693	−1.189	−1.167	0.318	0.473
	(4.44)**	(2.83)**	(2.78)**	(0.75)	(1.11)
Latin America & Caribbean	−2.745	−5.654	−5.619	−4.652	−4.520
	(8.66)**	(15.64)**	(15.52)**	(12.65)**	(12.19)**
Middle East & North Africa	−2.316	−3.452	−3.376	−2.398	−2.056
	(4.42)**	(6.44)**	(6.32)**	(4.54)**	(3.81)**
South Asia	−3.321	−5.576	−5.763	−5.316	−5.261
	(13.51)**	(19.94)**	(20.53)**	(18.73)**	(18.09)**
Sub-Saharan Africa	−3.408	−6.032	−5.911	−4.642	−4.659
	(11.07)**	(17.71)**	(17.28)**	(13.33)**	(13.23)**
Foreign Firm		0.801			0.582
		(3.57)**			(2.45)*
Exporter			0.176		−0.427
			(0.95)		(2.10)*
Small				1.710	1.721
				(8.00)**	(8.00)**
Medium				2.274	2.347
				(8.34)**	(8.46)**
Large				2.382	2.473
				(8.54)**	(8.65)**
Very large				1.848	1.894
				(7.24)**	(7.01)**
Constant	11.634	14.477	14.464	11.681	11.543
	(49.97)**	(49.55)**	(49.33)**	(34.24)**	(33.49)**
Observations	24163	22521	22190	21051	20703
R-squared	0.04	0.06	0.05	0.05	0.05

Note: Absolute value of t statistics in parentheses.
*significant at 5 percent; **significant at 1 percent.
All independent variables are dummies. Private local survey company is the omitted category.

Table A3.5

Firm Survey Fixed Effects on "Total Days Spent with Officials from Tax Inspectorate"

	Total Days Spent with Officials from Tax Inspectorate				
Government Agency	3.736	1.662	1.923	2.420	2.307
	(12.68)**	(4.31)**	(4.94)**	(6.24)**	(5.87)**
Private Int'l. Survey Firm	4.675	4.622	4.714	4.872	4.803
	(7.69)**	(7.45)**	(7.58)**	(8.03)**	(7.90)**
Europe & Central Asia	−0.927	−3.490	−3.388	−1.859	−1.752
	(2.19)*	(6.75)**	(6.53)**	(3.55)**	(3.30)**
Latin America & Caribbean	−0.550	−3.195	−3.040	−1.303	−1.252
	(1.42)	(6.59)**	(6.25)**	(2.61)**	(2.48)*
Middle East & North Africa	−1.185	−1.647	−1.788	−0.806	−0.628
	(2.86)**	(3.83)**	(4.16)**	(1.88)	(1.45)
South Asia	−3.927	−5.229	−5.283	−4.646	−4.368
	(13.07)**	(15.39)**	(15.42)**	(13.69)**	(12.48)**
Sub-Saharan Africa	−0.065	−2.473	−2.138	−0.927	−0.969
	(0.18)	(5.66)**	(4.87)**	(2.06)*	(2.13)*
Foreign Firm		1.533			0.904
		(5.07)**			(2.77)**
Exporter			0.849		−0.444
			(3.41)**		(1.63)
Small				0.819	0.900
				(2.55)*	(2.77)**
Medium				2.006	2.087
				(5.18)**	(5.27)**
Large				2.854	2.904
				(7.32)**	(7.21)**
Very large				3.885	3.913
				(10.52)**	(9.89)**
Constant	5.354	7.829	7.645	4.863	4.762
	(18.19)**	(18.80)**	(18.16)**	(9.32)**	(9.02)**
Observations	15982	14740	14502	13895	13615
R-squared	0.04	0.04	0.04	0.05	0.05

Note: Absolute value of t statistics in parentheses.

*significant at 5 percent; **significant at 1%.

All independent variables are dummies. Private local survey company is the omitted category.

Table A3.6

Firm Survey Fixed Effects on "Days on Average to Claim Imports from Customs"

	Days on Average to Claim Imports from Customs				
Government Agency	1.372	0.513	0.406	−0.162	0.114
	(3.31)**	(0.95)	(0.74)	(0.29)	(0.20)
Private Int'l. Survey Firm	−5.077	−4.526	−4.770	−4.702	−4.150
	(4.00)**	(3.50)**	(3.68)**	(3.57)**	(3.17)**
Europe & Central Asia	2.991	0.444	0.724	−0.499	−0.735
	(2.27)*	(0.32)	(0.51)	(0.34)	(0.51)
Latin America & Caribbean	4.169	1.925	2.200	1.422	1.462
	(8.08)**	(2.86)**	(3.24)**	(1.97)*	(2.01)*
Middle East & North Africa	2.842	1.250	1.903	1.334	1.071
	(7.72)**	(3.12)**	(4.60)**	(3.09)**	(2.39)*
South Asia	3.292	0.877	1.748	1.527	1.192
	(7.48)**	(1.54)	(3.05)**	(2.54)*	(1.95)
Sub-Saharan Africa	3.944	1.938	1.745	1.456	1.111
	(8.03)**	(3.10)**	(2.76)**	(2.20)*	(1.66)
Foreign Firm		−2.583			−2.341
		(9.51)**			(7.91)**
Exporter			−2.088		−1.665
			(8.54)**		(6.19)**
Small				−0.654	−0.473
				(1.32)	(0.95)
Medium				−1.621	−1.089
				(3.00)**	(1.99)*
Large				−1.942	−1.104
				(3.68)**	(2.06)*
Very large				−2.430	−1.326
				(4.85)**	(2.56)*
Constant	5.845	8.675	8.655	10.187	10.810
	(13.80)**	(14.30)**	(14.04)**	(13.03)**	(13.62)**
Observations	9735	9072	8726	8297	8003
R-squared	0.05	0.06	0.06	0.06	0.07

Note: Absolute value of t statistics in parentheses.
*significant at 5 percent; **significant at 1 percent.
All independent variables are dummies. Private local survey company is the omitted category.

Table A3.7
Firm Survey Fixed Effects on "Days on Average to Clear Customs for Exports"

	Days on Average to Clear Customs for Exports				
Government Agency	2.054	2.074	1.939	1.548	1.815
	(6.65)**	(4.97)**	(4.47)**	(3.56)**	(4.04)**
Private Int'l. Survey Firm	−1.462	−1.108	−1.444	−1.383	−1.080
	(1.09)	(0.81)	(1.04)	(1.01)	(0.79)
Europe & Central Asia	0.630	−0.694	0.129	−0.689	−0.454
	(0.46)	(0.48)	(0.09)	(0.48)	(0.31)
Latin America & Caribbean	1.634	0.480	1.063	0.503	0.740
	(4.21)**	(0.93)	(1.98)*	(0.92)	(1.31)
Middle East & North Africa	−1.931	−3.247	−2.524	−2.623	−2.821
	(6.28)**	(9.78)**	(7.18)**	(7.57)**	(7.67)**
South Asia	2.825	1.355	2.254	2.286	2.203
	(9.11)**	(3.27)**	(5.22)**	(5.33)**	(4.92)**
Sub-Saharan Africa	1.452	0.374	0.737	0.332	0.527
	(3.36)**	(0.69)	(1.31)	(0.59)	(0.91)
Foreign Firm		−2.135			−2.023
		(9.61)**			(8.40)**
Exporter			−1.147		−0.929
			(5.54)**		(4.25)**
Small				−0.184	−0.052
				(0.41)	(0.11)
Medium				−0.254	−0.034
				(0.54)	(0.07)
Large				−0.816	−0.473
				(1.77)	(1.01)
Very large				−0.823	−0.311
				(1.87)	(0.69)
Constant	3.570	5.200	4.989	5.240	5.821
	(11.43)**	(11.26)**	(10.33)**	(8.39)**	(8.98)**
Observations	8499	7691	7313	6903	6583
R-squared	0.03	0.05	0.04	0.05	0.06

Note: Absolute value of t statistics in parentheses.
*significant at 5 percent; **significant at 1 percent.
All independent variables are dummies. Private local survey company is the omitted category.

Table A3.8

Firm Survey Fixed Effects on "Optimal Level of Employment Compared to Current Level (%)"

	Optimal Level of Employment Compared to Current Level (%)				
Government Agency	−4.406	2.686	1.761	3.612	2.769
	(5.99)**	(3.19)**	(2.04)*	(4.04)**	(2.97)**
Private Int'l. Survey Firm	32.311	32.397	31.801	30.693	30.147
	(33.66)**	(33.84)**	(33.11)**	(31.82)**	(30.99)**
Europe & Central Asia	−24.731	−13.875	−14.021	−14.643	−14.672
	(21.74)**	(11.00)**	(11.01)**	(11.32)**	(11.11)**
Latin America & Caribbean	15.635	26.532	25.848	25.416	24.953
	(17.42)**	(25.24)**	(24.31)**	(23.03)**	(22.06)**
Middle East & North Africa	23.763	27.616	28.695	25.063	26.626
	(26.52)**	(29.41)**	(30.33)**	(26.14)**	(27.14)**
South Asia	−3.649	4.838	5.397	3.487	4.391
	(4.66)**	(5.39)**	(5.94)**	(3.75)**	(4.55)**
Sub-Saharan Africa	8.207	17.749	17.191	17.097	16.764
	(8.29)**	(16.20)**	(15.54)**	(15.03)**	(14.44)**
Foreign Firm		−0.678			2.234
		(1.01)			(3.07)**
Exporter			−2.754		0.531
			(5.06)**		(0.86)
Small				−5.119	−5.064
				(8.12)**	(7.89)**
Medium				−9.683	−9.826
				(11.90)**	(11.75)**
Large				−12.171	−12.522
				(14.44)**	(14.30)**
Very large				−14.120	−14.763
				(17.99)**	(17.51)**
Constant	97.630	86.792	87.952	94.922	95.165
	(132.65)**	(93.78)**	(93.58)**	(88.49)**	(86.27)**
Observations	26657	24927	24262	23373	22634
R-squared	0.09	0.11	0.11	0.12	0.12

Note: Absolute value of t statistics in parentheses.
*significant at 5 percent; **significant at 1 percent.
All independent variables are dummies. Private local survey company is the omitted category.

Table A3.9

Firm Survey Fixed Effects on "Days of Power Outages/Surges from Public Grid"

	Days of Power Outages/Surges from Public Grid				
Government Agency	−22.998	−32.970	−33.039	−32.984	−31.998
	(24.25)**	(25.21)**	(25.10)**	(24.69)**	(23.86)**
Private Int'l. Survey Firm	−16.348	−16.200	−16.319	−16.471	−16.366
	(18.49)**	(17.75)**	(17.92)**	(17.98)**	(17.84)**
Europe & Central Asia	5.191	−5.488	−5.307	−5.673	−5.009
	(4.51)**	(3.60)**	(3.47)**	(3.66)**	(3.23)**
Latin America & Caribbean	−9.723	−20.354	−20.187	−20.089	−19.381
	(10.34)**	(14.95)**	(14.79)**	(14.34)**	(13.80)**
Middle East & North Africa	22.942	22.224	22.364	22.419	22.046
	(24.83)**	(20.86)**	(20.83)**	(20.66)**	(20.22)**
South Asia	31.075	27.727	28.925	28.193	28.412
	(30.74)**	(23.97)**	(24.59)**	(24.02)**	(23.78)**
Sub-Saharan Africa	15.523	5.547	5.318	5.490	5.918
	(13.64)**	(3.73)**	(3.55)**	(3.60)**	(3.87)**
Foreign Firms		−1.420			−0.590
		(2.00)*			(0.78)
Exporter			−2.097		−1.638
			(3.72)**		(2.64)**
Small				−2.364	−2.245
				(3.81)**	(3.61)**
Medium				−3.313	−3.072
				(4.04)**	(3.69)**
Large				−2.530	−1.974
				(2.91)**	(2.23)*
Very large				−2.877	−2.091
				(3.57)**	(2.44)*
Constant	20.774	31.527	31.667	33.528	32.966
	(25.36)**	(24.60)**	(24.57)**	(24.56)**	(24.06)**
Observations	20343	18830	18650	18383	18229
R-squared	0.11	0.11	0.11	0.11	0.11

Note: Absolute value of t statistics in parentheses.

*significant at 5 percent; **significant at 1 percent.

All independent variables are dummies. Private local survey company is the omitted category.

Table A3.10

Firm Survey Fixed Effects on "Days of Insufficient Water Supply"

	Days of Insufficient Water Supply				
Government Agency	−0.713	−2.372	−2.542	−2.907	−2.673
	(0.99)	(2.40)*	(2.55)*	(2.89)**	(2.64)**
Private Int'l. Survey Firm	1.255	1.466	1.267	1.106	1.264
	(1.73)	(1.94)	(1.68)	(1.46)	(1.67)
Europe & Central Asia	1.610	−1.621	−1.372	−2.288	−2.242
	(1.69)	(1.24)	(1.04)	(1.72)	(1.68)
Latin America & Caribbean	3.386	0.228	0.417	−0.259	−0.144
	(4.32)**	(0.19)	(0.35)	(0.21)	(0.12)
Middle East & North Africa	15.652	14.062	14.606	14.215	14.253
	(17.26)**	(13.71)**	(14.11)**	(13.67)**	(13.63)**
South Asia	5.883	3.685	4.172	4.018	3.839
	(8.33)**	(4.09)**	(4.56)**	(4.39)**	(4.15)**
Sub-Saharan Africa	18.382	15.486	15.271	15.113	15.001
	(18.12)**	(11.64)**	(11.37)**	(11.12)**	(10.97)**
Foreign Firm		−2.040			−1.432
		(3.48)**			(2.31)*
Exporter			−1.035		0.019
			(2.22)*		(0.04)
Small				−2.004	−2.063
				(3.79)**	(3.90)**
Medium				−3.260	−3.243
				(4.74)**	(4.67)**
Large				−3.020	−3.047
				(4.22)**	(4.16)**
Very large				−3.606	−3.359
				(5.44)**	(4.77)**
Constant	2.505	5.843	5.686	8.339	8.354
	(3.67)**	(5.24)**	(5.02)**	(6.84)**	(6.82)**
Observations	19064	17670	17493	17365	17222
R-squared	0.03	0.03	0.03	0.03	0.03

Note: Absolute value of t statistics in parentheses.
*significant at 5 percent; **significant at 1 percent.
All independent variables are dummies. Private local survey company is the omitted category.

Table A3.11

Firm Survey Fixed Effects on "Days of Unavailable Mainline Telephone Service"

	Days of Unavailable Mainline Telephone Service				
Government Agency	−4.001	−3.671	−3.557	−3.855	−3.690
	(3.91)**	(3.46)**	(3.36)**	(3.61)**	(3.46)**
Private Int'l. Survey Firm	0.076	0.009	0.087	0.135	0.067
	(0.15)	(0.02)	(0.16)	(0.26)	(0.13)
Europe & Central Asia	−1.497	−1.418	−1.426	−1.598	−1.383
	(1.37)	(1.27)	(1.28)	(1.43)	(1.24)
Latin America & Caribbean	−2.038	−1.982	−1.960	−2.261	−2.067
	(2.00)*	(1.90)	(1.89)	(2.16)*	(1.97)*
Middle East & North Africa	20.298	20.143	19.896	20.322	20.328
	(24.37)**	(22.60)**	(22.14)**	(22.62)**	(22.44)**
South Asia	4.969	4.710	4.624	4.277	4.327
	(8.17)**	(6.99)**	(6.77)**	(6.29)**	(6.29)**
Sub-Saharan Africa	12.854	12.712	12.290	12.389	12.222
	(12.05)**	(11.67)**	(11.30)**	(11.30)**	(11.13)**
Foreign Firm		0.649			0.812
		(1.57)			(1.87)
Exporter			−0.381		−0.725
			(1.12)		(1.96)
Small				0.235	0.273
				(0.64)	(0.74)
Medium				0.531	0.625
				(1.09)	(1.27)
Large				1.045	1.112
				(2.04)*	(2.12)*
Very large				0.363	0.496
				(0.76)	(0.98)
Constant	5.165	5.053	5.169	4.939	4.772
	(5.26)**	(5.02)**	(5.17)**	(4.81)**	(4.64)**
Observations	17355	16700	16516	16426	16295
R-squared	0.06	0.06	0.06	0.06	0.06

Note: Absolute value of t statistics in parentheses.

*significant at 5 percent; **significant at 1 percent.

All independent variables are dummies. Private local survey company is the omitted category.

Table A3.12

Firm Survey Fixed Effects on "Percent of Sales Lost Due to Power Outages/Surges"

	Percent of Sales Lost Due to Power Outages/Surges				
Government Agency	−0.083	−0.212	−0.213	−0.242	−0.229
	(1.09)	(2.37)*	(2.35)*	(2.62)**	(2.43)*
Private Int'l. Survey Firm	0.091	0.096	0.074	−0.004	−0.013
	(0.39)	(0.41)	(0.32)	(0.02)	(0.06)
Europe & Central Asia	0.674	0.492	0.548	0.350	0.386
	(5.57)**	(3.65)**	(4.08)**	(2.57)*	(2.80)**
Latin America & Caribbean	0.468	0.292	0.350	0.162	0.200
	(4.83)**	(2.59)**	(3.11)**	(1.38)	(1.68)
Middle East & North Africa	1.464	1.412	1.440	1.234	1.260
	(15.00)**	(14.08)**	(14.47)**	(12.04)**	(12.09)**
South Asia	1.984	1.841	1.917	1.724	1.783
	(24.20)**	(19.55)**	(20.36)**	(17.99)**	(17.91)**
Sub-Saharan Africa	0.615	0.485	0.525	0.341	0.341
	(5.98)**	(4.33)**	(4.67)**	(2.94)**	(2.90)**
Foreign Firm		−0.165			0.106
		(1.91)			(1.11)
Exporter			−0.367		−0.136
			(5.38)**		(1.75)
Small				−0.164	−0.173
				(1.94)	(2.02)*
Medium				−0.631	−0.639
				(6.11)**	(6.07)**
Large				−0.675	−0.681
				(6.51)**	(6.38)**
Very large				−0.890	−0.874
				(9.01)**	(8.36)**
Constant	1.390	1.580	1.585	2.062	2.049
	(18.15)**	(16.38)**	(16.41)**	(17.34)**	(16.94)**
Observations	14413	13821	13587	12293	12019
R-squared	0.06	0.06	0.06	0.06	0.06

Note: Absolute value of t statistics in parentheses.
*significant at 5 percent; **significant at 1 percent.
All independent variables are dummies. Private local survey company is the omitted category.

Table A3.13

Firm Survey Fixed Effects on "Percent of Sales Lost Due to Insufficient Water Supply Last Year"

	Percent of Sales Lost Due to Insufficient Water Supply Last Year				
Government Agency	1.016	0.575	0.573	0.665	0.653
	(4.96)**	(2.37)*	(2.34)*	(2.64)**	(2.59)**
Private Int'l. Survey Firm	0.191	0.173	0.197	0.140	0.149
	(0.58)	(0.52)	(0.59)	(0.42)	(0.44)
Europe & Central Asia	−0.486	−0.963	−0.930	−0.856	−0.881
	(2.73)**	(4.37)**	(4.25)**	(3.83)**	(3.91)**
Latin America & Caribbean	0.068	−0.407	−0.373	−0.383	−0.402
	(0.38)	(1.84)	(1.70)	(1.70)	(1.77)
Middle East & North Africa	−0.986	−1.030	−0.968	−1.073	−1.046
	(6.02)**	(6.10)**	(5.60)**	(6.22)**	(5.96)**
South Asia	0.000	0.000	0.000	0.000	0.000
	(.)	(.)	(.)	(.)	(.)
Sub-Saharan Africa	−0.861	−1.307	−1.315	−1.194	−1.243
	(3.43)**	(4.62)**	(4.61)**	(4.08)**	(4.22)**
Foreign Firm		−0.295			−0.235
		(1.57)			(1.15)
Exporter			0.044		0.264
			(0.34)		(1.86)
Small				0.194	0.164
				(1.38)	(1.15)
Medium				0.125	0.089
				(0.71)	(0.50)
Large				−0.037	−0.098
				(0.20)	(0.51)
Very large				−0.383	−0.461
				(2.05)*	(2.27)*
Constant	0.987	1.481	1.421	1.342	1.361
	(6.64)**	(7.49)**	(7.24)**	(6.42)**	(6.43)**
Observations	2281	2191	2172	2164	2153
R-squared	0.04	0.04	0.04	0.05	0.05

Note: Absolute value of t statistics in parentheses.
*significant at 5 percent; **significant at 1 percent.
All independent variables are dummies. Private local survey company is the omitted category.

Table A3.14

Firm Survey Fixed Effects on "Percent of Sales Lost Due to Unavailable Telephone Service Last Year"

	Percent of Sales Lost Due to Unavailable Telephone Service Last Year				
Government Agency	−1.068	−1.081	−1.029	−0.852	−0.844
	(4.62)**	(4.67)**	(4.44)**	(3.48)**	(3.42)**
Private Int'l. Survey Firm	−0.157	−0.147	−0.158	−0.273	−0.276
	(0.48)	(0.46)	(0.49)	(0.84)	(0.85)
Europe & Central Asia	−1.557	−1.583	−1.532	−1.430	−1.420
	(9.09)**	(9.13)**	(8.92)**	(7.99)**	(7.75)**
Latin America & Caribbean	−0.768	−0.793	−0.754	−0.699	−0.691
	(4.64)**	(4.73)**	(4.55)**	(3.87)**	(3.76)**
Middle East & North Africa	0.000	0.000	0.000	0.000	0.000
	(.)	(.)	(.)	(.)	(.)
South Asia	0.000	0.000	0.000	0.000	0.000
	(.)	(.)	(.)	(.)	(.)
Sub-Saharan Africa	−1.798	−1.805	−1.725	−1.519	−1.511
	(7.98)**	(8.01)**	(7.53)**	(6.28)**	(6.18)**
Foreign Firm		−0.162			0.043
		(0.96)			(0.24)
Exporter			−0.216		−0.013
			(1.73)		(0.09)
Small				0.187	0.186
				(1.06)	(1.05)
Medium				−0.323	−0.325
				(1.58)	(1.57)
Large				−0.383	−0.386
				(1.83)	(1.80)
Very large				−0.456	−0.463
				(2.21)*	(2.07)*
Constant	2.028	2.065	2.057	2.035	2.028
	(14.36)**	(14.10)**	(14.47)**	(12.15)**	(11.93)**
Observations	1685	1685	1685	1677	1677
R-squared	0.06	0.07	0.07	0.08	0.08

Note: Absolute value of t statistics in parentheses.
*significant at 5 percent; **significant at 1 percent.
All independent variables are dummies. Private local survey company is the omitted category.

Table A3.15

Firm Survey Fixed Effects on "Percentage of Average Cargo Value Lost in Transit"

	Percentage of Average Cargo Value Lost in Transit				
Government Agency	−0.080	−0.203	−0.183	−0.191	−0.176
	(1.12)	(2.85)**	(2.56)*	(2.59)**	(2.37)*
Private Int'l. Survey Firm	−2.051	−1.623	−1.629	−1.628	−1.629
	(14.06)**	(12.77)**	(12.80)**	(12.71)**	(12.71)**
Europe & Central Asia	1.477	0.871	0.908	0.913	0.905
	(14.58)**	(8.92)**	(9.31)**	(9.16)**	(9.02)**
Latin America & Caribbean	0.194	−0.091	−0.064	−0.040	−0.056
	(2.41)*	(1.12)	(0.79)	(0.47)	(0.66)
Middle East & North Africa	0.317	0.075	0.098	0.093	0.066
	(4.29)**	(1.13)	(1.48)	(1.33)	(0.94)
South Asia	0.075	−0.107	−0.102	−0.075	−0.115
	(0.84)	(1.28)	(1.21)	(0.87)	(1.30)
Sub-Saharan Africa	0.204	0.000	−0.013	0.020	−0.008
	(2.47)*	(0.00)	(0.17)	(0.24)	(0.09)
Foreign Firm		−0.143			−0.181
		(2.45)*			(2.77)**
Exporter			0.089		0.153
			(1.88)		(2.86)**
Small				0.046	0.037
				(0.75)	(0.60)
Medium				−0.003	−0.020
				(0.04)	(0.27)
Large				0.064	0.041
				(0.86)	(0.54)
Very large				0.003	−0.039
				(0.04)	(0.52)
Constant	0.941	1.132	1.074	1.060	1.075
	(13.55)**	(15.43)**	(14.66)**	(12.00)**	(12.09)**
Observations	17335	15924	15783	14712	14477
R-squared	0.02	0.02	0.02	0.02	0.02

Note: Absolute value of t statistics in parentheses.

*significant at 5 percent; **significant at 1 percent.

All independent variables are dummies. Private local survey company is the omitted category.

Appendix 4

Table of $z_{\alpha/2}$ Distribution Corresponding to Different Levels of Confidence α

α	$z_{\alpha/2}$	α	$z_{\alpha/2}$	α	$z_{\alpha/2}$	α	$z_{\alpha/2}$
68.3%	1	86.4%	1.49	94.0%	1.88	97.7%	2.27
68.8%	1.01	86.6%	1.5	94.1%	1.89	97.7%	2.28
69.2%	1.02	86.9%	1.51	94.3%	1.90	97.8%	2.29
69.7%	1.03	87.1%	1.52	94.4%	1.91	97.9%	2.30
70.2%	1.04	87.4%	1.53	94.5%	1.92	97.9%	2.31
70.6%	1.05	87.6%	1.54	94.6%	1.93	98.0%	2.32
71.1%	1.06	87.9%	1.55	94.8%	1.94	98.0%	2.33
71.5%	1.07	88.1%	1.56	94.9%	1.95	98.1%	2.34
72.0%	1.08	88.4%	1.57	**95.0%**	**1.96**	98.1%	2.35
72.4%	1.09	88.6%	1.58	95.1%	1.97	98.2%	2.36
72.9%	1.1	88.8%	1.59	95.2%	1.98	98.2%	2.37
73.3%	1.11	89.0%	1.60	95.3%	1.99	98.3%	2.38
73.7%	1.12	89.3%	1.61	95.4%	2.00	98.3%	2.39
74.2%	1.13	89.5%	1.62	95.6%	2.01	98.4%	2.40
74.6%	1.14	89.7%	1.63	95.7%	2.02	98.4%	2.41
75.0%	1.15	89.9%	1.64	95.8%	2.03	98.4%	2.42
75.4%	1.16	90.1%	1.65	95.9%	2.04	98.5%	2.43
75.8%	1.17	90.3%	1.66	96.0%	2.05	98.5%	2.44
76.2%	1.18	90.5%	1.67	96.1%	2.06	98.6%	2.45
76.6%	1.19	90.7%	1.68	96.2%	2.07	98.6%	2.46
77.0%	1.2	90.9%	1.69	96.2%	2.08	98.6%	2.47
77.4%	1.21	91.1%	1.70	96.3%	2.09	98.7%	2.48
77.8%	1.22	91.3%	1.71	96.4%	2.10	98.7%	2.49
78.1%	1.23	91.5%	1.72	96.5%	2.11	98.8%	2.50
78.5%	1.24	91.6%	1.73	96.6%	2.12	98.8%	2.51

α	$z_{\alpha/2}$	α	$z_{\alpha/2}$	α	$z_{\alpha/2}$	α	$z_{\alpha/2}$
82.3%	1.35	91.8%	1.74	96.7%	2.13	98.8%	2.52
82.6%	1.36	92.0%	1.75	96.8%	2.14	98.9%	2.53
82.9%	1.37	92.2%	1.76	96.8%	2.15	98.9%	2.54
83.2%	1.38	92.3%	1.77	96.9%	2.16	98.9%	2.55
83.5%	1.39	92.5%	1.78	97.0%	2.17	99.0%	2.56
83.8%	1.4	92.7%	1.79	97.1%	2.18	99.0%	2.57
84.1%	1.41	92.8%	1.80	97.1%	2.19	99.0%	2.58
84.4%	1.42	93.0%	1.81	97.2%	2.20	99.0%	2.59
84.7%	1.43	93.1%	1.82	97.3%	2.21	99.1%	2.60
85.0%	1.44	93.3%	1.83	97.4%	2.22	99.1%	2.61
85.3%	1.45	93.4%	1.84	97.4%	2.23		
85.6%	1.46	93.6%	1.85	97.5%	2.24		
85.8%	1.47	93.7%	1.86	97.6%	2.25		
86.1%	1.48	93.9%	1.87	97.6%	2.26		

Source: Rea and Parker 1997.

Appendix 5

Table of Random Numbers

7766	8840	8661	9670	7875	2977	2194	1237	6611	5342
7481	5371	1661	5913	3302	2595	9237	0318	4626	3786
0588	2012	1045	8022	3870	9411	2202	0837	7487	4904
0579	7695	6900	4870	6014	5311	0657	0626	6031	0674
7998	7098	9794	5599	4404	7589	6950	6403	9668	1789
5509	7915	1156	6588	0816	9695	3317	6045	8131	5046
7919	1649	9908	8001	5635	4142	7258	2039	3353	8526
2870	1206	7102	3450	3016	8358	3998	8401	2785	1735
5444	5359	3444	4993	6175	1987	3493	8516	1879	6594
9369	3143	9393	7739	7240	6632	9086	6588	4119	3686
2494	6541	6464	9513	4697	4312	8602	7950	6790	1419
0407	6701	5903	2737	8320	1782	1180	4608	3268	6026
6724	6338	7653	2914	0247	7031	2088	2431	1465	2335
6906	9051	4894	8977	4166	5460	6695	4673	7659	2005
6656	2091	6148	9173	9880	9694	4509	9321	9040	0301
3648	0201	8894	2008	0764	0884	2641	2554	4365	8224
6293	8557	1206	0788	2237	0384	8069	9329	2234	6788
9401	557	7198	4726	5899	7211	6993	2246	7252	7562
5294	1897	8249	7684	8683	0527	5327	1640	9434	8186
2743	7839	7117	1672	4337	6073	8341	3132	6105	3789
4600	1971	6306	7527	0157	5961	8670	3335	5477	8138
2958	0144	3962	8316	9746	3127	2743	6766	3508	8634
1931	8079	6347	8056	0071	0617	4970	2675	5543	4684
0252	3123	7412	1662	2119	7663	3343	1716	9600	4250
0600	1363	5737	5183	4558	2101	0289	8807	7432	2187
7184	7511	6759	5868	5882	3186	572	6780	0717	2777
5303	1777	7720	3326	1776	3497	2738	9829	4887	9410

4694	3749	8090	7967	6811	505	4648	8041	9757	6185
8419	1226	6768	2864	3548	3254	8389	5906	2664	4831
7148	5893	906	1180	1738	4855	8443	1915	7249	2935
8950	2714	2008	8494	1097	4638	6323	8662	4332	1552
7931	1476	3638	4119	1930	5546	4686	5007	1026	6696
5050	4902	7768	5939	2570	5703	6062	6720	5565	8794
2456	9038	3484	8709	2590	4033	8477	0657	7875	0600
2116	5291	9382	8136	4527	7955	4223	6178	7026	0420
0193	8067	9122	7735	1245	2806	0333	8267	1504	4244
3838	2705	9429	3924	9273	1294	9710	1580	4041	0520
9087	6103	9635	9027	1197	3679	9198	4046	1803	7159
4849	8586	6334	892	3783	8668	0896	3808	2683	7869
4503	3955	5137	8928	4668	4722	0701	5000	0536	7813
1471	6670	3756	6138	5505	2347	9451	8565	9249	8731
0210	5175	242	4484	5118	1807	1996	9551	6277	1873
3893	889	7898	7729	5549	5555	2251	4253	2664	8323
1756	9782	0237	2753	6799	9267	3463	8867	8475	2270
3095	8249	0420	0891	1146	6260	9657	2475	4158	4325
9616	7652	8895	4913	2182	8584	1901	0364	7491	5092
0122	0438	4559	9192	5320	8675	1812	3015	4428	2273
4411	3822	8231	0146	0589	3644	1407	2580	8004	0677
2687	1533	9055	7113	9331	0730	2159	7141	7703	4704
4910	3376	7024	3533	1969	4117	6048	7872	2123	4424

Source: Kish 1965.

Appendix 6

Information Disclosed in
Survey Introductions

	Percent
1 Research organization	85.9
2 Study director's name	82.1
3 Research topic	80.8
4 Sponsor	44.9
5 Confidentiality	42.3
6 Anonymity	25.6
7 Purpose	25.6
8 Future data use	24.4
9 Sampling technique	20.5
10 Survey length	12.8
11 Participation voluntary	10.3
12 Sample size	3.8
13 Consent signature	3.8

Source: Sobal 1984.

Appendix 7

Minimum Field Work Log Data

ID	Strata	Super-visor	Visits	Non Response	Response	Post Stratification
			1st	REF = Refuse	AGR=agree to participate	(final strata)
			2nd	OOS = Out of scope	F1 = Form partially completed	
			3rd	NC = No Contact	FF = Form fully completed	
					FV = Form validated	
					FE = Form entered	
1	A	JM	12–Dec	OOS		A
2	A	JM	13–Dec		AGR	C
3	B	JM	14–Dec		AGR	B
4	B	GI	13–Dec	REF	AGR	B
5	C	GI	14–Dec		F1	A
6	C	GI	14–Dec		FF	C
....	....	....	....	....	....	....
....	....	....	....	....	....	....
....	....	....	....	....	....	....
....	....	....	....	....	....	....

Index